PASSAGES

IN THE

LIFE OF AN ENGLISH HEIRESS

OR,

RECOLLECTIONS

OF

DISRUPTION TIMES IN SCOTLAND

By

Lydia Miller

ISBN: 978-1-905787-95-1

INTRODUCTION

By Elizabeth Sutherland

Lydia Falconer Miller, the author of this novel published anonymously in London by Simpkin, Marshall & Co in 1847 when she was aged 35, was the wife of the famous Hugh Miller of Cromarty, stone-mason, geologist, writer and newspaper editor. The subtitle, ***Recollections of Disruption Times in Scotland***, points to her main purpose in writing it, which was to explain the creation in 1843 of the Free Church of Scotland. The book is important also for the light it casts on the character and formidable intellect of a remarkable woman, whose place in Scottish history was overshadowed by that of her husband.

Baptised in Inverness on 25 January 1812, Lydia was the daughter of Elizabeth Lydia Macleod, a descendent of the Mackenzies of Redcastle, a heritage of which both were justly proud. Her father, William Fraser, described by Peter Bayne, Hugh Miller's biographer, as *notably handsome in youth and famous in Strathnairn as a deerstalker*, was to die as a bankrupt Inverness businessman in mysterious circumstances in 1828, when Lydia was only sixteen, a vulnerable age at which to suffer such a loss. The theme of beloved father and devoted daughter is recreated several times in her novel, in which her heroine, Jane Hamilton Legh, appears first as a recently orphaned daughter age 18.

Lydia was well-educated from the age of eight, first at the Inverness Royal Academy where she excelled in French, Italian, mathematics, and music taught by the well-respected elderly Keith Thomson. Probably on his advice, at the age of thirteen, she was entrusted to his half-brother George Thomson, a leading Edinburgh musician, who, with his wife, ran a small establishment at 140 Princes Street, for 'young ladies' to attend classes in the arts and learn the social graces of conversation and dancing. Here she became known to, and petted as 'little Lydia' by many Edinburgh luminaries including the writer, Mrs Anne Grant of Laggan, George Hogarth, father-in-law of Charles Dickens, William Tennant, professor and poet, and the landscape painter, the Reverend John Thomson. Three year later, in 1828, she was invited to stay with wealthy relatives called Dobinson in their substantial mansion, Egham Lodge (now demolished) in Surrey, where she may well have helped to educate the Dobinsons' four young children. These, despite the loss of her father, were happy times for Lydia when she was able to develop and practise social accomplishments and learn how to be at ease in society. Egham Lodge may well have been the model for her heroine's idyllic English home, Chesterlee. Meanwhile her widowed mother, described as *a lady of strong will and an unusual force of character,* had moved from Inverness for financial reasons to set up a new family home in Braefoot Cottage, Cromarty. Lydia joined her there in 1829.

Cromarty was a busy lively community with plenty of distractions for a pretty young girl. With warships at anchor in the bay, there were dancing parties, picnics and breakfasts to enjoy, for the officers were great favourites ashore. Like the rest of the community, Lydia fell under the spell of the minister, the Reverend Alexander Stewart, whose sermons were keenly anticipated, and, as Lydia herself recalled, *formed the topic of conversations with high and low, even in casual forenoon visitings.* Lydia set up a girls' school in the cottage. She enjoyed teaching and was clearly popular with the girls. It was through her interest in education that she was first to notice Hugh Miller.

She and her mother visited a nearby school to observe the teaching methods and Hugh was present. Although she was *greatly struck by the thoughtful look of his countenance,* he did not notice her. Later that summer, however, Lydia joined some friends who were admiring a sundial he had made. Hugh was to write of that first meeting, *though in her nineteenth year at the time, her light and somewhat petite figure, and the waxen clearness of her complexion, which resembled that of a fair child than of a grown woman, made her look three to four years younger.* He considered her to be *light-hearted and amiable, but somewhat foolish and affected.* He was soon to change his opinion after he met her *sauntering on a still and lovely evening* reading *an elaborate essay on Causation.* Although they did not acknowledge each other in passing, *her face and figure...haunted me for several days after.* He was soon to discover that Lydia *was highly accomplished and no fool, she drew finely, sang beautifully and possessed at least the endowments of a just taste in poetry and belles lettres.* As he got to know her better he noted that she was *by far the most intellectual of her companions.* He also became aware of her anxiety to please and her credulity. As one of her pupils told him, *I never saw anyone like Miss Fraser. She believes everything we tell her.* He also saw that she was *in no slight degree self-willed, and yet not at all self-confident...and from her want in confidence in herself - from something in her manner which at times approached to affectation, and yet so much was she the reverse of being thoroughly affected that she was in general too open and too natural.* Hugh was sure that *her intellectual faculties were of the first order and that her reasoning mind was alike powerful and acute,* but that *all her pleasures must be of a positive not a negative kind and she cannot indulge in indolence without becoming unhappy.* These characteristics are apparent in her novel. Like Lydia, her heroine was well able to argue philosophical propositions and discuss abstruse Biblical doctrine and was never afraid to speak her mind, while her naivety is evident here and there, especially in the high-flown concluding chapters.

Hugh, although at the time convinced that marriage was not for him, began to fall in love. And Lydia with him, convincing herself that *Hugh was essentially an aristocrat of the aristocracy of genius.* However, nothing in her life so far had prepared her for the relationship that existed in Cromarty between her middle-class friends and the working-class stonemason, so much so that she discussed the situation with her mother's landlord. He assured her, *there was not a lady of the place who might not converse, without remark, as often as she liked and pleased,* with Hugh. But the apparent class difference between them perhaps troubled her more than she would admit, for the heroine of her novel, Miss Legh, although at ease with all classes, mixes socially only with aristocrats.

Lydia's mother, when she realised that her daughter might be falling in love with Hugh, was worried that he was never going to earn enough to keep her in suitable comfort and forbade them from meeting. However, they eventually persuaded her in November 1833 to agree to an engagement, even though marriage would be a long way off. And it was a long engagement. Hugh was offered a job in the new Commercial Bank in Cromarty, but this entailed a fairly lengthy separation as he went south to Edinburgh to train as an accountant.

Her almost daily letters to him reveal not only the depth of her feelings for him but also her interest in religion, in science and also in public works for the benefit of the community, an interest which was to last all her life, for she left some money to improve the drainage system in part of Inverness. This interest in what the Reverend Thomas Chalmers called 'the Godly community' was to become one of the major themes in her novel.

Even after Hugh returned to Cromarty, there were several more years before they were married, during which Lydia continued to teach. She also was able to visit relations and get to know many of the most influential ministers of the north, including the charismatic Dr John Macdonald, called in his biography *The Apostle of the North*, who had a particular vocation for evangelism. Thus she was able to write knowledgably about all aspects of ministry. Also with Hugh's encouragement she began to write herself, in a modest way, *for the annuals*.

They married on 7 January 1837, possibly her twenty-fifth birthday, and set up a home next door to Hugh's mother in Miller House, a substantial establishment built, but never lived in, by Hugh's skipper father and now housing the Hugh Miller Museum owned by the National Trust for Scotland. This was perhaps the happiest time in Lydia's life. Never particularly domesticated, she could call on her mother and mother-in-law for advice when wanted. They had many friends. Hugh was trying to make a name for himself, and some additional income, as a writer, and his book, *Scenes and Legends of the North of Scotland*, had been a success. Their first adored child, Elizabeth Logan, was born in November of that year.

This happiness was, however, to be short-lived. 'Little Eliza' died in August 1939, a devastating and defining moment in their lives. At the same time, the Church of Scotland entered a crisis in which they were both to become deeply involved and which was not only to alter the religious landscape of Scotland but also to change their own lives forever.

The national church in Scotland had at times in its history come into conflict with authority, both ecclesiastical and political, as in the Reformation of 1560, the Glorious Revolution of 1690 and the Secession Church of the 18th century. The ultimate split in the established Church of Scotland came after a ten year conflict in 1843 and was to be known as the Disruption, when the Free Church of Scotland was established. The crux of the matter was the Patronage Act of 1712 which gave local lairds, the Crown, burgh or university the right as patron to appoint a new minister to a parish regardless of the wishes of that congregation, which the civil courts could enforce. The 'Moderate' party was content to accept this imposition by the state and the landowners. The 'Evangelical' party, however, was not. A new party emerged out of the Evangelicals calling themselves the 'Non-intrusionists'. As their name implied, they were solidly against the intrusion of 'patronised' candidates into parishes against the will of the congregations. The climax came at the General Assembly of the Church of Scotland held in Edinburgh in 1843, when out of the 1,195 clergymen in the Church of Scotland, 454 (38.1 per cent) resigned their parishes and on the same day entered the Free Church of Scotland, with The Reverend Dr Thomas Chalmers elected as their first Moderator. The Disruption, as Chalmers saw it, was not another secession. It was, he believed, a tragic rupture between the true Church of Scotland and the British State. It was also both an astonishing act of faith and an enormous logistical undertaking. It required a huge financial commitment to provide some 750 new Free Church congregations each with a church, minister, manse and parish school.

For Lydia, as for all the Evangelical Non-intrusionists, the Free Church now represented the national establishment. Her novel sets out to preach its gospel of the true Christian commonwealth under the leadership of the Reverend Doctor Thomas Chalmers, who was, perhaps, if not the hero of her book most certainly its inspiration. He was born, the son of a baker, in Anstruther in 1780. He entered St Andrews University at the age of eleven, later became assistant to the Professor of Mathematics in 1823, Professor of Moral Theology in St Andrews, Professor of Divinity at Edinburgh in 1828 and Moderator of the General Assembly in 1832. It was, however, his dedicated development of pastoral care in the true Calvinist sense of self-help, rather than state aid, in his parishes in Kilmany and the Tron, Glasgow, that was to make him beloved; his contribution to the expansion of popular education that was to make him important, while his charismatic preaching made him popular nationwide. At the same time, his leadership of the Evangelical party and the Church Extension Committee made him famous as the inspiration behind the formation the Free Church of Scotland.

Lydia and Hugh had met Chalmers in 1839, before the death of their daughter, in Cromarty where they heard him preach for the first time. Both Hugh and Lydia, partly inspired by their local minister, Alexander Stewart, had been taking a close interest in the development of the conflict in the Church, although they had not become actively involved. But Hugh had long looked up to Chalmers as *the man of largest mind that the Church of Scotland had ever produced.* Lydia too was impressed. He paid them a forenoon call, and, like Hugh, she was *struck with the goodness, the large humanity, which only a near interview in private made one fully sensible of.* In her novel, Miss Legh meets him socially and notices that, *simplicity pervaded every movement, and even communicated itself... to the very dress which he wore...the folds of his neckcloth, and the very tie upon it, without an indication of eccentricity told of a toilet devoid of concentration...But there was a charm in this simplicity quite beyond the reach of imitation.* Miss Legh was struck too by his *remarkable beauty...as well as the size of his head.* Subconsciously, or perhaps consciously, Lydia could be describing her own husband.

When, in Parliament in May of that year, Lord Brougham openly declared that the opinion of parishioners regarding the choice of minister had always been a mere formality, *comparable to the actions of the champion's horse at the coronation ceremony*, Hugh felt he could not remain silent. Following a sleepless night, he *sat down to state my views to the people* in the form of an open letter addressed to Lord Brougham. The result was a masterpiece of reasoned language and flowing argument which conveyed the indignation, pain and outrage Hugh felt on behalf of his Church. The repercussions were unexpected and of huge significance. Hugh was invited to become editor of the proposed new Evangelical newspaper, **The Witness**. This would involve a move to Edinburgh, a much larger salary and a complete change of lifestyle. Both Hugh and Lydia thought long and hard about it. Hugh was the more reluctant, realising that the twice-a-week demands of a national newspaper would take up most of his time and interfere with his passion for geology which he was able to indulge in the spare time afforded him from his bank job in Cromarty. Lydia, who loved Edinburgh, saw the offer as a great opportunity for her husband to fulfil his potential as a writer. The offer was accepted, and Hugh moved to Edinburgh in December.

Lydia joined Hugh in Edinburgh after the birth of their second child, Harriet, in the spring of 1840. They rented a house on the south side of the Meadows and life settled into a busy routine. She helped Hugh where she could by assisting *in the editorial department first with paste and scissors, then with pen, as contributor of reviews of books.* Hugh was delighted after breakfasting with Dr Chalmers; when the great man complimented him on one of *The Witness* critiques, and he had *never felt so proud in his life as saying it was by his wife.*

During the next five years, while Hugh built *The Witness* into one of the most popular newspapers of the day, Lydia had three more babies, William, Elizabeth (Bessie) and Hugh, and started to publish on her own account, but concealing her identity. We know of seventeen books written by her for children, four of which were published before her novel, and all under the pseudonym of Mrs Harriet Myrtle. These books sold well being very much in the Victorian tradition of moralising and teaching, but the settings and themes are full of variety. The same might be said of her novel.

Living, as she had done, through the Scottish Church's momentous struggle to free itself from patronage and state interference, knowing socially the major characters who were to engineer the devastating break-up of that Church and on fire with zeal for the new doctrine, she was inspired to put the case for the Disruption into fictional form. This was an enormous challenge. Firstly she had to consider the Calvinistic outlook of the Free Church which considered that fiction was *simply a lie and as such intrinsically immoral...Fiction corrupted the reader, it inflamed the passions and made vice interesting.* Therefore her romantic imagination had to be curbed.

But Lydia was not writing first and foremost for a Free Church audience. She was writing to instruct and persuade not only the 'Moderates' in Scotland but also an English readership of the merits of the Disruption. The Church of England, in her opinion, was as much in need of reform where patronage and state control were concerned as the Church of Scotland. In true Calvinistic style, she also believed the Church of England to be in danger of a take-over by Roman Catholicism, not without some cause, for the Oxford Movement, with its belief in a return to the original purity of the apostolic church with its 'high church' ritual, had been the subject of many of Hugh's articles in *The Witness*.

Her orphaned heroine, the eighteen year-old Jane Hamilton Legh, is half English, in that her late father and mentor, Sir Arthur, was a baron and Member of Parliament with an English estate and Whig tendencies. Though a religious man, he had taught his daughter her duty towards his tenants on the basis of ethics rather than religion. He had, in fact, created out of his estate Chesterlee a veritable Garden of Eden which Jane was left to manage. Her mother came from a west Highland estate called Rosemount which Jane too eventually inherits. Thus her worldly and her spiritual interests lay on both sides of the Border. This enabled Lydia to comment, and comment she does, on Dr Chalmers' 'Godly commonwealth' which consisted of an ideal religion matched by an ideal political system both for Scotland and for England.

But Miss Legh is more than a mouthpiece for her creator's preaching zeal and moral outlook. Clever and beautiful, she is also curious, didactic and formidably intelligent, fortunately saved by an endearing sense of humour and an ability to laugh. Lydia herself shines through the character of Miss Legh, her opinions, her outlook on life, her appreciation of beauty and her passionate belief in the Free Church principles.

The main plot is simply told. The orphaned Miss Legh goes to stay with her uncle in his near bankrupt Ross-shire estate where she meets other landowners and learns about the controversy over patronage in the Church. She then goes to stay with well-to-do cousins in Edinburgh and there meets and marries the older General Maitland, widowed father of a beautiful daughter whom Jane befriends. The General is a devout non-Intrusionist. He introduces her to the main personalities of the Disruption, including Dr Chalmers. Jane, in turn, introduces her new husband to her English estate of Chesterlee where they celebrate the birth of Arthur, their son and heir. Here Jane finds that the local Church of England parson is a Roman Catholic in disguise and has decimated the congregation. She realises that the Church of England is in danger not only of state control but also of a return to Catholicism. Meanwhile the General inherits an earldom, and Jane her uncle's Highland estate. They inaugurate in the Highlands and in England, Chalmers' ideal of a Godly commonwealth.

There are several subplots that follow the fortunes of Jane's young servant May Morrison, a handful of Highlanders, and the lives of various ministers and crofters. Each character is skilfully drawn to reflect the behaviour and opinions of the day. The reader is introduced to the aristocracy and landed gentry, mostly Moderates, such as Miss Legh's blasé uncle and her young mad-cap cousin who are unwilling to part with past privileges. The Edinburgh set includes fashionable but kindly young people and the somewhat holier-than-thou General Maitland himself. Among the Highland ministers, we meet the saintly Dr Blair and his worthy ordained son, both sharply contrasted with the degenerate Reverend George Macdonald and his crass unworthy offspring who is intruded into Dr Blair's parish against the will of the congregation, thus causing a riot. At the other end of society, the reader becomes involved with the actions and opinions of a Highland catechist of rustic nobility, and some crofters evicted from their glens by landowners to make room for sheep, including the fiery youth, Kenneth Ore, whose description suggests he is partly modelled on Lydia's 'stalker' father, with whom May falls in love. They and their counterpart English tenants are all depicted with a loving, if over-idealistic, pen.

As Lydia makes clear in her own Preface to the novel, she is describing people, scenes and incidents of which she had personal knowledge, and she excels in her descriptive scenes and dialogue. With the authority of experience, she is equally at home in a Highland croft and at an Edinburgh dinner party. Skilfully she introduces the reader to the Court of Session, takes him up a Ross-shire mountain shrouded in mist or into an English summer garden. She compares a homely Highland manse with one that has been turned by its unworthy occupant into a filthy hovel. Her crowd scenes are convincingly handled, especially the Glenmore riot which she may well have based on a similar uprising in the parish of Resolis near Cromarty. Occasionally, in her enthusiasm, she over-indulges in sentiment, as in her description of Arthur, infant son of Jane, now Countess of Lentraethen, in his *mother-of-pearl cradle shaped like a nautilus* or in her triumphal return to the Highlands *robed in white, with a white crape* [sic] *bonnet wreathed with roses entwined with heather* as the new owner of the Rosemount estate.

The final added chapter entitled *A Few Thoughts on Chalmers' Burial-Place* is a clue to the inspiration behind the novel. It consists of a paean of praise to the founder of the Free Church. She was not alone in her admiration. Thomas Chalmers died aged 67, worn out, on 30 May 1847. After an impressive funeral service in St Andrews Free Church in the presence of the Free Church General Assembly and delegations from Free Churches in England and Ireland, 2,000 mourners processed through the city to the Grange Cemetery. The route was lined with 100,000 silent spectators, and, though the weather was gloomy and raw, the surrounding fields were filled with mourners. Hugh was to write in **The Witness**, *Never before in the memory of man did Scotland witness such a funeral...it was the dust of a Presbyterian clergyman that the coffin contained and yet they were burying him amid the tears of a nation, and with more than kingly honour.* Sadly, Hugh's own funeral, nine years later, was to echo that of his friend. Thousands of citizens lined Princes Street and followed his coffin to the same Grange Cemetery. After twenty years of an anxious, overwrought and tireless widowhood, Lydia, too, was to be buried in the Grange Cemetery on 20 March 1876 without the crowds present, perhaps, but surrounded by the love and admiration of those who had cared for her.

We do not know how soon after the Disruption Lydia started to write her novel. Nor do we know whether Hugh knew exactly what she had in mind when, as seems probable, she consulted him about the drafting of some passages. But it seems he had no part in the final text. Only one, anonymous, review is known, which appeared in **The Witness** of 1 January 1848. It was probably written by Hugh himself,. It ran to nearly 4,000 words and treated the novel with a proper respect. After apologising for the delay in printing a critique, the writer made the point that *there are cases in which the novel may be the best vehicle for conveying instruction; and we are also persuaded that the subject of this work is to unfold the causes and character of the Disruption, especially to the English mind.* This being the aim of the book, *the conception of the work was not more happy than its execution is successful.* The reviewer made one small criticism, which seems to confirm that he, if it was Hugh, had not seen it in final form before publication. *There is especially at the opening of scenes, a want of artistic arrangement; and now and then a slight formality of style;*

but these are very minor matters, and may, with a little trouble, be corrected in future editions. The rest is glory and congratulation on the author's ability to surprise, and her powers of observation. Others, too, must certainly have thought so for the novel went into a second edition.

The book is important, for what it reveals of Lydia herself, her relationship with her husband, her attitude to religion and her undoubted creative talent. In it, her formidable intelligence and her touching naivety, her strong beliefs and convictions are laid bare before the reader. It is important, too, for what it adds to the cannon of knowledge collected over the years regarding Hugh Miller himself, of his family and professional life, both in Cromarty and in Edinburgh. Many of the theories posited in the novel had been aired in **The Witness**, and probably discussed at length in their private conversations. Its prime importance, however, lies not so much in the story or its telling as in the theme. Historically, it accurately reflects a first-hand knowledge of the characters, outlook and events that were to have such overwhelming repercussions for Scotland. Moreover, it was to be the first and only time, as far as is known, that the Disruption and formation of the Free Church were to be the central themes in a work of fiction. Although its literary quality could have been improved had Lydia taken time to rework some of its passages, its zeal is touching and its 'truth' persuades the reader to turn the page. Whatever its flaws, **Passages in the Life of an English Heiress** is a revealing and educative read fully deserving its re-publication for the light it sheds on a period of Scottish history which is still a matter of debate.

Lydia might well have written more and better-crafted adult novels had Hugh not taken his own life in December 1856, thus leaving her to support and educate his four children and to make herself responsible for the posthumous publication of his daunting backlog of works. Hugh's subsequent fame depended to a large extent on this unselfish task. It was an enormous undertaking which tested her knowledge of geology and her intelligence to the limit and found her equal to the task. But it meant that she never achieved her own place in the ranks of well known Victorian female writers. When Lydia's great-great-grand daughter, Marian McKenzie Johnston (who died in October 2009) embarked on her research into the family background, the results of which I was able to use in my biography of Lydia, she was given by the National Library of Scotland a photocopy of the somewhat tattered copy of the novel in their possession (believed to be one of the only two copies surviving, the other being in the British Library). Marian's husband, Henry, has obtained the Library's permission to have the text of the novel reprinted for charitable use. As a memorial to his wife, he has reproduced the text from this photocopy, not attempting to make a facsimile but retaining the spelling, punctuation, italics and capitalisation as in the original, and has met all the cost of printing. It will now be sold in Cromarty and the proceeds given to the charity **The Friends of Hugh Miller**, which has as its objects *to advance the education of the public concerning the name and work of Hugh Miller in the fields of Scottish science and literature, and to develop increased public interest in Scotland's heritage by supporting the Hugh Miller Museum and Birthplace Cottage in Cromarty*, which are owned and run by the National Trust for Scotland. Henry and I both feel strongly that the name of Hugh Miller should embrace that of his wife who herself did so much, particularly in her widowhood, to make sure that it was never forgotten. I am glad, at Henry's request, to have been given the opportunity to provide this introduction to explain the background to the theme of the novel and Lydia's purpose in writing it.

Elizabeth Sutherland. October 2010

PASSAGES

IN THE

LIFE OF AN ENGLISH HEIRESS;

OR

RECOLLECTIONS

OF

DISRUPTION TIMES IN SCOTLAND

LONDON
SIMPKIN, MARSHALL, AND CO.,
STATIONERS' COURT
MDCCCXLVII

PREFACE

A few words are necessary in explanation of the following pages. If they have any value, it is as a faithful record of personal experience. In the earlier chapters I have not introduced a character which I had not familiarly known, and scarce an incident which did not occur in real life. But although these characters, as living realities, are in so far indentified with their several parties, it by no means follows that they are so with the events narrated in the concluding chapters. Those events were of public interest – and it is only names in connection with them, conspicuous enough to have become the property of the historian, with which a writer of the present day has any right to meddle. To drag forward, even under a fictitious disguise, those who were concealed behind the scenes, would savour of private scandal, and be at once indelicate and improper.

But, while avowing that I hold the individuals whose characters I have chosen to delineate, to be true representatives of at least large sections of their parties, I grant it possible that the experience of others may have differed from mine. The Moderate and Evangelical parties in the Church of Scotland, as it formerly was, might be not inaptly compared to the sides of a parallel ruler drawn asunder and placed upright. The one side ascends much higher – the other descends greatly lower than the other, while there is a middle, though not very considerable region, where a real parallelism exists. Thus it is no wonder that one whose lot may have fallen in this latter sphere, should doubt the fidelity of pictures whose originals he has not seen. Is it just, then, it may be asked, to draw representations from two extremes? The reason is this – that only in connection with their peculiar parties could these extremes possibly have a being. Moderate opinions cannot produce the piety, zeal, and unbending principle of the higher section of Evangelicals; nor in connection with the latter could the lower section of Moderates be suffered to exist. The equalization in the middle, is but the effect of that balance of human character which Nature always produces; the extremes are the results of principles fully acted out.

I have ventured to introduce to the reader a class of humble individuals with whom he has probably heretofore had but little acquaintance. They are the relics of a primitive age – extinct everywhere except in those parts where a different language has preserved the manners and customs of the olden time from the inroads of change. Marked by peculiarities, assuming in some districts, it has been said, a less agreeable aspect than in others, I am far from advocating their support or encouragement when the necessities of the past have ceased to exist. Certain it is, however, that they have lent most material aid in evangelising the Highlands of Scotland; and that were any one intimately acquainted with them to be asked where he could point to the noblest specimen of a Christian peasant, he would, in all probability, select one of the "the men" of the northern Highlands.

In conclusion, I would fain ask the indulgence of the Christian reader. I have not attempted the high task of giving a full-length portraiture of a perfect or ideal Christian. With regard to the principal character in this book, the light of divine truth is but making gradual way into her mind from the beginning to the conclusion of the passages in her life. And as the Christians most frequently met with in the world are those who have not already attained, but are pressing onwards to perfection, I do not feel that I have erred in endeavouring to portray the life of one under divine teaching as having, in common with that of others, some portion of light and shadow; or, in other words, in drawing from a living, though defective model, instead of from a piece of ideal sculpture. But if, on the other hand, I have misrepresented principles, or contributed to bring upon them any measure of contempt, may God forgive the wrong! I can be consoled only in believing that these principles, which are as immutable as the eternal laws of God, must outlive alike the mistaken efforts of friends, and the misrepresentations of enemies.

CHAPTER I

"May it not be that these noble spirits, to whom their very superiority may be the commencement of a revelation, perceive dimly that in the midst of their amiable virtues, virtue itself is wanting?"
Vinet's Discourses

JANE HAMILTON LEGH was the lineal and only remaining descendant of an ancient race of Barons, who, since the Conquest, had resided in one of the midland counties of England. She thus inherited their property, while the title went in the male line to a distant branch of the family. Her father, Sir Arthur, had been highly esteemed throughout a wide district of country, as an accomplished gentleman, and an upright magistrate. He had once sat in Parliament as the representative of his county; but being a man of peculiar political opinions, and an inflexible conscience, he found no party with whom to co-operate heartily. He therefore took the first opportunity of resigning. As a professed advocate of the rights of the people, he was attached to the Whig interest; yet, he was wont to say that he would like to work out his Whiggism by a wholly different set of means from any he saw in operation; but for which he then perceived no materials in the Legislature. He alleged that the golden age of politics was yet to come; that opinion upon religious, moral, and social rights must be transmuted into principle, before the Legislature, which ought to be founded on these rights, could be anything but precarious. And *the right* he imagined would yet be rendered apparent by a series of providential dispensations, too palpable to be overlooked; and then would a better state of things have its beginning. Nevertheless, he continued to give his interest to the Whigs, not because of his admiration of their government machinery, but because, on the whole, it went on in the right direction.

Had Sir Arthur been in the habit of broaching these notions frequently, he might have been called eccentric. He was content, however, with working them out in the shape of practical good within the limits of his own domains, while he was always ready to explain the principles upon which he acted to those who took the trouble to inquire into them.

Such was the father of Miss Legh, who was spared until her eighteenth year. She had lost her mother at her birth, and Sir Arthur never contracted a second marriage. He became the tutor and friend of his only child, who knew almost no other companion; and, as might be anticipated, the principles upon which he conducted her education partook in some measure of the peculiarities of his political views. Strange as it was, he made the science of ethics the basis of all her acquirements — the centre from which all other knowledge radiated. Two questions he constantly kept in view as the grand problems of life, "What is in itself good?" and "What is the method of producing the greatest amount of practical good in any given circumstances?" He asserted that position in society in no way altered the obligation upon every human being to the pursuit of these grand topics; but in his daughter's position, he considered that obligation much enhanced. "Every intelligent creature for whom you have to think," he often said to her, "and for whom you are therefore in so far responsible, renders the application of your whole energies to this subject the more imperative." This mode of education must be taken in connection with the fact, that Sir Arthur employed no substitute in the management of his extensive property; he was his own overseer — the literal head of his own estate; and it was his most earnest desire that his daughter should walk in his footsteps, for he considered the care and intelligence of a proprietor the natural birthright of all who were dependent on him. "It is the real feudal service you owe to your country for your tenure of her soil; not to discharge it to the utmost of your ability involves you in the deepest guilt." In this manner he would address his future heiress.

With all this, Sir Arthur did not give his daughter a religious education, and herein he greatly erred. Religion was to him a grand and solemn thing, to which he intended to turn all the faculties of her mind when they should have arrived at maturity — a time which appeared to him later than the current opinion would warrant. That period, however, for him, never arrived. He was killed by a fall from his horse, without having made any preparation for the event of his death. Thus it was that the young mind of the heiress, naturally strong and reflective, imbibed a more vigorous tone of thinking than is usual with her sex; her sensibilities, however, were cast in a more delicate mould than those of many who threw a sneer at her pursuits as being of too masculine a character. The accidents of fortune conspired with those of nature in her behalf. It happened that a Scotsman of the name of Hamilton, connected with the family of Legh by some marriage tie, had been compelled, through misfortune, when beginning life, to throw himself on the bounty of Sir Arthur, then just come of age. The young baronet had freely lent him his protection and assistance, and finally had procured for him a cadetship. Hamilton, on his part, out of gratitude to his early patron, executed a will, whereby, in case of his decease without heirs of his own, he vested all his property, "whatever that might be, in Sir Arthur and his successors, upon condition that they should connect the name of Hamilton with their own, and invest part or the whole of his money in an estate in Scotland." He never contracted any tie, and died in the rank of General, shortly before Sir Arthur, leaving a large fortune.

Miss Legh had still nearer ties than this to the Scottish soil, her mother having been the sister of a northern baronet, whose estate lay in the western part of Ross-shire. Had Sir Arthur looked forward to his death as a probable event, he would have made more special inquiries than he had ever done respecting the character of his daughter's maternal uncle, whom he knew only as a man of polished manners and fine taste, who paid him a visit at distant intervals upon his way to or from the Continent. And the result would have been, an express provision against the chance that the child over whom he had so tenderly watched should be in any measure thrown upon that uncle's protection. As matters stood, Sir Duncan Ross lost no time, after his brother in-law's death, in going, with all the kindness of which his nature was capable, to bring his young and beautiful niece to his Highland mansion-house, whither he was then on the eve of betaking himself.

Sir Duncan's nature, indeed, had been originally frank, kind, and hospitable, and still continued so in so far as it was not corrupted by the life of a thorough *roué*, spent for the greater part amid the most dissipated scenes of Paris and Rome. He was a man upwards of fifty, a bachelor, and still handsome; consequently a desirable *parti* in the eyes of those mamas who had daughters to settle; indeed, so pleasing were his manners, and so insinuating his gallantry, when he chose, that in not a few instances he might have been regarded in the same light by the young ladies themselves. He now began, however, to be looked upon as hopeless, except by those who had unlimited confidence in their own abilities at a *coup-de-main*. Indistinct rumours there had been of broken fortune; but as it was known that he could always command some thousands by the sale of a few of his splendid pictures, it was not doubted but that, keeping up his expensive habits, he would be able to make the day and the journey alike. The grand object of his life, next to the indulgence of his pleasures, had been the accumulation of the finest specimens of art, with which his mansion in London was nearly glutted. These he had himself collected on the Continent, with a discrimination not always exercised by British travellers. His northern seat of Rosemount where he was now residing, was the receptacle of what he considered as only his second-rate foreign pictures; but it contained some choice specimens of the English masters. Every inch of wall, from the staircase, the public rooms, and the dancing-saloon, to the smallest dressing-room, was covered with paintings, a surprising number of which were of the most superior character.

Thus furnished, and having a fine library, and noble grounds, Rosemount would have had many attractions for Miss Legh, if it had possessed that first and greatest — congenial society. Sir Duncan, it is true, treated her with the most profound respect, and with more consideration for her feelings than he was at all in the habit of manifesting for those of others. Still, her mind being full of that tender and ennobling friendship which she had enjoyed with her departed father, she could not help feeling that her new guardian was in thought and sentiment all *outside*; while his admiration for her beauty, to him the most meritorious of all qualities, she did not know whether to consider as most ludicrous or disagreeable. There was no other resident in the house for the time being, except a young mad-cap Highland cousin, a relation of the —s of —, and possessed of a large share of those personal advantages for which his family was always remarkable.

One afternoon, several months after Miss Legh's settlement at Rosemount, and when the early spring had begun to give a kind of coquetting promise of its favourable intentions, the heiress, after passing the day in solitude, stood at the window of the small drawing-room which had been allotted for her use, looking at the landscape outside, under the effect of the still early sunset. The fine chain of hills which stretched away to the westward were bathed near their summits in a clear purple light, which took its tint more, however, from the cold blue of the sky, than from the beams of the sun. The departing luminary stood like a coronet of gold above one of the loftiest peaks of the range, darting his rays directly down upon it like a glory, and kindling its purple into a glowing bronze. The gloom of evening had already settled down at the bases of the hills; but, below the height on which the mansion stood, there was a small lake, which, with the rising ground beyond it, lay without the shadow, and caught up a faint reflection from the brightness in the western heaven. The leafless twigs of the trees growing on the farther side, and drooping here and there over the edge, seemed drawn as with a pencil against the sky, and were reflected with the same distinctness in the water below. It was a sweet and solitary scene; but its very solitude brought a sense of pain to the heart of the lovely orphan. The hour of sunset was that at which, from her earliest childhood, she had wandered with her father through her own woods of Chesterlee, and visited with him some one or other of their numerous tenantry. It was the time at which Sir Arthur had sought to lay aside from his manner everything that might not have belonged to the tenderest mother, the most devoted friend; and when, in return, he had won all the artless confidence of his child's heart. No wonder, then, that the orphan wept bitterly at the recollection, or that the world appeared to her a dreary solitude, which she wondered how she was ever to pass through. This feeling often pressed heavily on her mind, but, with a courage natural to her, she used all her efforts to subdue it. In society she was successful, for she was aided by the feeling that it was an injustice to others to press her peculiar sorrows upon them; but in her solitary hours the pursuit of literature, or even severer study, failed to banish a sense of desertion and loneliness from her spirits.

  At this moment, however, the sound of her cousin Harry's bounding footsteps on the staircase made her hastily dry her tears; and scarcely had she done so, when the said Harry burst into the room, glowing with exercise and the mountain breeze. "What *are* you moping for here, cousin Jane?" said he. "We have had a glorious day's sport — you should have been with us; it's a shame that women don't fish and shoot as well as men." "Why they do sometimes, Harry," replied Jane. "there was Lady H — wasn't she a capital shot? — but you know tastes differ." "Well, you study politics and meta — what is it? something about physic? Ah, *I* should leave out the first part; — if there isn't a volume of political economy lying on the table! Harriet Martineau?— Pooh! it's a woman's. I dare say you will not be greatly the worse for it after all." "Nor would you, I suspect," said Jane, laughing and putting the book into its place; but did I not hear a carriage drive up?" "You might have heard two. There are two sets of arrivals — the Grants of Granton, and the Frasers of Auchtertyre; so make haste and get dressed for dinner — the ladies are in their rooms. Will you honour me by taking my arm, Miss Hamilton ? Let's see how we look together in that pier-glass;" and the young rattle, marching up the room with his cousin on his arm, surveyed himself rather than her, in a large mirror at the farther end. "I'm a handsome fellow, aint I? even beside you, Jane, which is saying a great deal." Jane looked up in his face and laughed — there was no resisting it. Harry looked down and laughed, and it seemed to strike him as a truth which he had alluded to without properly comprehending it, that his cousin was certainly very handsome. "What a superb head and neck you've got, Jane," said he, looking first at her, and then at her reflection in the mirror; "it reminds one of an Arabian horse; and what a beautiful small foot; and you are rather tall too!" "Come, that will do," said Jane, withdrawing her arm; "I thought you were merely going to admire yourself; I had no expectation of attracting any share of your notice." So saying, and nodding to her cousin, she tripped away to her dressing-room. "A magnificent girl that," said Harry, looking after her; "a spice of mischief in her, too. There's a great family likeness between us," he continued, as he stepped up to the glass and recommenced a survey of his person; "the same *air distingué*" — he drew himself up, and threw back his head; "the same fine chiselling," as uncle would say, "about the nose and mouth; the same open bland forehead" — he put his hair gently back; "the same depth, clearness, and delicate shadowing," as uncle says again, "about the eyes, though of course Jane beats me there. I am to have my regimentals in a week. I shall ride up to — Church on the Sunday after, on purpose to stand in the front gallery. "Good morning, sir," said he, bowing to the glass in conclusion of his soliloquy, "Your *tout ensemble* ought to make you the envy of — of both sexes." So saying, he adjourned to the mirror in his own room.

Jane found the company in the drawing-room to consist of the two lairds, of whose arrival she was apprized, their wives, and two pairs of daughters. Grant of Granton was a cold, proud man, who spoke little, and was not over-well informed, except in the genealogies of the neighbouring families; and Fraser of Auchtertyre resembled him, at least in the latter respect, but he had more of the warmth and hospitality of the genuine Highlander. Both had abundance of that feeling of feudal aristocracy, which the longer continuance of the feudal system has probably kept up among proprietors in the Highlands, especially in those of them who have not travelled or devoted much time to the cultivation of their understandings, though even to such as have enjoyed these advantages something of the ancient feeling still clings. Miss Legh did feel sometimes at a loss to know why a piece of land which was mountainous, should impart a more awful dignity to its possessor than other pieces of land, situated in countries which were rich and level; and now that all the appurtenances to feudal state were departed, she thought the pretension to superiority from such a cause somewhat out of date; but it was an assumption which she had too much real dignity either to dispute or to ridicule. When she entered the drawing-room, she found Auchtertyre engaged in a dispute with her uncle, the subject of which it was easy to divine. "I say, sir," he exclaimed, in a strong Highland accent, and with an aspect which betokened a desire to carry fire and sword into the dwellings of all who might differ from him — "I say, sir, that a gentleman that has the high Gaelic and the English, may stand before the king or the queen, as majesty is of the female gender at the present day." Sir Duncan, whose fault it was rather to despise his brethren of the soil, replied with a sneer, "I am afraid, Auchtertyre, her majesty would be but an indifferent judge of your Gaelic;" and he embraced the diversion occasioned by the entrance of his niece to resume a discussion on a print of one of the Cartoons which was lying on the table. He spoke to Mr. Davidson of Kilblair, a gentleman whose presence we have not yet announced, but who was no unusual guest at Rosemount, where he often stopped to dine on his way to or from the nearest town. "There is one thing very remarkable about these Cartoons, Davidson," said Sir Duncan, "and that is, that although you may imagine yourself well acquainted with them from the prints with which you are familiar, you are entirely deceived; they come upon you with as much novelty, as great originality, as if you had never seen a sketch of one of them in your life."

Auchtertyre. who cared little about the Cartoons, and whose pride had been offended in some degree, sought to console himself by fastening on Miss Legh. "You have never been at Auchtertyre, Miss Legh," said he; "it is worth your while to come, though it should only be to hear my piper; he has the finest collection of pibrochs in all the north country. We will keep an empty seat for you in the carriage the next time we are coming this way; and I hope you will stay some time with us." Thank you," replied Jane, "I shall be very happy to go to Auchtertyre, but I prefer riding. I never go in a carriage when I can help it" "No, indeed!" said Auchtertyre, "you are not of the same taste as old Lovat, then, who never found himself happy out of his carriage. He lived in it, Miss Legh; he ate, and drank, and slept in it. He often caused his people to drive him through the night, as he thought he slept better that way than any other; and he would not do either without his two footmen and his *gillie cas fleuch*; that is, a man that in that day used to run beside the carriage every step." Jane could not help smiling, "An instructive precedent," she replied, "without doubt." "Not just that either," said Auchtertyre, a little put out; "but I'll tell you an instructive story about *him*. You see he was a Catholic; Lovat is a Catholic family. Well, at the time of Lent, he thought he would send a present to a great Catholic lord in England, and he shipped to London twenty as fine salmon as ever were fished. Beautiful salmon they were! — every one with a stone in his mouth. What happened to the shipmaster, but he lost the address! The poor fellow didn't know what to do, for he knew Lovat's temper; and that none would dare to tell him of the accident; but being an honest man, he thought he would sell the fish at the London market, and try, when he had the money in his hand, if he couldn't get a word of Lovat himself. Well, the fish brought a pretty sum, you may be sure; but when the shipmaster came home, not a soul could he find that would speak a word for him to Lovat. At last, he bribed a servant to let him in at a little back gate into a road behind the house, where Lovat used to walk every day at a certain time when he was at home; and there he waited, pretty anxious you may be sure, till he saw Lovat coming, and went up and made his bow to him. Lovat wondered to see him there, and asked immediately if the salmon were all safe. His brow grew red, and he scowled terribly as the man told what happened the best way he could; but when the poor fellow, making his bow again, said, 'Here, Lovat — here's your twenty guineas for you,' he took the money in his hand, looked at it, and then lifting his arm he threw it at the man's head as hard as he could draw, saying, 'Keep the twenty guineas to yourself, you rascal, and — ' I needn't say it all. Miss Legh." "Was not that the person," asked Jane, a strong and unpleasant association crossing her mind, "who presented Donaldson to the parish of Aird?" A shade of displeasure passed across the face of Auchtertyre as he heard the great Highland chieftain designated as the *person*; but he replied, "The very same." "That *is* instructive," said Miss Legh, gravely.

The conversation was here interrupted by the sound of the dinner gong; and Mr. Davidson of Kilblair came forward and offered his arm to Miss Legh. This Mr. Davidson was, perhaps, the most remarkable man of the party. Of south country origin and unknown descent, he had come to that part of the country with money sufficient to make him one of the largest proprietors in the county, though the manner in which his money had been acquired, remained for ever a mystery. Of a restless enterprising disposition, continually employed in some scheme of business activity, whether for good or evil, he contrived by his monied and landed interest, and by taking the lead in county matters, for which his energy and a certain kind of shrewd business sagacity well fitted him, to place himself at the head of the country gentlemen of the district, though without that descent which they of all things most highly valued. He had the merit of forwarding local improvements, thereby giving himself a real value in the county; but his temper was tyrannical, and his impatience of contradiction so great, that he was constantly involving himself in law-suits which ate away a great part of his property. Above all, by engaging at different times in transactions of a dubious character in a moral point of view, and likewise by meddling with the affairs of the Church courts, he had involved himself in hostilities with the greater number of the clergy in his district. He never wanted a hobby; and at the period of his present visit to Rosemount, the *Church question* as called in Scotland, or the controversy between reforming and anti-reforming clergy, was the theme continually uppermost in his mind. "You go to hear that fellow Blair, Miss Legh?" said he, as he led the young lady to the dining-room. "Who do you mean?" asked Jane, with some surprise. "Not the venerable Dr. Blair?" "Yes, the venerable Dr. Blair!" said Mr. Davidson, mimicking as nearly as politeness would let him the manner of his fair companion, "You're taken in, Miss Legh — you're humbugged. They're a humbugging lazy set these clergy — the whole of them, between you and me; though the Moderates have something more of gentlemen about them; as for the others, they're gone mad." "Is Donaldson much of a gentleman?" asked Jane with simplicity. "No, no; not he; but the most of them, though by — there's some of them beginning to be infected with the plague spreading from the other side." "My dear sir," said Sir Duncan, "suppress all topics of discussion till after dinner; there's a haunch of particularly fine venison coming; pray, don't spoil your appetite."

"I always talk when I eat," said Davidson testily; "I hate your American fashion."

"Oh yes," joined in the young ladies, who had all been carrying on a flirtation with the young soldier to be, "it's much better to be social." Granton professed he didn't understand the Church question, and never meddled with it; and the married ladies declared he "was quite right."

"I don't know much about those parties," said Jane, "and should be glad to have information. In what do the superior gentlemanly pretensions of the Moderates consist?"

"Why," said Davidson, "they don't meddle with what does not concern them. They can sit quietly while their superiors stow away a couple of bottles or so (though I hold that to be too much for them, as the times go at any rate); they can sing a good song, take a hand at whist, and, in short, be friendly and social in their way: and then, you know, it is natural that, after all that, they should tip the wink at certain gentlemanly follies." He winked at Sir Duncan as he spoke.

"You have enlightened me on the subject of Moderatism, and on that of *patronage* too" said Jane, her eye giving out an indignant flash, as it was wont when she detected anything radically false and hollow, but giving no other sign of emotion. "But you will pardon me," continued she, "if I think that those accomplishments you have mentioned are not the chief ends of a clergyman's life"

Davidson saw that he had gone too far. He had been sure of the rest of his company, and had counted upon Miss Legh's opinions as being very unformed, and upon her prejudices as an Episcopalian in favour of Church and State, against popular influence. Although a man of too much temper to be always politic, he would not have given the view he had of Moderatism, and its recommendations to a certain portion of the aristocracy, in any large and mixed company, because he knew that the plague he had spoken of as spreading from the other side rendered it obnoxious to the general taste, and that in this way he would but strengthen the hands of the enemy. He was, on the present occasion, far from wishing to disgust his young friend whom he knew to be possessed of money to be invested in Scotch property, which, it was extremely probable, she would purchase in that part of the country, more than one estate in the neighbourhood, being then in the market.

" My dear Miss Legh," he replied, "I do consider the investment of a small part of the public money in the clerical body a very good thing. I dare say I have said more than 1 meant — I often do. It is, upon the whole, a provision for a very respectable body of men, who sometimes even have the honour of having the relations of good families amongst them, if nothing better occurs, and who are paid for being moral, and I think ought to be kept so, in order to set a good example to the lower orders." "Ay, the rascal multitude," began Sir Duncan.

"I have not been accustomed to speak of the *rascal multitude*," interrupted Jane, with a good-humoured smile, for she saw that it was in vain to feel strongly, since there was an utter want of all common ground on which to argue between herself and her friends. "Who" continued Sir Duncan, "have left us since the Reformation, as it is called, scarce a decent place of Christian worship? Churches are certainly ornamental things, when architectural taste is displayed in them. We might have boasted of some as fine as any in Europe, if that same rascal multitude had not made them places to play bo-peep in. I never can go to church with comfort, except on the Continent — I never attempt it here, the whole thing is so deplorably bald."

Sir Duncan was half a Catholic on the Continent, and nothing at home.

"It seems to me," said Miss Legh, "that the Scotch multitude have suffered more abuse for the breaking down of those stone walls than the French have done for all the horrors of their Revolution. And, after all, they were guilty of no more than you, Sir Duncan, would be if, seeing a snake creeping out of that piece of Dresden china, you threw a stone to kill him, without minding whether you broke the china or not. You might possibly reflect afterwards that the snake might have been killed and the china preserved; but surely you would excuse your haste, as very natural. Now, if as the moral and religious feelings of the Scotch came to be awakened, they *did* connect the existence of Popish places of worship with Popery itself, I do not see that the mistake was very fatal. Nay, perhaps they might even be justified in a philosophical point of view; for association has unquestionably a powerful effect in leading the mind back to its old track. As for the Reformers themselves, I think no candid reader of history can consider them as the instigators of those deeds; the utmost with which they can fairly be charged, is some degree of indifference regarding them. It is the fault of great minds, in the pursuit of great objects, to view other things which are good in themselves as comparatively trifling. This perhaps is a necessary consequence of human weakness. The object of the Scottish Reformers was to build a great temple to the Supreme Being in a nation whose morality should be pure and stable, as being founded on a religion which was so."

Miss Legh spoke with great animation. She remembered having conversed on this subject more than once with her father, and she almost fancied herself for the time engaged with him in one of those discussions which she had so much loved. The illusion, however, was soon dispelled.

"My very beautiful niece," said Sir Duncan, assuming an air of mock gravity, "with the greatest respect for the animation which lights up your countenance to so much advantage, allow me to say that I consider *morality* a disagreeable sort of word. I think it ought to be banished from polite society. What say you, Davidson?" Mr. Davidson thought it was a very good *thing* in its own place. "Pshaw!" said Sir Duncan, "I don't mean the thing, but the word."

The conversation which had been carried on with great volubility by the other two parties separately, viz, the married people and the young people, here became in some measure general. They had all caught Sir Duncan's last proposition. "Oh, yes," said one of the Misses Grant, "I think it so stiff and formal." "Quite old-maidenish," said one of the Misses Fraser. "I think," said Mrs. Grant, who was considered a *sensible* woman, "that young ladies should not meddle with things which it is not to be expected they can understand." "Unless they want to be called *blue stockings*" said Mrs. Fraser, a little spitefully. "Ah! the old times were the best," said Auchtertyre, "when the ladies *span* their stockings, instead of *dyeing* them," and he laughed heartily at his own joke.

"Quite right," said Jane, rather mischievously misconstruing the old gentleman's meaning, in order to have a hit at his prejudices,

> 'When Adam delv'd and Eve span,
> Where was then the gentleman?'

You know the old English distich, Mr Fraser?"

Auchtertyre was going to enter into a disquisition, illustrated by sundry examples to show that they were *bona fide* ladies who did their maids the honour of superintending their spinning operations and taking part in the same, when Davidson, who stuck like a bur to any subject which had possession of his heart, — or *spleen*, as the old synonyme was, — for the time, renewed his attack on Miss Legh, as he had begun it, with, "I say, Miss Legh, you are humbugged; that old fellow, Blair, is humbugging you. You could not have those ideas otherwise." "I assure you", replied Jane, "that my ideas are but the result of the principles I have been accustomed to entertain and of such observation in this country as I have had. Dr Blair I am but little acquainted with. I do not pretend to be well informed on the subject of religious controversy as connected with your Church; but I intend, if possible, to make myself so."

"Well, well; but my dear Miss Legh," resumed Davidson, "you do not see the secret springs of the thing, I mean of this movement, as I do. There is as much intriguing carried on in every one of those presbyteries and synods throughout the country, for the purpose of getting votes, strengthening parties, and carrying certain measures, as there is in Parliament itself, any day. The whole drift of the highfliers is to gain popularity — to get unlimited influence over the minds of the simple people. There now, the spokesman of your *unco gude* bodies goes to Dr. Blair, and says. 'Oh, Doctor, we're in a great defeecoolty. Who do *ye* think would be suitable for *such* a parish? We're in a strait between Mr. *so-and-so* and Mr. *so-and-so*" And the venerable Doctor puts in a word against the one and against the other, and then he says, I'll tell you, Saunder's just the man for you. There's a grand preacher from the south yonder;' — and so he goes on humbugging the man, while all the time the old boy has a sly eye to the Church court, or to some measure that he wants to get carried."

"Why," said Jane, laughing, as everybody else did, at the drawl with which this was spoken, "I really think there must be some slight caricature in all that, for the peasantry here are so shrewd and well-informed in religion, that I think they would soon perceive any sinister motive where it existed — though I don't know that the recommendation of a man who preaches the doctrines to which the people are attached, and who would in all probability concur in measures for their benefit, can exactly be called *sinister*. At the same time, if intrigue is ever employed for the accomplishment of any end, it cannot surely be too strongly condemned. As to the general influence of the clergy, it seems to me that there is a natural influence possessed by men of exemplary worth, and a proper deference which is paid to their judgment. I observe, for example, that Dr. Blair has it, while Donaldson totally wants it."

"The short and the long of it is, Miss Legh," said Davidson, losing patience, "that the Church may go to the — bottom, before I lose my patronages. Did I not pay £400 only two years ago for Cambusnethan and Kilrathy? It is downright swindling to speak of it." "Nothing else," responded Sir Duncan. "Heyday!" said Jane, with a small affectation of simplicity, "I am sure you, Mr. Davidson, would spend a great deal more in a law-suit only in trying to prove that somebody had called you something; and you dear uncle, would you not give as much for fine pictures in a single day? And why not generously concede as much to popular rights, if they are such?"

No one else, who knew Davidson's violent temper, would have ventured so far; but the young English heiress had been bred to a feeling of her own independence.

Davidson's face grew alarmingly black; and the veins in his forehead swelled. He struck the table with his clenched fist, and wished that a very fearful consequence might ensue to himself if he acceded to anything of the kind. "I tell you," continued he, "there's not a boor of them shall get living of mine without pledging himself against this *non-intrusion* humbug. We are not so helpless as you think us. We can make compacts as well as our enemies; and there are excellent fellows among the Moderates," continued he, sobering a little, "who are doing all in their power to help us. It were odd if they didn't, since we gave them their livings and have got those of their sons in our hands. What between our power and their art, we must gain over the young ones by shoals. Yet it is inconceivable how obstinate the scoundrels are, as my friend Dr. Bremner tells me. Ah! he should have been a cardinal, at least, that man. It cannot continue; this cursed majority must be swamped at last."

"In how many minds," thought Jane, "does an attempt at reason just resolve itself into passion!" but she said nothing; she could not stoop to reply to such an outbreak. Bowing to Mrs. Grant, therefore, she rose to leave the gentlemen; but she felt that she owed something to Mr. Davidson for having occasioned him such a loss of temper. She went to him with her hand outstretched, and with a smile of such sweetness as few could resist.

"We shall not see you in the drawing-room, I suppose, Mr. Davidson?" said she; "but you will, I hope, soon return and we shall talk over the subject by ourselves. You know I may probably have a stake in the question of patronage as well as you." So saying, she shook him kindly by the hand, while he bowed with that respect which so much beauty, wealth, and talent could not fail to inspire.

"I don't care for that Miss Hamilton Legh," said Miss Matilda Grant to her mama, as they drove away directly after tea. "She makes one feel so *inferior*; and I don't know why *we* should feel inferior to anybody. Besides, the gentlemen always seem as if they thought no one else worth paying attention to when she is present."

" She is very rich, my dear," said her mother laconically, and the conversation dropped.

When Miss Legh retired to her chamber on that evening, she felt sad and dejected; and when her heart spoke to her in solitude, as it was often wont, that communing drew tears to her eyes. "*Morality* a. word unfit for polite society! — a very good sort of thing in its way! Ah," thought she, "the pursuit of good has been a reality with me. I once thought it was so with all the world. But is not a *reality* the object of our cares, thoughts, schemes? Is it not what most readily excites our hopes and fears? What is my uncle's reality? A fine picture — very good in its way. But will the immortal spirit be satisfied for ever — *for ever* with *painted canvass*? And poor Davidson's reality? — power, pride, revenge. And were it to go by a majority of votes would *my* reality — what I have been taught to consider such — be real after all? Is it indeed then so? Is this great science of the greatest possible moral good, *the* reality — *the chief end of existence*? — or is it, after all, but an amiable delusion?" While her mind was thus occupied, she almost unconsciously rung her dressing-room bell. The little Highland girl whom it summoned, did not loiter in replying to her mistress' summons. She had now been an inmate of the mansion-house for some months, and from her gentleness and intelligence, had in a great measure superseded the smart English woman whom Miss Legh had brought to Scotland as her waiting maid; but this advancement in her lady's favour, was the cause of bringing on her considerable persecution below stairs, which the poor child felt severely, as it was the first unkindness she had ever known. Her greatest happiness, therefore, consisted in being as much with her mistress as possible.

"Did you want to undress, ma'am?" said she, going up to the couch on which Jane lay reclining, with her face half buried in a pillow, and in the rich tresses of her own hair. "Yes, May," said her young mistress, half rising, and laying her hand upon the chestnut locks of the girl, whose colour heightened at this silent expression of kindness. "May, *What is the chief end of man's being?*"

She had unconsciously framed her question in words with which the child was very familiar.

"*To glorify God, and to enjoy him for ever,*" she replied, gazing with her eloquent hazel eyes into her mistress' face. "Where have you learnt that? who taught you that?" said Jane quickly, and looking intently upon the girl. "I learnt it in the Shorter Catechism — I used to say it to my grandfather," replied little May Morrison. "Fetch me that book, my child. I wish to see it," said Jane, and she threw herself again on the sofa "You may go now," said she, after May had brought her the book, "I shall undress by myself." Before Miss Legh retired to rest, she perused and re-perused the questions and answers in the worn and half dirty pamphlet which had been brought her by the girl; that from which poor May had learnt from her earliest years. "Those are extraordinary views," said the young lady, as she finished reading the pages for the third time, "and extraordinary peasantry they are who hold them. They do love good. I feel that they pursue it more earnestly and constantly than I do myself. It is with me as writing on a slate, which may be effaced; which is always ready to be effaced. It is engraven somehow on these people's hearts."

When her knee was bent that evening in prayer, she felt an awe come over her which she had never experienced in the same duty before.

It had flashed across her mind like a sudden light, as the girl answered her question as she did, that GOD himself was the *great truth* of all existence. This idea, not yet clear to her — like the sun just rising above the horizon, ere it has banished the shades of night from the landscape — was distant, but beautiful and full of promise. God as *the whole* of existence was a sublime thought! It did not banish that *summum bonum* of moral good, which she had found so subtle and evasive; it gave to it life, completeness, permanence. Her whole mind was full of it. She felt as if she had seen for the first time *the first principle of living*.

CHAPTER II

*"Wolves shall succeed for teachers — grievous wolves
Who all the sacred mysteries of Heaven
To their own vile advantages shall turn
Of lucre and ambition,"*

MILTON

Nowhere have our country and it inhabitants undergone a greater change, within the last two centuries, than they have done in that part of the Highlands where our sketches open. The *clans of Ross* are singled out as particularly obnoxious, in an act passed so late as the reign of James VI, for the suppression of theft, riot, and oppression. And although there were some remarkable men who preached a pure Gospel in this very district about the middle of the seventeenth century, the mass of the people were yet unenlightened, when in 1678, hordes of Highland savages were brought down on the low countries to persecute and trample down the peasantry there, who were devoting their lives to the cause of religious truth and freedom. But when Christianity was freely preached in simplicity and purity, its effects were singularly marked. The people possessed a large share of those virtues said to be best developed in the semi-barbarous condition — courage, fidelity, and hospitality; and these they retained in no degree impaired by the new element of a pure faith, while their ignorance was exchanged for sound religious intelligence — their ferocity, for a peculiar gentleness and high tone of moral feeling. And here, especially in those parts where a mercenary intercourse with strangers has not corrupted the simple manners of the inhabitants, Reformation principles, and their noble practical fruits, still exist in all their ancient vigour. Nowhere is the power of evangelical *Presbyterianism* to produce high intelligence and morality, even in the most unlettered minds, better exemplified; accordingly, nowhere is attachment to the Presbyterian Church more deeply seated, or the cruel self-interested policy which attempted the religious ruin of Scotland, by introducing the secular and irreligious into the appointment of her pastors, more bitterly felt. Remarkable as the attachment of the Highlander has always been to his country, his regard for his Church is still stronger, and among the peasantry, there are many whose being seems so identified with her welfare, that their solicitude for her prosperity most evidently surpasses what they ever feel for their own. In the following pages, we purpose bringing the reader acquainted with a few individuals of this class; and with this view, we shall introduce him into the humble dwelling of our friend old John Morrison, a few evenings before his decease, which happened several months *previous* to the date of our last chapter.

On the side of a hill, overlooking one of the most extensive valleys of Wester Ross, a full quarter of a mile above the line at which cultivation ceases, there stood, in the year 183—, a small turf cottage, built within the angle of a projecting rock, which served the double purpose of supporting part of the tenement, and of sheltering it from the bleak winds. This little habitation could scarce be distinguished at a short distance from the hill above. It was covered with vegetation a-top; and, both outwardly and in its internal arrangements, was ruder than most of the cottages on the lower grounds. It had but a single apartment, with a wooden partition at one end, which left space enough for a small sleeping place. Its furniture consisted only of a wooden bedstead, a deal table, with a few rude benches, and one old arm-chair by the fire-side. The floor was of earth and the fire-place, instead of being in the centre, as is still the ruder style of Highland cottages, was at the further end, having stones at the back to protect the turf wall, and piles of stones at the sides, built in the form of buttresses sloping backwards, for the purpose of conducting the smoke towards the chimney — or rather the wooden box which served for a chimney — a-top. Outside the cottage, sloping downwards on the moor, was a piece of potato ground that had been forced to supplant the heather, an imperfect enclosure to which was formed of furze intertwined with sticks; — all above, a wide heath stretched upwards and onwards, till it appeared to meet with the sky. Towards the middle of November, in the year of which we write, heavy falls of snow had taken place in the uplands, so that they already appeared white with their winter covering. The season had been cold and wet and part of the crop yet lay out upon the ground. In the clear frosty evenings, the full moon might be seen from the door-step of the hut, shining upon the harvest-fields that covered the lower slope of the hill, where the corn lay; in some parts gathered into stacks of sheaves, in others still uncut, and all covered with a white hoar-frost and a sprinkling of snow, that made them glitter and sparkle in the moon-light. At the height of the cottage itself, the snow lay in masses in those hollows where the sunshine of a few fine days had not been powerful enough to melt it; — higher up there was nothing to be seen but an unbroken surface of the most dazzling white, which, as the eye wandered around the horizon, was seen to be repeated on peak after peak of the more distant mountains.

It was on one of those evenings that old John Morrison rose from his bed for the last time. His little grand-daughter, May, a girl of twelve years old, the only inmate of the hut besides himself, had assisted him to get up, as she usually did at the same hour; for old John had been too feeble for a long time to be out of bed during the day. She seated him on his chair by the fire-side, and put his large coat, of a coarse blue cloth, which he wore as a mantle, around his shoulders, and his stick into his hand; and as John bent forwards over his staff, his grey hair falling down upon his shoulders, he looked a very venerable and patriarchal figure. The traces of great intelligence and sober thought were plainly discernible in the lines of his large wrinkled forehead, although age had in some measure dulled the expression of his features. Of such men, perhaps, were the seers and bards of his country in the olden time.

When May had set everything to rights, she sat down to read — as she frequently did in the winter evenings — beside her grandfather, after having placed upon the table a small oil lamp. A very old and yellow book it was which the light of the lamp fell upon, as, shading her forehead with her hand, she began to read in a clear sweet voice. It was *"The Cloud of Witnesses"* a volume which preserves the dying testimonies of the Scottish martyrs of the time of Charles Stuart, in favour of those truths for which they suffered. The greater part of them were men no higher in station than the dwellers in that humble cottage; but they were all able to leave, in clear and forcible language, their reasons for preferring the scaffold to such submission of conscience as had been required of them; and these reasons old John, and even little May, could well comprehend. As the reading proceeded, John's face brightened; he drew himself erect, and listened with compressed lips and knitted brow; but when the oppressed people came to relate how within their prisons they had found their faith strengthened, their hopes exalted — how sweet they had felt communion with God to be, and how they were as willing to lay down their lives for the kingly dignity of Christ, as if death were nothing but honour and joy — John would raise his eyes, and clasp his hands, as if in silent prayer.

On that evening May read how Margaret M'Lauchlan and Margaret Wilson — the first an elderly woman, the second a girl of twenty three — had been tied to stakes in the sea below high-water mark, and how the younger had been dragged out senseless when the waves flowed in around her, and pressed, on her recovery, to save her life by taking the oath of the king's supremacy over Christ's Church; — which she and the other both constantly refused till they died. After May had finished this history, she threw back her light brown curls, and looking up with her hazel eyes into her grandfather's face, said, "I think, grandfather, I could do that." A smile of complacency passed over old John's countenance, which he in vain tried to suppress; but he replied "Ah! May, it is easier to think we could die for Christ, than to conquer one sin; we must 'die daily,' and it is the slaying of our daily sins that will show whether we are willing to give up our frail breath for Him if needful." May dropped her eyes on her book, and proceeded. "What is *Erastianism*, grandfather?" she asked, after she had passed the word several times.

"My child," answered John, "Erastianism is a word of which every man, woman, and child in this kingdom ought to know the meaning. I shall ask you a few questions before explaining it to you. Who is the head of the Church on earth?" "Christ Jesus," answered the girl. "How can you prove that?" "Because the Church is Christ's spiritual kingdom, and he tells us himself that he is its king. He say, 'My kingdom is not of this world;' and he said before Pilate that he was a king, although he knew that he would be put to death for it." "Did Christ make laws for his kingdom?" "Yes; everything that he said was a law to his people, and everything that he did too, because he was always doing the will of his Father in heaven. He says, 'If ye love me, keep *my commandments*;' and, 'If ye know these things, happy are ye if ye do them;' and —"Yes," said John — "*my* commandments, these sayings of *mine*; not the commandments or sayings of earthly kings and rulers, although we are bound to give them all due honour in temporal things. Now, if Christ died rather than deny that he was a king, (yes," said John, with eyes uplifted, as if speaking to himself, "to deny that he was a king, would have been to deny his own cause, his Gospel, and his authority over his people. Blessed be his name, he did not do *that*); but does not that show, May, that he thought his kingly dignity a *great* thing?" "Yes," said May, thoughtfully; "surely he would have thought it a sin to give his life for a little thing; and he showed that he did not seek death, because he often hid himself for fear of the Jews." "Then if Christ thought it worth *his* while to die rather than deny that he was a king, does it not become his followers to do the same?" "Surely, grandfather," said May, "or else they would not be his followers at all." "Well, child," said John, "*Erastianism* is the putting of another in Christ's place as *king*. Charles Stuart, a very wicked man — but that is not to the purpose, for who is to be compared to the glorious Redeemer? — Charles Stuart sought no less than to be put in the place of the divine person of Christ. He sought to make the Church subject to judges and magistrates; and it was for disowning that Erastian doctrine, and the prelates and curates who held that doctrine, that many of the martyrs were put to death." "Surely, grandfather," said May, "if that was the way, there could be no true religion at all; for kings and judges must die like other people; and I dare say there are seldom two of them of the same mind. Now, if I were to believe what one king desired me at one time, and another king at another time, I could believe nothing at all. And surely, grandfather," said May, becoming more earnest, "the Holy Ghost does not teach truth that changes; surely, grandfather, the truth cannot change."

"Come here, May," said old John, with a voice not quite so steady as it had been. May drew near her grandfather as she was desired, and John, putting his stick into his left hand, placed his right upon her head. "Child of my old age," he said, "receive my blessing. May the blessing of the eternal Father rest upon you! May the eternal Son, the KING of the Church, reign in your heart! May the Holy Ghost, the eternal Teacher, take of the things of Christ, and show them to your soul! May he work in you the faith that changes not!" John kissed the forehead of his grandchild, put his arm round her, and drew her towards him. May began to weep, for there had been great solemnity in the old man's manner, and the tenderness he had shown was unusual with him, who, in general, was somewhat austere in his carriage, although kind and considerate. "Do you know, May," said John after an interval of silence, "that the Church of Scotland is doing battle again for the headship of Christ?" "I know," said

May," that the good ministers are refusing to put in men to parishes when the people are sore against them." "Yes," said John again, speaking as if to himself, "blessed be His name! that I have lived to see the day when the root of bitterness is about to be taken out of Zion — when Erastian patronage shall be digged out and cast away; though it will not be without a struggle," continued he, speaking more inwardly; "when it is taken out of the devil's hands, he will keep it with his teeth. But I have seen the combat begun, and now I desire to say, with Simeon, 'Let thy servant depart in peace.'" "Is *patronage* Erastian?" asked May. "*Is* it Erastian? repeated John, with more vehemence and sternness than he had hitherto spoken with. "If the Papist, and the unbeliever, yea, the blasphemer, and the drunkard, are to put in ministers according to their minds, is not that taking to themselves the very keys of the kingdom of heaven? Is not that the straight way to change the truth of God into a lie? We know them, we know them — we know their fruits," said John, raising his voice so loud that he might have been heard outside the cottage. May felt frightened, for she had never seen her grandfather go to extremes of any kind as he had done to-night. She answered timidly, "Yes I am sure that is true, for Mr Donaldson is a bad man. He gets drunk, and is of no use to anybody, and it was a Papist that put him in. If all the ministers were like him, as I dare say the patrons might have them, if they chose, there would be no good in having any ministers at all."

"Do you know how that man was settled?" said John, changing his voice to a low key. "I know," replied May, "that it was sore against the people's will." "I shall try to give you the history of that settlement," continued John, with much emotion, and a trembling voice, "though from that day to this the mention of it has never crossed my lips, May — it cost you a mother, and me an only child! An only child she was at that time, for the Lord saw meet to take away my sweet boy when he was but fourteen years of age. Yet he, though young in years, was old in grace. From a child the law of God was his delight, and his loving temper made my own heart tenderer during the years of his life than it ever was before. Bad years came, and crops failed, and we were straitened in our means. The boy entreated to be let go and work at a road which was making a mile down from this; he was killed by the falling in of a bank before he had brought home his first week's wages. But the Lord supported me under *that* trial, and I was enabled to say from the heart, 'The Lord gave, and the Lord hath taken away, blessed be his great name!' But your mother, May, was not like her brother; she was a bold-spirited girl, so that I often thought the woman's nature had gone into the boy, and that what should have been his in the ordinary course, as it were, had taken possession of her. She had been gifted with great beauty of person, too, so that strangers would come from a distance to see Ellen Morrison; all which made her more vain and headstrong; yet for all that I had the sinful folly to be proud of her. Yet open-hearted and open-handed she was, and would give the morsel that was to go into her own mouth to them that needed it; and wherever was the right, Ellen was sure to stand by it. My poor Ellen! right or wrong, it was all headstrong nature with her. When her brother had been dead four years, and she was in her twentieth summer, for she was a year older than him, she was to be married to a well-doing lad in the neighbourhood, and all things were going on well, when the young folks quarrelled, I never could tell how, and the young man, in a fit of anger, listed with a party of soldiers. Ellen cried night and day, for she was soft-hearted when it came to the push. She met her sweetheart by chance, or rather, I think, she watched to meet him; they made it up together, and, in spite of all that we could say or do, she married him, and got herself billetted to go along with him. Her poor mother never got above that; and when she was taken away, I was left, as I thought, alone in the world. But it was ordered otherwise. Ellen was soon to come back to me. Her husband fell into bad health, and died on a march, when she had been a year and a half married; so she returned with you at her breast a sucking infant. She was spent and thin, but her spirit was still the same.

About that time our worthy minister, an honoured servant of the Lord, was called to rest from his labours; and it was understood that the patron was to present Donaldson, whom all knew to be an ungodly man, to fill his place. We met and petitioned; but it was of no use. High words went about the parish: it was said there would be blood before Donaldson got in. Blood there was. Little did I think whose it was to be. Seeing that all was vain, I did my best to calm the tumult; but the people got the key of the church and blocked up the door with stones, nor could any thing prevail on them to give it up. On the first Sabbath that Donaldson was to preach, the men gathered early and surrounded the church; but the patron had his party of soldiers ready, which it so maddened the people to see, as they marched by the cottage doors, guarding Donaldson in the midst of them, that by the time the soldiers reached the hollow where the church stands, the very women had poured out to the heights above, to shower down stones upon them. Ellen having gone to a neighbour's house, joined the multitude unknown to me; for had I known, God is my witness, I would have used force rather than let her go. But it was not so disposed. Ellen pressed into the very front of the crowd. And after the soldiers had cleared a window, and forced Donaldson in at it, their blood got heated with the insult that was poured upon them. Several fired upon the people. My Ellen was the mark set. A bullet passed through her very heart. When the messenger of calamity came, I was at home wrestling, as was most beseeming, in the cause of the poor Kirk, little thinking of the trial of faith that was appointed for me. And oh! it was heavier than all the trials that ever befell me. The Lord's people were kind, and many a precious promise was poured into my ear; but they did not reach my heart. I thought I could have spared my Ellen if she had been called to testify for Christ, and if, without offence or violence, she had chosen death rather than deny the kingly dignity of the Lord that bought her; but I feared, I feared that she was still in a state of nature, though she *had* been inquiring more of late than formerly. Long, long did I rebel against that decree; but at length I was brought out of the furnace, and enabled to say, 'Good is the will of the Lord' "

This narrative was not given so connectedly as we have written it. John often interrupted himself, breathing heavily, and seeming to appeal inwardly for strength from on high. May was frightened, too, to see that the muscles of his face worked as if it were beyond the power of his will to control them. She kept looking at him, till she saw his eyes close, and he fell heavily back in his chair. The poor child thought he was dead. She began to cry, and to clasp the old man's body in her arms, kissing his hands and face. She attempted to move him, but could not. At length, when she had composed herself a little, she succeeded in laying his head on her bosom, and then she felt his breath coming and going on her cheek. She had never felt so utterly lonely and helpless. She was a long quarter of a mile from any human dwelling, and she feared that if she left her grandfather to go for assistance, he would fall upon the floor. She felt as if she herself were going to faint with terror and distress, when suddenly there came into her mind a verse of the psalm which had been sung that morning at their family worship:

"What time my heart is overwhelm'd.
And in perplexity,
Do thou lead me unto the Rock
That higher is than I"

The child felt her courage renewed; she was assured that God would not forsake her; and she silently poured forth a prayer for relief such as only hearts in extremity can utter. She then recalled all her senses, and casting about what she should do, determined that, if any length of time elapsed and nobody came, she would fearlessly leave her grandfather to the care of the Almighty, and hasten for the nearest aid.

CHAPTER III

*"Tread softly, bow the head,
In revrent silence bow:
No passing bell doth toll,
But an immortal soul
Is passing o're"*
     CAROLINE BOWLES

  A long half hour passed in this manner before described. May had made up her mind to leave her grandfather, though her tears gushed out afresh as she gently withdrew her shoulder from its burden, when the distant bark of a dog struck upon her ear, and made her heart leap within her bosom. She heard the dog's bark change into a whine as it came close by the cottage, and a few seconds afterwards a footstep approached, as if coming down from the moorlands. "Are you within, May?" asked a voice at the little window. "Oh, is that you, Mr. George?" said May; "come in, come in — make haste; God has sent you." "Your door is fastened in the inside," said the person without, going to the door and trying to open it. "Never mind," said May, "it's only with a string — break it. I can't leave this spot. Grandfather's dying — oh, I'm afraid he's dying," said the poor girl with a burst of weeping. The door was burst open with a strong jerk, and a short, thick-set, dark young man entered, having a plaid across his shoulders, and a gun in his hand. His dog, making way between his legs, ran, wagging its tail, towards the fire-place. " Hech Machullin! what's the matter here?" said the lad, standing still as the scene inside presented itself to him. 1 hope old John's not dead," he continued, coming forward and stooping over the old man's face. "Oh, no; the breath's in him yet When did this strike him?" May gave the best account she could in which her grandfather had been seized, leaving out, however, all mention of the narrative which had preceded it; for the person she addressed was none other than Mr. George Donaldson, the son of the parish minister, who, having been out grouse-shooting all day, had stopped at the hillside hut for refreshment on his way home. "Come, lassie" said he, when she had done, "make down your bed. I'll soon give your grandfather a lift for you." So saying, he took the old man, heavy and strong-boned as he was, in his arms, and, as May obeyed his directions, laid him down upon the bed. "Now," said he, turning to May, "I should have a kiss for that; but we'll say nothing about it just now," he added, seeing that she looked deeply distressed. "Come, cheer up, my bonny lass; get me a snack of bread and cheese, and I'll go and send up some of the town folks to you. Who do you want?" said he, sitting down in the chair which John had lately occupied, drawing it close to the table, where the old book still lay, and, by way of signal to expedite the bringing of the viands, going through the motion of chucking in pieces of bread and cheese at the distance of nearly a foot from his mouth — the manner in which he usually ate.

Poor May laid the bread and cheese on the table with her eyes swimming in tears, but without being in the least shocked at the want of refined feeling in her guest, for her heart was full of thankfulness at what she considered a great and providential relief; and she told simply who she thought would be best to come and sit by her grandfather. There was Donald Matheson, the catechist of the parish; and his wife, if it were possible for her to come; James Ross and Daniel M'Gillivray, crofters in the neighbourhood; and Angus Munro, a shopkeeper in the hamlet. All these were old and tried friends of John Morrison; and May knew that if he himself were able to tell it, they were those whom he would wish to have beside him in his last moments. Each name, as it was announced, was received by Mr. George with a groan, indicative of irony, which he would not have ventured on had John been able to hear, but which he reckoned on May's simplicity for not understanding; for, though the young man himself was on good enough terms with the class to which they belonged, as his coming into the hut in the way he did sufficiently showed, yet as the persons named never went to the parish church, and were regarded as the chief agents in keeping up a higher standard of religion than the minister liked, they were of course looked upon by the minister's family in the light of secret enemies. The lad, however, who was neither malicious nor ill-natured, promised to lose no time in summoning them to the bed-side of their dying friend, and after satisfying his hunger, he bade May a good-night, whistled away his dog, and called, as he went out at the door, that he would look up to-morrow and see how matters went on.

May, poor child, when she had taken a long and earnest look at her grandfather, who still lay with closed eyes, and with no other sign of life than that he breathed, went patiently to make her little preparations for her expected guests. And until these appear we shall take the opportunity of glancing shortly, for the reader's information, at the character, not so much of the individuals, as of the class to which they belonged.

Types or representatives of *The Men*, as they are called, *par excellence*, are perhaps to be found in every parish of Scotland, though they are unhappily becoming less numerous than they at one time were; but it is only in its more northernly districts that they form what may be regarded as a fourth estate in the Church — the lowest order of the religious, representative opinion of the people; ministers, elders, and deacons, being the three higher. They are usually men both of distinguished piety and of more than ordinary powers of eloquence, who, after they have acquired the confidence of the people, by the consistency of their conduct, and manifested their "gifts," as it is called, by the earnestness and power displayed in their addresses at the throne of grace, are then so far countenanced by the clergy as to be permitted to take a share in the more public exercises of the Church. Upon sacramental occasions there is a day expressly set apart for "the men" to give their thoughts upon the more experimental passages of Scripture; and this day is found extremely profitable, and its privileges are highly valued by the pious of all ranks. Tradition does not go back to the rise of this class into the position which they have occupied in the north of Scotland; but names of such an ancient date are preserved of distinguished individuals among them, that it is highly probable it had its beginning at the time of the Reformation, since we find express provision made both in the Book of Common Order and in the First Book of Discipline for persons of such description.

"Every week," says the former, "once the congregation assemble to hear some place of the Scriptures orderly expounded; at the which time it is lawfull for every man to speake or inquire as God shall move his heart," &c.

Again, in the Book of Discipline: "To the end that the Kirk of God may have a tryall of men's knowledge, judgements, graces, and utterances, ... it is most expedient that there be a time in one certain day every week appointed to that exercise which *St. Paul calls prophesying.* .... This exercise is a thing most necessarie for the Kirk of God this day in Scotland; for thereby, as said is, shall the Kirk have judgement and knowledge of the graces, gifts, and utterances of every man within their bodie." Then follow regulations for the preservation of order in these exercises, in case of strife, debate, or error arising, when the matter was to be immediately referred to a minister or elder.

This was an order of things exceedingly well adapted to the times of primitive Christianity in the first formation of a Church, whensoever that might be; for when preachers were few, and the field to be occupied great, it was of the utmost consequence that the church should come to the knowledge of her most gifted members, that so she might encourage and use, for the advantage of her whole body, those talents for the ministry which God had placed at her disposal. Neither is this a small proof of the parity of the genius of Presbyterian government with that condition of things which prevailed in the days of the apostles. The scheme of a brotherhood, where all should devote themselves to the common weal of the Church in measure and degree as God gave them ability, seems the grand leading idea of both.

The custom to which we have referred has now fallen into desuetude throughout Scotland, except in the Highlands, where it is kept up only on sacramental occasions, and is practised in very close accordance with the rules laid down in the First Book of Discipline. Elders are frequently made choice of from among "the men," as they are found to possess a great religious influence within the parishes where they reside — sometimes even for a considerable distance beyond. Their sympathies are more accessible to the mass of the people than those of individuals in a higher station can be; their modes of expression are more familiar; and being always superior men, their attractive influence is the more powerfully felt that the square of the distance is, as it were, so much diminished. Being the immediate representatives of the religious opinions of the country, so they aid materially in giving shape and consistency to those opinions; their judgment is always consulted, and great weight is attached to it in every matter affecting the spiritual welfare of a parish; especially in that most important of all points, whether, as they themselves would express it, a minister has grace as well as gifts; in other words, whether to talents sufficient for the discharge of his ministerial functions he adds that effectual calling of the Spirit of God, without which they have the fullest scriptural authority for believing no man to have a valid title to the sacred work of the ministry. And although, as fallible beings, they are liable to error, it is certainly the case that in at least nine instances out of ten their judgment is correct, and that for very simple reasons; — first, They are themselves generally possessed of what they would judge, which is the spirit of devotional piety; secondly, Their interests are exclusively spiritual, which could not certainly be premised of any order of patrons, whether lay or clerical. Such men have greatly assisted in elevating the moral and religious standard in the districts where they reside. But we are digressing too far from our narrative.

Our little friend had not long completed her preparations, when the door of the hut was gently opened, and the catechist appeared on the threshold. He was an elderly man, probably between his sixtieth and seventieth year, but hale and elastic; his form was well set and muscular, rather than bulky; his constitution had evidently not begun to break down; and he appeared as able to travel on missions of consolation and instruction throughout the bounds of a wide parish, as he had been at any time of his life. His countenance — seen to advantage as the light of the cottage lamp fell upon it when he took off his broad blue bonnet, and stood for a moment in the doorway — was strikingly prepossessing. It indicated a most happy temperament and pleasant humour; while its lines were strongly expressive of what is called sagacity, or that mental sense which dwells most in the results of thought and observation, and appropriates them with a peculiar force and conviction. His forehead was square and full, his grey hair growing thickly back from it. His countenance was weather-beaten; but its features, somewhat of the Roman type, were fine and regular, and there lurked around his mouth, even in his gravest moods, the curves where smiles were wont to play. He stepped forward as the girl rose to meet him, and laying his large hand upon her head pronounced impressively in his native language, the single word "Blessing." His companions, who had been whispering together for a few moments outside, followed him, and each in turn saluted May with some expression of feeling or interest. First came a thin pale man, with a quiet, mild face, and a shy retiring manner; then another, cast in a rougher mould in whose aspect there lingered some traces of the warlike Highlander, and whose spirit, in the event of insult having been offered, would evidently have been the first to take fire, and the most difficult to subdue, These were the crofters. The shop-keeper was a worthy-looking person, distinguished from the others chiefly by his wearing a less peculiar dress — the place of the bonnet being supplied by a hat, and the coarse light-blue broad-skirted coat with one of finer material and more ordinary make. There was impressed upon the aspect of the whole of them, at this moment, a deep reverence for the presence of death; and it was more by signs and looks, than by words, that they inquired the circumstances which had preceded the fatal stroke. May told her story with more freedom than she had done formerly, and when she had finished, the catechist, raising his eyes to heaven with an expression which gave a momentary sublimity to his countenance, said, without other remark or comment, "Let us pray." He then knelt by the bed-side, while his three friends and the girl followed his example, and gave utterance to a prayer which, while it was characterized by extraordinary vigour and fluency of language, was pervaded by that lofty and earnest tone which always distinguished the addresses of the fine old man at the throne of Deity, and which was now rendered more intense, by the feeling that a kindred spirit, with whom he had for many long years held intimate communion, was about to pass into the presence of its Maker. He seemed at times overwhelmed with a realizing sense of the purity, and holiness of the divine nature, as contrasted with the sinfulness and misery of man, but these passages were always followed by a gush of blessing towards that Saviour, in whose righteousness alone the spirit may venture to appear before its Creator.

    When the prayer was ended, the little party went and seated themselves at the table, upon which May had previously placed the large Bible that her grandfather had been accustomed to use at their family worship, and prepared to engage in the religious exercises of the night. These consisted almost entirely of prayers by the alternate members of the group, relieved by the reading of a chapter and the singing of a psalm. Nor would those exercises, even to one not imbued with their devotional spirit, have proved devoid of interest. Each prayer was well marked by its own individual character. Of the catechist's we have already given some idea. James Ross, the most retiring, and bashful of the party, gave vent to the breathings of a deeply pious and chastened spirit — of a heart well acquainted with its own deceitfulness, and accustomed to go for strength and support to the Fountain of all grace. The aspirations of the other crofter, Donald M'Gillivray, were of a more fervid and impassioned kind. They abounded in bold poetical images and sudden transitions. His prayers, too, were always the longest, as, from the full suggestive quality of the speaker's mind, at every expected close would burst forth with fresh vigour. He was followed by the honest shop-keeper, who was plain, concise, and practical.

All through the silence of that night, till the moon-light was succeeded by the grey dawn of morning, there might be heard from that cottage, first, the subdued, monotonous sound of Scripture reading; then the tone of earnest pleading, as of one pleading with Him who had the power of life and death; then a burst of wild plaintive psalmody, so sweet in its cadences, that if it fell on the ear of the traveller, as he journeyed on the mountain, he might fancy, even were he unconscious of being near a human dwelling, that it was music to greet the ear of a dying saint, after all other intercourse between the world and his senses had ceased for ever. Towards the middle of the night, the catechist's wife, a well-conditioned sensible-looking woman, came softly in, and took her place among the worshippers, without causing any disturbance or interruption. She brought with her some simple refreshment, which they stopped for a short time to partake of, while she assisted May to undress the old man and lay him down with more appearance of comfort. Nor did the little party separate until the morning broke, when the men rose to go to their several occupations; promising, however, to come back at noon, and the catechist telling his wife to stay at all events till somebody came to relieve her. Before noon-day came, a number of the villagers had gathered into the room. The catechist, who returned as early as possible, sat close by the bed-side, and, assisted by some of the younger "*men*," who were now present, again engaged in occasional prayer, and at intervals entered with them into serious conversation, to which the villagers listened with deep attention.

Not more than an hour had passed in the manner described, when the entrance of another visitor caused somewhat of a sensation, A lady, young and beautiful, whose appearance indicated high birth and breeding, stopped, after she had crossed the threshold of the door, looked kindly around the circle, and returned their respectful salutations with heightened colour, as they all rose to greet her; and then, seemingly acquainted with the customs of the country, where the *forms* of politeness and friendship are more common between the respectable poor and the rich man they are elsewhere, advanced with extended hand towards the catechist, and addressed him and some of the other people whom she knew, in kindly inquiries for their welfare. It was, as the reader will have guessed, the young English heiress, who had already begun to put into practice, in her new home, her habits of familiarity with the peasantry around her; and who found, in so doing, one of her highest mental resources and enjoyments. She sought out little May, of whose relationship to the sick man she had heard, patted her on the head, and told her not to lose courage, for her grandfather might possibly recover, "Has any medical man been here?" said she, turning to the catechist. Samuel replied, with one of his peculiar smiles — which seemed to insinuate, "My dear lady, you don't know what you say" — "that they were ten miles from any town where a medical man could be found, and that though such a person might be very willing to visit the poor within a reasonable distance, he could not be expected to go ten miles without remuneration." "Indeed!" said the lady smiling in turn, "then the doctor will perhaps visit me without any fear for his fee;" so saying, she gave some orders to an attendant who remained near the door, and who had set down a heavily laden basket on the floor, and returning, seated herself as if she meant to remain for some time, and begged Samuel to go on with the conversation in which she had interrupted him.

"We were just speaking on that passage in John which says that the sheep know the voice of the good Shepherd, and will not follow the stranger, but will flee from him; and we were about to read the chapter in which it is so said," replied the catechist, turning over the leaves of the Bible on the table before him. "It was the remembrance of the severe trial that befell worthy John Morrison that led us to it."

"May I ask," inquired Miss Legh, "what that was?"

"Well," said the catechist, looking towards John, who lay with his eyes closed, and who was now breathing heavily, "John seems to be slumbering, and I will go over it shortly, for I would not wish (seeing he may understand more than we wot of) that he heard us dwelling on that subject;" so saying, he, in an under-tone, made the lady acquainted with the chief details of Ellen Morrison's fate, as old John, on the night before, had told them to his grandchild.

Scarce had he finished the tale, when there walked into the midst of the group, inquiring for John in a loud voice, the earliest guest of the preceding evening, Mr. George Donaldson. He was proceeding to greet some of the persons present in a boisterous and patronizing manner, when perceiving the lady, his colour changed, and his manner assumed an air of more awkward embarrassment than had been shown by any of the peasantry. The young lady merely noticed him by a slight bow, in which more *hauteur* was apparent than from her manner to the cottagers, it might be thought she could assume. But suddenly the attention of the whole party was directed towards old John, who had been supposed, until the entrance of Donaldson, to be in a deep slumber. The tones of the young man seemed to strike acutely on his ear, and in the mysterious way in which, when an impression is made upon a single sense, it serves to awaken all the others, his whole frame seemed about to be quickened into life. He opened his eyes — gazed in a bewildered manner at the persons near him, until by degrees the haze of imperfect apprehension passed off from his face. He looked earnestly towards the catechist, and began to struggle for the power of speech. His vision then slowly wandered over the other individuals of the company, and at last fixed upon Donaldson. As with the overpowering force of a master-feeling, the bonds in which his spirit had been held were broken. His look assumed an inexpressible intensity of meaning. He raised his head from the pillow, and repeated, in a voice which was like the echo of speech and memory after speech and memory had departed: "*He that entereth not into the sheep-fold by the door, but climbeth up some other way*, THE SAME IS A THIEF AND A ROBBER." Nature was exhausted by the effort, and the old man instantly fell back and expired.

A chilling awe passed through the little assembly, in which every eye was fixed upon the figure in the bed, as if it were expected to raise its head and speak again. It seemed as if the king of terrors had touched the living with his icy fingers as he passed: so suppressed was the breathing, and so motionless the attitudes of the whole group for a time. George Donaldson was the first to break the awful silence; he moved to depart, and the "good day" with which he bad adieu to the party, jarred strangely on their sense of hearing. "My friends" said the catechist, when he was gone, "a soul has entered into its rest. There is no cause to mourn on earth, when there is rejoicing in heaven. Let us adore the Lord who reigneth." When he had thus spoken, he rose, while the rest kneeled, and among them the high-born lady who had witnessed the scene, and a prayer was poured forth of such fervour, such holy joy and confidence in the Father of spirits, and in Him who said. "I go to my Father, that where I am there ye may be also," that when the company arose from their knees, they felt as if they had been for a time in the immediate presence of God — as if the love of the world were crushed for ever in their hearts, and they were prepared to go forth hating the evil, and having their whole conversation above.

The lady now prepared to depart, and went to take leave of the catechist by gently putting her hand within his. Tears were in her eyes, and it would seem as if others had found their way down her cheeks. "May shall go with me," she said; "1 will take care of her." "Well, my dear young lady, since the Lord has put it into your heart," said Samuel, "I will not be a hindrance; but my wife and I intended to take her home with ourselves. John Morrison's child should not want a piece bread as long as we had it, but you may be able to do for her when we are gone. The Lord be with you." "Perhaps the girl will feel more comfortable with you till the funeral is over," said Miss Legh in a low tone looking towards May, who stood weeping and trembling; "when that is the case, your wife will, I am sure, take the trouble to bring her to me." She took a kindly farewell of the cottagers, who were conversing together, in an undertone, in knots of two and three, and departed.

CHAPTER IV

*The spirit of God promised alike, and given
To all believers.*
                                    MILTON

In the course of this spring the half-yearly celebration of the sacrament of the Lord's supper took place in the parish of Glenmore, where the house of Rosemount was situated. The catechist and his friends resided within the boundaries of the neighbouring parish of Aird; but as they could derive no benefit from the ministrations of Mr Davidson,, they preferred walking six miles every Sabbath (which is, indeed, considered but a short journey in the Highlands, if undertaken for such a purpose), in order to attend the more edifying pastoral instructions of Dr. Blair. The consequence of this procedure was, that they, together with some others of their more serious fellow-parishioners, were obliged to communicate in the church where they heard sermon, as tokens of admission to the Lord's table would have been refused by their own clergyman on account of their non-attendance on his ministry. On all sacramental occasions in the Highlands, numbers of people flock from adjoining, or it maybe from more distant parishes, to hear the services in that church where the communion is to be held. One circumstance contributed at this time to attract an unusually large number of strangers to Glenmore. Dr. Blair, a man revered for his worth and celebrated for his pulpit eloquence, had been for many months labouring under a painful and protracted disorder, which confined him to the house; and as he was now far advanced in life, it was feared he never again would be able to resume his public duties. It had got rumoured abroad, however, that he was now to make an effort to address his people, for it might be the last time; and many persons, in the hope of hearing divine truth once more from his lips, crowded to his parish, from the distance of even thirty and forty miles. They depended for lodging and sustenance, during the five days the sacramental duties lasted, upon the hospitality of the inhabitants of Glenmore, or of any friends within walking distance from its church.

Upon such occasions as these the ancient manners of the Highlanders are seen to blend well with their more recently acquired Christian character. Hospitality has been with them from the most ancient times a sacred rite. And Christianity does not destroy — it refines the rude virtues of the savage. Among the many crowded households assembled expressly for religious purposes, no vestige of riot, intemperance, or the once fiery temper of the country could be discerned. The days when a Highlander ate his meals with *the dirk* stuck into the table beside his plate were no more; but courtesy of manner, warmth of friendship, and a liberality unlimited, except by the means of bestowing it, remained — softened, indeed, but still unimpaired. Nor was any one ever known to involve himself in pecuniary difficulties by his willingness to share what ever his means afforded on such occasions. On the contrary, the habits of decency, sobriety, and forethought, engendered by this social religious communion, had a most salutary effect on the worldly affairs of the peasant throughout the year.

No household afforded a more characteristic picture of a scene which was repeated with little variation on different scales throughout the neighbourhood, than did that of our worthy friend the shopkeeper. He had, in addition to his shop, a small but very excellent farm, which was laboured principally by his own children, and he was thus a wealthy man in his way, and an excellent specimen of that worthy class which the remorseless spirit, misnamed *improvement*, has so nearly swept from the country. His farm not only supplied the means of plenty to his family, but helped to purchase a yearly stock of miscellaneous merchandise, the profits of which were thus clear and unembarrassed. The premises he inhabited consisted of a single row of small rooms, beneath a thatched roof, the end nearest the village being appropriated to the business of the shop. The front of this long low building presented no less than three doors of entrance. There was the shop door, the lower half of which was kept shut, in the Flemish style, while the upper opened like a shutter; another which led to the kitchen; and a third opening on the landing place, which divided the two principal rooms from each other. These latter were sufficiently humble, although they possessed their own share of homely comfort. Their floors were simply sanded, and they had both old-fashioned square bed-steads; but that in the best room doubled up curiously in the manner of an opera bed, leaving the top, with its frilled and fringed hangings, projecting in the midst like a canopy. Here, too, there were Dutch tiles within the fire-place, and a few curious ornaments on the top of the wooden mantel-piece; there was an old clock, which pursued its dull tickings incessantly; and there were oaken chairs, and a chest of drawers of black heavy Spanish mahogany.

Such was the apartment in which, on the Friday evening before the communion, our friend the catechist, and a few more of "the men" from various parts of the neighbouring country who had spoken in the course of the day, were met over a social cup of tea. In this room only, and in that opposite, was there tea provided for the guests. For the poorer class, who were lodged to the number of thirty or forty in the kitchen and out-houses, ample provision was made in more substantial but coarser fare. When the *grace* had been pronounced by the catechist, and tea accompanied by oaten-cakes, butter, and cheese, had been handed round, conversation commenced in a serious but animated strain. It was carried on in English, out of deference to one or two of the company who understood Gaelic but imperfectly, and mostly, too, by the elderly persons present, the younger, with but one exception, presently to be noticed, rather listening in order to learn than presuming to speak. The Bible and the pulpit formed the only literature of the speakers, and the discourse turned almost exclusively on points of theology, illustrated either by *notes* preserved from the sermons of remarkable preachers, for it might be many generations by-gone, or by anecdotes of the olden time relating to remarkable men in their own sphere of life.

The young person we have mentioned, who presumed to enter into debate with his elders, was the eldest son of the host, who had just completed his third year at college, and who was generally looked upon as a very promising aspirant to the rank of a clergyman: that rank, when worthily filled, being far more sacred and honourable in the eyes of this company than any secular title could possibly be. Evan Munro's personal appearance was strikingly handsome; even in his father's house he looked as if he belonged to a grade of society different from that in which he moved. He had formerly been celebrated for taking the lead among all the young men of the village in every rustic sport. He had even carried athletic exercises, and his fondness for a certain kind of waggish drollery, so far as to give pain and displeasure to his worthy father, whose ideas were formed, in some measure, on the severe model of the old Covenanters. But all at once his mind had taken a sudden turn, as his friends expressed it. He had become fond of books, serious and reflective, and had urged his father to send him to college, with the view of studying for the Church. What share the desire of an awakened intellect for the exercise of its powers, and the aspiring wishes of an energetic temperament, might have had in this direction of his views for the future, we do not know. It is certain that his father did most anxiously set himself to ascertain whether a desire for benefiting the souls of men — that only motive which the Scottish Church and its better people recognise as the lawful one in such circumstances — was the animus of his son's desires; and when he at last consented to let Evan follow the bent of his wishes as to the manner of his education, it was under the express condition, that if he were not fully satisfied as to the thorough and radical nature of the student's religious beliefs, some other profession than the clerical one should ultimately be chosen. Every year Evan returned from his studies with an increase of knowledge, and an expanded mind; and every year, at the same period, he underwent a close examination by his father, as to the progress which divine truth, *in the love of it,* had made in his heart. His friends regarded Evan with the same hope, without, perhaps, the same mixture of fear. He had, for some years, loved serious conversations, and to be heard with respect is pleasant to the aged. He had, to be sure, sometimes broached opinions, picked up *without* the little circle of his home — neither immoral nor heretical, but at which the old men would shake their heads in such a manner as to say, "Deeper experience of human nature and of God's truth will show you that matter in a different light; but that will come by-and-by."

One or two such opinions Evan was led to border upon on the Friday evening of which we write. The subject on which "the men" had spoken during the day, and which was indeed a very frequent one for discussion on the like occasions, was "the marks of a true Christian," given by each of them from their own experience or their observation of Christian character. Evan, in allusion to this subject, asked, with that turn for the speculative which distinguishes young and enquiring minds, how far a man who had once appeared to possess the marks of a true Christian could fall into sin without conveying to others the certainty that his belief had never been genuine? A man from a parish at some twenty miles distance, of a very pleasant expression of countenance, and with much even of that bland Christianity in its maturer stages scarce ever fails to impart, took up the discussion of the question with young Evan, by disclaiming the power of ultimate and decisive judgment in the matter at all. Evan had for his Scripture authority the saying of our Saviour, "By their fruits shall ye know them." His opponent, Simon Anderson, brought forward that other equally imperative text, "Judge not that ye be not judged." "But," said Evan, "the passage I have quoted with its context *implies* judgment 'Men do not gather grapes of thorns, or figs of thistles;' does not that imply a comparing of the fruits with the tree? — of the works with the individual who produces them? There are surely no contradictions in the Bible."

"There are no contradictions in the Bible, my young friend," replied his antagonist mildly; "But the people of God may be situated so differently at different times as to require various directions, even in relation to the same point of conduct. In my opinion, the passage I have brought forward is intended for the general guidance of Christians in their private judgment of their fellow-Christians; while they are to disapprove of and hate the sin, as tried by the standard of the Word of God, they are to entertain hope for the backslider, even unto the end. But, again, there are times when the interest of our own souls and those of others depends upon the right exercise of judgment in regard to some individuals' spiritual state. You will find, if you look at the passage to which you have referred, which occurs in the 7th chapter of Matthew, that it was spoken by our Lord to the multitudes assembled to hear his sermon on the mount, and that it refers to their right of judgment in regard to their spiritual teachers. 'Beware,' says he, 'of *false prophets*, that come to you in sheep's clothing, but inwardly they are ravening wolves;' and then follows that which you have quoted. Is it your opinion that I am right?" said Anderson, looking towards Samuel, and the other men of weight who were present. They all signified their fullest approbation of what he had spoken. Evan was still unwilling to depart from his own view of the question. He granted that the more immediate application of the passage was to the selection of spiritual teachers; but he contended, that as all Christians were in one sense teachers, lights set on a hill, it applied to them likewise.

"Well, well," said the catechist, "to set the matter at rest, I will tell you what I heard an old Christian say upon it. He belonged to the time of great Christians, who were much given to prayer. He was old when I was young, but I still remember the saying, and it has more than once come to the support of my own mind in my course through life. There was a man mentioned in his hearing, who had been a great professor, but who had fallen into grievous sin. A person present called him a *hypocrite*. 'O,' said my old friend, with a look of deep humility, although his own life had been spotless for fifty years, 'O,' said he, 'let us not judge him — *let us pray for him*.' "

Every one was pleased with this little anecdote, and felt the justness and beauty of the spirit it exhibited more than they could have been demonstrated by any argument. Some remarks were introduced upon the nature of prayer, and those promises of Scripture in which much is promised in answer to it. "I recollect," said a woman present, "a note of a sermon of Mr. Lachlan M'Kenzie. I do not know if any here heard the sermon; it was preached at a communion in the parish of — thirty years ago, at the time of the making of the Caledonian Canal. You all know," continued she, "nothing was lost with Mr. Lachlan. 'Oh' says he, 'you may think with yourself what is the use of *my* poor prayers ? Surely they are too weak to bring down any blessing from heaven. Did you ever see the people working at the great canal, which is to stretch across the country? How is it made? Just by digging out the ground in spadefuls. Every man throws out his spadeful of earth, and perhaps his own work appears to him small enough. But what is the consequence? A communication will be opened from the sea on the one side of the country to the sea on the other side, and ships will carry their goods into the very heart of the land. Now, that is the way with your prayers. *Persevere* in earnest prayer, and a passage will be opened from earth to heaven, through which the blessings of grace and mercy will be poured upon your souls.'

"Ah, he was indeed a wonderful man, Mr. Lachlan," said M'Gillivray, who was present. "The Lord raises up instruments to do his work, and tempers them in his own way. It is said he had a great gift of poetry, and that he used it in a singular way. I dare say the story of Black Kate is well known to some of you, at least, and I need not repeat it." Some said they were acquainted with it, but a few of the young people, who were not, signified their wish that M'Gillivray should relate it; which he accordingly did as follows:

"This *Kate* was the very worst character in all the parish of Lochcarron. Some said she received the name she went by from the darkness of her complexion; and others, that it was from the blackness of her crimes. It was said there was no commandment which she had not broken, except the one against murder. As for the ordinances of religion, she laughed them to scorn, so that some thought it impossible she could believe in a future state at all. Mr. Lachlan had often tried to get at her by means of conversation, but without effect. As Kate grew old in years she grew hardened in sin, till at length it was doubted whether she was not beyond the reach of mercy. But God is sovereign in his dealings with sinners. It struck Mr. Lachlan to write a poem, in which he would enumerate all Kate's sins, and at the same time mourn over them, in a tone of pity. This poem he caused some young lads to learn, with instructions that they should sing it in Kate's hearing. And the arrow struck the mark. 'Is it possible that I am such a sinner as that?' thought Kate. 'O what a wretch I must be!' The poor creature got into a state of mind bordering on despair. For two years she mourned night and day, and it was said, that if tears could wash sin out, she would have washed hers away. But her eyes were opened to see that nothing would do for them but the blood of Christ. When Mr. Lachlan was convinced of the genuineness of her convictions, and when Kate had at last found peace, he endeavoured to prevail on her to come forward and make a public profession at the Lord's table. But she still thought herself unworthy to partake of the body and blood of her Lord. I remember well, on occasion of a communion in the parish of Lochcarron, a time which the Lord wonderfully blessed with his presence, when the last of the tables in the out-door congregation was about to be served — it was a fine summer's evening, and the light of the sun in his going down was striking slant-ways upon the table — the singing of the psalm was proceeding, and every now and then Mr. Lachlan stopped to invite any intending communicant who might still be lingering behind, oppressed with doubts, to come forward in the strength of the Redeemer. He was about to begin the communion-service, when a sob of distress was heard from a distant part of the congregation. Mr. Lachlan well knew the voice. He made his way through the crowd, and taking poor Kate by the hand, he seated her himself at the table.

And O, then, what a view did he give of the riches of redeeming love, and of the free grace of God! Oh," said M'Gillivray, changing his dialect into that in which he could best give expression to his feelings, "is it not beautiful, that grace of God which can make the heart of an old sinner like the heart of a little child? Is it not precious, the blood of Christ, which can make the blackest sins as white as snow?"

The conversation continued in this strain for some time longer, when one of the young people of the family came in to announce the arrival of a woman who had come to ask for a night's lodgings, and who was accordingly met and welcomed by the host and hostess, and conducted into the opposite apartment. It happened that she was well known to all the persons whose conversations we have been relating; but the news of her arrival elicited no symptoms of pleasure; on the contrary, it was apparent that a shade of disapprobation passed across the countenances of many of them. No remark was made, and a pause of a few moments ensued. This woman was known as one who was much addicted to ill-natured gossip; her tongue and her temper were equally sharp. She had even got herself engaged in several disagreeable broils in the village where she resided, and had made shipwreck of great part of her means in a law-suit, in which she had foolishly involved herself with a neighbour. Nevertheless she was very constant in her attendance at the sacraments; indeed, she never missed one within the circuit of twenty miles from the place where she dwelt.

Evan was the first to break the pause which followed her announcement, and it was with a regret that anyone should cause the way of truth to be evil-spoken of. The elders of the company made no reply. A man who might be either somewhat more or somewhat less than thirty years of age, of a lively expression of countenance, remarked that it was a pity any one should seek the bread that perishes, rather than the bread of eternal life. This individual was looked upon as a rising Christian. He often prayed in such meetings as the present, where, indeed, the first appearances of "the men" were generally made; but he was not considered to have acquired sufficient experience to speak in the more public meetings on *the day of the men* in the church. "Well," said the catechist, in answer to his remark, "the Lord sometimes meets with those who are not looking for him. It is not the first time that the blinded mind, wrapped up in the things that perish, has been trysted with a sight of His glory. There is a story that comes to my recollection, and as it seems to me suitable, I will tell it to you. In the time that followed the persecution, when there were few faithful ministers in any part of the north country, in the whole of that which lies between the Cromarty and Beauly Friths, which we call the Black Isle, there was no one minister who preached the Gospel. And few there were either, who had any relish for it, although the Lord preserved here and there a faithful witness for the truth, who, in preaching Christ crucified, got in some measure the fulfilment of the promise: 'And if I be lifted up, will draw all men unto me.' Among the rest there was that great man Mr Fraser of Kincardine; and among those who went to hear him, there were two men from the Black Isle, who crossed the water every Sabbath and travelled to Kincardine to get the gospel from his lips. There was a poor woman, an acquaintance of these men, who made many enquiries why they went so far and took so much trouble every Lord's day; and she questioned them as to whether they got *any treasure* in payment of their long journey. They replied to her, that they did get a precious treasure, for which they were willing to part with all they possessed. 'O', says the woman, 'would I get any of it if I went with you?' 'Who knows?' said the men; 'at any rate if you come with us you will not lose your reward.' Next Sabbath the woman went to Kincardine and heard the sermon, and on coming home, although both the men were poor, they joined together and gave her half-a-crown. This they continued to do for three or four weeks, she always supposing that she got but a small share of their riches. But one Sabbath afternoon, after hearing a powerful sermon from Mr. Fraser, when they came to prepare for their journey home, the woman was nowhere to be found. They inquired of her at many houses in vain; at last she was seen sitting by herself behind a large stone in a lonely place, and weeping bitterly. Her eyes had been opened to see that the treasure which the men sought was infinitely more precious than silver or gold, and she never could be over bewailing her own blindness which had never seen this before. At parting, she was offered the half-crown as usual, but the sight of it overwhelmed her with sorrow and shame. 'No, no' said she, 'little would I care for a *peck* of half-crowns now. If I get but treasure in heaven, willingly would I part with all I have in the world.' That woman became a distinguished Christian."

In such conversation as this the evening wore away, and was concluded by a solemn act of worship, the catechist and the master of the house jointly conducting the services. In other parts of the household the conversation partook of much the same character, varied, of course, by individual recollections and experience. Not that the whole of the persons assembled were animated by exactly the same love of religious subjects, although it might be safely asserted that they were so very generally, as it was the professed love of religious intercourse which drew them together; but if there were any who would have sought to introduce less serious topics of discourse, they were overborne by the presence of persons of weight and authority; and it was felt, besides, that such topics would be disagreeable to the general taste. In all the different apartments where the people were met, and even in the barns and out-houses, worship was conducted by some one of "the men;" and when this duty was over, the guests were disposed of for the night, with all the attention to comfort which circumstances permitted. In the interior of the house, beds were laid upon the floor, stores of blankets and linen, which had lain quietly in their keeping-places for the last half-year, were drawn forth, and in this manner the males were accommodated in one apartment, and the females in another. The same arrangements were preserved in the out-houses, except that in them the beds were either of straw or heather.

Scarcely had the next morning dawned when some of the men withdrew from the company of sleepers, and, for the sake of privacy, sought the different solitudes in the neighbourhood, in order to prepare their minds, by communion with God, for the sacred duties of the solemn occasion. It was no rare sight throughout the parish of Glenmore, on these mornings, to see a solitary individual in some little hollow beside a mountain streamlet, in the sheltered corner of a field, or in some spot shaded by a tuft of bushes or trees, kneeling on the ground, and, with eyes turned towards the heavens, which were yet but dimly lighted by the sun, earnestly pleading with the Holy Spirit, for his heavenly influences of grace and love.

Are there indeed persons of refined sentiment who can find something poetical in the worshipper of the East, who pays his morning adoration to the first beams of the newly risen sun, with forehead bent to the earth, and who yet can discover nothing beautiful in the contemplation of an immortal spirit thus holding early and earnest communion with that glorious and all-perfect Nature, whose worshippers, if they are such in spirit and in truth, must, by an immutable law, be approximated, in their spiritual natures, towards his own?

Chapter V

Precepts divine their awful station keep
Fencing the holy table: at its head
Now stands the servant of the Lord; while sleep
All feelings, thoughts, emotions, save the dread
Sublime of love to Him who liveth and was dead.
ANON

The next Sabbath dawned on the parish of Glenmore, a day of uncommon brightness and beauty. It was what is rarely witnessed in the northern part of our island, a genuine spring-day — balmy, clear, and soft. There the seasons do not always vindicate their names. "Winter in the lap of May" is a poetical figure which in that region is thoroughly understood. But upon this 16th day of April, its every hill and valley rejoiced in unclouded sunshine. The snowy summits of the mountains shone with a bridal splendour, the pastures wore their softest tints, the stems and branches of the budding birch trees were decked in silver and pearl; and the rivers, as they struggled through the deep gorges of the mountain ravines, tossed upwards their noisy waters to the sunlight, crested with sparkling foam. But although nature thus rejoiced in her own beauty, there was a quietness abroad, which seemed to proclaim it a Sabbath morning. The streams brawled onwards, and the little birds poured out their songs at intervals from tree and brake; but this language of solitude was addressed only to the blue heavens. Quiet as these mountain pathways were at all times, they could not, on a week-day, be traversed without encountering signs of human movement and labour; but upon the early Sabbath, the cottages on the hillsides and in the hollows were all carefully closed. If, however, the traveller approached the rude walls, and stood beside one of the little windows, almost hid beneath their roofs of turf, he might discover not unfrequently, proceeding from within the sounds of Bible reading or prayer.

As the morning advanced, a group of two or three persons might now and then be seen wending their way down the glens. Gradually the number of these groups increased, until at length the pathways became studded with them as far as the eye could reach; and they were all evidently taking their journey in the same direction. There were patriarchal men with staff in hand, wearing the blue bonnet; and sober decent-looking women, dressed in hooded cloaks, with a simple kerchief of silk or muslin tied over their heads. Here and there might be descried an old woman with the tartan plaid or *screen*, which had served her ancestors for many generations, falling in folds over her head and person, and fastened at the bosom with a silver brooch of equal antiquity with the plaid itself. The young men wore the *trews* of tartan — kilts being now seldom seen among the Highland peasantry — and had very frequently a shepherd's plaid thrown across their shoulders. There was a manly vigour in their limbs, and a firm elasticity in their tread, peculiar to the mountain races. The young maidens trode lightly beside them barefooted. Their shoes and snow-white stockings, to be put on as they approached the church, they carried in their hands, both to keep them unsoiled by travel, and for the sake of coolness and lightness on their journey. They were bareheaded as well as barefooted, and were sometimes distinguished by the snood of blue ribbon tied around their simply parted locks, although this pretty and poetical custom seemed to have worn a good deal out of fashion. Such were the groups which emerged at different times from the cross pathways upon the high-road leading through the parish of Glenmore, and which, as they appeared in sight, after having climbed the steep ascent above some little glen, with its streamlet, its rocky sides, and its clustering birch and hazel; — or, as they just turned the corner of some cliff which had before hidden them from view, would have afforded rich materials for the pencil of the artist.

It is customary on sacramental occasions in these northern parishes of Scotland, to have double services performed; that is, service both within and without the church. This is necessary in the Highlands, where the same language does not serve for the whole of the parishioners. The out-door services are performed in Gaelic; and the congregation met in the open air being thus composed of the native population, is usually much more numerous than that assembled within doors. It was not so, however, at this time, in the parish of Glenmore. Some expectation prevailed that the English sermon was about to be delivered by Dr. Blair himself, and consequently the church was crowded to excess in all its parts, and even around the windows on the outside, immense masses of people were congregated.

But Dr. Blair was too feeble to undertake such an arduous duty; — another able and popular preacher occupied his place. Among the audience in the front gallery, Miss Hamilton Legh sat an interested and attentive hearer. Sir Duncan Ross, too, was there; — he had probably accompanied his niece either from curiosity or *ennui*. After the sermon was ended, what is called the *fencing of the tables* began — an address intended to impress the persons about to partake of the communion with just views of the solemnity of that holy ordinance, and to deter any one from coming forward to it with either levity or profanity. The Scripture authority for this proceeding is taken from the Apostle Paul's warning address to the Corinthians, and from his enumeration of those characters who are unfit to take their place at the Lord's table. Miss Legh, to whom all this was new, felt her mind much impressed, in spite of a slight degree of prejudice and a different religious habit. Her heart confessed that this was not an unsuitable preparation for the sacred rite, which was to follow.

When the address was nearly concluded, a movement was observed among the crowd nearest the door. Every eye turned in that direction, and the throng in the passage opened with difficulty in order to make way for some one about to enter. Their aged pastor then came forward with slow and feeble steps, assisted by two of his elders, upon whom he leaned for support. It had been his ardent desire to commemorate his Saviour's death once more with his beloved people — to partake with them yet once of that heavenly manna with which he had fed them for forty years, ere the place that now knew him should know him no more. Yet Dr. Blair was a man of no weak or sentimental caste of intellect. There had been a vast deal of thew and sinew, if we may use such an analogy, in the constitution of his mind. A vigorous philosophical sense, by which he had been accustomed to seize strongly upon the judgment and understanding of his hearers, had always made itself felt both in his conversation and his discourses. His views were always based upon broad principles. With him there was but the *right* and the *wrong*, without any shadowing off or merging of the lines of either into each other. Beneath this staple of his character there dwelt warm feelings, ever ready to burst forth upon occasions of moral excitement, and which, if they were rather repressed than displayed, had, by the very strength of their sincerity, a powerful effect on the minds of others. The outward appearance of the man was in keeping with the mental character we have endeavoured to portray. His tall and masculine frame seemed to have broken down, from the rapid advance of old age and disease, both coming suddenly upon it without previous decline. His well-marked features were at the first glance almost harsh in their outline, but ever and anon a light would spring up — a softer shadowing would appear, till, as the gazer continued to look, the countenance became one to love as well as to revere.

Such was the man who now stood at the head of the table where the communicants were already seated, and who began to address them in a voice at first tremulous, but which gained strength as he proceeded. He began with a touching allusion to that saying of our Saviour to his disciples: "With desire I have desired to eat this passover with you before I suffer." The subject seemed to open the flood-gates of feelings and mental perceptions which had quickened and deepened in intensity in hours of distress, and in the contemplation of approaching death. His first sentences were expressive of a deep and humble conviction of the efficacy of the sufferings which this supper preceded and prefigured. His whole soul bowed itself before this conviction. "The bread and wine," he proceeded to say, "was not a sacrifice — was not salvation; but typified these." How mighty and pregnant their meaning! That meaning he shortly and comprehensively unfolded; then stopping, he gave thanks in Christ's name, and after his example, the whole assembly rising up. He then gave to the communicants the bread and the cup, and paused till these had passed from one to another along the whole table. Then his voice was again heard with a vigour inspired, as it would seem, by the thoughts which had thronged upon his mind during the silence. Again he recurred to the expression, "With desire I have desired to eat this passover with you before I suffer." "What a wonderful condescension in the eternal Son of God — the Divine Nature — to take upon himself *our* nature! Not in that distant acquaintance which would have sufficed to make him in some measure *feel for us*, while the recollection of some dim consciousness passed across his divinity, even as breath passes from the surface of the mirror; but in all the fulness of our human hearts, in such intensity as that we might *feel with him*! — that our sympathies might be irresistibly attracted towards him, as the less is drawn towards the greater!"

"Oh, my friends," continued he, "it was no *dim consciousness* which the Son of Man carried home with him to his Father's bosom; and let us remember, that upon the amplitude of his human experience there is set the immutable seal of his Godhead. He cannot forget it; — all past consciousness is for ever present to the Eternal Mind. How nearly does language here fail to express the longing desire of our Saviour to enter once more into intimate social communion with those who had been his friends during his sojourn on earth! '*With desire I have desired* to eat this passover with you.' He took them not to the mount of transfiguration, there to be glorified with him, as if *that* were more congenial to his desires; he met them at the social table, and partook with them of that food which constitutes the support of frail mortality. And wherever there are two or three who believe in his name, met to commemorate his death through faith, there is he still present, with the same feelings of intense affection with which he partook of his *last supper* on earth with his disciples. What does he deserve from *you*, my friends? Is it not your very hearts? — No measured affection, no scrimp confidence, but your *hearts*, with all their treasures of faith and love. You may have a beloved partner, a child, a friend, whose integrity you would think it foul scorn to doubt, whom you deem worthy of all your heart's love can give them, and more if you had it. Where is there a friend like the Saviour of sinners? Oh, wrong him not by doubts of his wisdom, his power, or his love! I stand here an old man addressing to you what are, in all human probability, my last words as your pastor — as forty years ago, I stood before you in the vigour of manhood; and I leave you my most solemn testimony, that I have found Christ an *all sufficient* Saviour — that I have found him sufficient in temptation, in suffering, yea, even in my very darkest hours, as I hope to find him still sufficient in death and through eternity."

"Now before we part, my people — my beloved people, one word on a subject which presses on my thoughts. Some may call it *delicate*, but before the necessities of the conscience the frost-work of delicacy melts away. What I would say regards the succession to this pastoral office. You are all aware of the struggle which is now going on in our Church. I thank God I have confidence towards him that it will end in the purifying and establishing of his Zion in our land, however long the days of darkness may be. Now, in whatever way the subject may be presented to your minds — however it may be sought to involve it in perplexity — you well know, just because you *feel*, that the substance of it is this: Whether, when you ask for bread, you are to receive a stone; or whether, even of spiritual food, you are to get that kind which is best adapted for the nourishment of your souls. Now, my people, I do not speak to you for the purpose of telling you to *value* spiritual food; I know that to those of you at least who have tasted of the bread of life, I might as well leave my parting injunctions to care for the bread which is to support your mortal bodies. Of the one kind of food as well as the other you will feel the want. The desire for its supply will arise; but it is for this I speak to you — in case that days of persecution for the truth's sake may arise. Now, I would say to all of you, that while you use all honest and legitimate influence to procure for yourselves a suitable pastor — while you use it with much prayer, and stand firm against all worldly motives in a concern so momentous — never lose sight of this declaration of God's Word, that 'the wrath of man worketh not the righteousness of God.' You will possibly have great, and, as it may appear to you, *just*, cause of provocation; but the resentment which often appears to our natural minds justifiable or necessary when our rights of property are invaded, is especially forbidden on this sacred ground. Seek, O seek the aid of the Holy Spirit. Seek it powerfully, plentifully, efficiently, in its restraining and sanctifying influences. If it is permitted me to speak from personal motives, I would beseech you, on my own behalf, that you let it not be said (which it will, mark you, on slight enough grounds) that this parish, where I have laboured for forty years, presented, after my decease, a scene of riot and confusion, which caused the enemies of the truth to blaspheme. To some of you such a motive may be more forcible than any other; and to such I would leave it as my last request, that they disgrace not the memory of their pastor. And 'now unto Him that is able to keep you from falling, and to present you faultless before the presence of his glory with exceeding joy,' I would commit you, for time and eternity."

During this address, of which we have imperfectly preserved but a few sentences, there was scarcely a breath heard over the whole of the numerous audience. From the lifting of a head here and there to take a stealthy glance around, it might be perceived that the female part of the congregation were bathed in tears; and the quick drawing of a rough hand across many a weather-beaten face, showed that even the outward signs of emotion were not confined to the softer sex. Dr. Blair, after he had sat down for a few minutes to rally his exhausted strength, retired from the church in the way he had entered, just as the communion table was filling for the second service.

Sir Duncan Ross rose and left the church at the same time. Miss Legh, too, accompanied him, although she felt a very great wish to stay and hear the conclusion of the services. Upon their way home, Sir Duncan rallied her upon her gravity. "That church was a grave place," replied she mildly. "Why, my dear niece," said her uncle, "you actually look as if you thought yourself a sinner." "If a great deal that is deficient, to say the least of it, in conduct and character constitutes a sinner, I am afraid I am," replied Jane with a sigh, "Pshaw! child," said Sir Duncan impatiently; "we are surely what nature made us. In my opinion, the only real sin is unnecessary suffering. The world is beautiful; what have we to do more than to enjoy it?" "I begin to wish I were better than *nature made me*" answered Jane, and the tears started to her eyes. "My dear niece," said Sir Duncan, looking kindly into her face, "I do not love to see those beautiful eyes dimmed in that manner. Exert your fine understanding, and don't let a few fancies and the whining of an old man disturb your peace of mind. Why, I don't think," continued he after a pause, as Jane answered nothing — "I don't think Dame Nature has acted the part of a step-mother to you at all She has given you a face and person which I vow I never saw surpassed She has showered fortune upon you, and given you a rich and powerful mind. What would you have more?"

No sooner however did Jane find herself alone than she sat down to peruse her New Testament, internally forming the resolution, that until she understood it better, she would devote an undivided portion of her attention to that sacred volume every day. "It is surely," thought she, "the Author of my being, and not a creature like myself, who understands best my being's end and purpose. If I fulfil it not, I must needs be a worthless thing. Wealth, beauty, even intellectual pursuits, must in that case be only the ministers of self-love. What a detestable principle of living!" Miss Legh could not help at that moment earnestly longing for a friend with whom she might share the burden of her thoughts. She remembered her father — if, indeed, she could be said to remember one whose image never forsook her — and her tears fell. Some idea of the Saviour of the world, as he was represented by Dr Blair, full of the best and noblest human feelings, united to the majesty and glory of Godhead, passed through her mind. Might he not, though unseen, be a *real* friend perhaps present to her mind by some mysterious influence? and might not that friendship be of the most elevating character? But this was an ill-defined vision. She felt like a child whose teacher presents to him some abstraction, which he has not yet strength of mind enough to comprehend. It is not altogether meaningless, but he cannot give it a complete lodgement in his ideas, and he relinquishes the attempt.

Dinner was served at Rosemount at a somewhat earlier hour on that day than usual. This arrangement took place very generally of a Sunday, as Sir Duncan said he always felt hungrier then than on any other day of the week. As the evening twilight came on, the baronet lay stretched on a sofa in the drawing-room, with eyes half closed, reading the last new novel. Harry lounged in an arm-chair within the deep recess of a window, and with head leant back, and eyes wholly shut, seemed either asleep or absorbed in a reverie. He wore his new regimentals. Jane stood in the same window, looking at the tranquil evening light, as shade after shade of a deeper grey fell on the landscape without "Shall I act the part of the monkey, who looked into the puppy's eyes to see what he was dreaming about?" asked she at length of her drowsy cousin. Her mind had been full of other thoughts, but at this stage of her experience she could scarce communicate them to such an one as he. Harry gave out a sound of approbation. "Well, you are thinking," said she, "of the country beauties, who cast admiring glances on your red coat to-day in the church at — town." "By Jupiter," said Harry, sitting bolt upright in his chair, "you are right; you can't think how many pretty demure glances were sent upwards towards the gallery where I sat. But do come and take a stroll over the grounds, and I'll tell you all about it. It is not late yet, and in spite of my red coat, I feel dreadfully mopish." Jane obliged her cousin by putting on her bonnet and going out with him. But she then proposed that, instead of staying in the grounds, they should walk as far as the parish church, as she had heard that there was to be an evening service, which would last till eight or nine o'clock. Thither accordingly they proceeded, Harry entertaining his fair companion by the way with anticipations of his own future prowess, which he said "was to raise the reputation of the garb he wore; with accounts of the many breaches he was to force," and the great execution he was to make among the enemy in all sieges and battles, as well as among the fair sex, by way of *entremets* between the courses of his grand warlike entertainment. Jane would have preferred some other conversation; however, she listened with that quiet good-nature which she always gave to the follies and absurdities of others; — with which, nevertheless, she had not yet learnt to contemplate their meannesses and vices. In this she reversed the manner of many, which is to treat folly with impatience, while they can perfectly tolerate vice.

"Hush, Harry! what is that?" said Jane, as they passed over a plank thrown across a small rivulet at no great distance from the church. They paused and listened. The full moon had now arisen, and its light streamed on the broken, uneven ground around them and on the church spire, which rose white and tall above a belting of low trees, by which the churchyard was surrounded. The sound of a single voice singing, as it appeared, the first measure of a psalm tune, was borne towards them on the faint evening breeze down the rocky declivity over which the streamlet they were crossing had just taken its course. Immediately the air was filled with the chorus of several thousand voices singing the same tune in wild but inexpressibly sweet measure. It was evident that a congregation were in this manner concluding their evening devotions in the open air. Our travellers instantly began to ascend the rocky pathway which led upwards by the side of the stream; and they had only reached the top of the nearest eminence, which was crowned with furze and broom, when a sight burst upon their view as picturesque in itself as, to Jane at least, it was novel and extraordinary.

The banks of the stream, which were pretty high, here receded, from each other; and, from their slope and the nature of the ground, afforded convenient sitting room to the multitudes who were clustered on its sides, to the number, as it appeared, of several thousands. They were distinctly visible by the light of the high full moon, even to the bottom of the little valley; and the more thinly scattered groups and figures on the upper edges of the acclivity stood out in fine relief against the bright clear sky. Jane listened with inexpressible delight to the grave sweet melody, which seemed to ascend like incense to the skies, from the hearts and voices of the assembled multitude. Although gifted with a fine musical ear, she felt that it would be difficult to follow the tune, even after having heard it repeated several times. It was simple in its scale, like the melodies of all primitive people, but rapid and involved in its transitions; and often when the measure seemed about to close, it swelled out anew in what, but for the perfect time kept by so many voices would have seemed an extempore cadence introduced according to the fancy of the moment. The rugged, picturesque character of the landscape, the clear loveliness of the moonlight, the devotional aspect of the people, and their wild sacred music, had all an inexpressible charm; and Jane's heart, at all times alive to the beautiful and good, swelled within her bosom. "Strange!" said she, speaking to her companion, yet as if without heeding whether he listened or not — "I never saw a scene so much in keeping with the holy calm of this light before. Who could look at that sky, with the moon gliding silently through the depths of its serenity, without thinking of something more intensely pure, yet more intensely loving, than any thing belonging to this earth? Yet if the earth does hold any thing that can accord with them, well, it is surely the devotion of humble hearts ascending, without artificial medium, to Him whose ineffable being is but faintly shadowed forth in all things beautiful and pure." The music ceased; a farewell blessing was pronounced by the preacher in a tone which, though not loud, was distinctly audible amid the silence of the evening, and then the multitude rose to disperse. The cousins, too, retraced their steps down the rocky height which they had ascended.

"I don't think the old boy will last long, Jane; do you?" asked Harry, as they returned homewards. "Who do you mean by *the old boy?*" asked Jane, in return. "Why, Dr. Blair, of course," was the reply. "Dear Harry," said Jane, "don't speak in that manner of an old man of so great worth. It really jars on my ear like a false note in music." "Well, then, to please your fancy, I'll call him the *old gentleman*," retorted Harry; "but do you think he'll last long? that's the question." "I am afraid not," replied Jane, "from all that I hear." "Then," said her cousin, "my one-eyed friend, George Donaldson, will be soon ready for license, and he is to have the parish." "What do you mean?" asked Jane, looking into her cousin's face with no pleasant surprise. "This is what I mean," he replied; "George Donaldson and I were college companions. In some sport I rammed a fork into his eye, and I was deuced sorry for it. I can assure you his life was in great danger. I watched by his bed-side for a week without pulling off my clothes; and I can tell you it was a considerable relief to me when he was pronounced out of danger. And really he did bear his loss with wonderful good-nature. So you see I owe him something. The presentation to Glenmore belonged at one time to Sir Duncan; but on some occasion when he wanted money, he sold it to my father, and I made him promise, as soon as he got it, that it should be offered to George Donaldson if it happened to be vacant when he wanted a living; so that if Dr. Blair were to pop off in six months or so, it would be, as the Irish say, *mighty convanient*."

All that passed through Miss Legh's mind upon hearing this short narrative, it would be impossible to describe The scene she had witnessed in the course of the day — that she had just left — returned with a kind of double meaning upon her recollection. She thought of her visits to the cottages of the honest religious poor, with whom pastoral instruction such as they could relish formed the staple of their mental enjoyment, and was a vital part of their moral and religious being. And could she doubt that this George Donaldson, of whom she knew more than her cousin supposed, was immeasurably inferior, both morally and intellectually, to many of her humble friends! notwithstanding his crude college education unaccompanied by any spontaneous operations of a thinking or elevated mind? Her heart was so formed as to make its own all the best feelings of others. Her cheek flushed, and her pulse beat more quickly; yet she could hardly define her own emotions. She did not yet see the subject in the whole of its bearings: so she made no immediate reply. There was an embarrassing mixture of generosity, too, in her cousin's purpose, and she knew that he possessed a considerable share of obstinacy, especially when this one-sided generosity was engaged on its behalf. The latter conviction was uppermost in her thoughts, as she at length laid her hand gently on his arm, saying, "Dear Harry, don't do this rashly. Recollect there are high and sacred interests to be considered. Let us at least talk the subject over occasionally, and try to come to a right understanding about it This is surely a case in which, above all others, *the greatest amount of good ought to be produced to the greatest number*." "No, no," said Harry, "no talking over. I shall not be talked out of my senses by anybody. I am as fixed as — as — as Atlas." Miss Legh sighed. She saw little hope indeed of talking Harry into his senses on such a subject. Here was a vain, reckless, generous boy, with few ideas of any kind, with scarcely a first principle of reasoning; and the interests of thousands — interests which she did feel to be immeasurably superior to any secular interest whatever — were his to tamper with as his fancy might dictate. Her indignation rose; — but it was against a system whose false and guilty nature she began to discern, more than against her poor hair-brained kind-hearted cousin.

Chapter VI

How often have I loitr'd o'er thy green
Where humble happiness endear'd each scene;
How often have I paus'd on every charm!
GOLDSMITH

Viewed from some little distance, the manse of Glenmore appeared embosomed in trees which permitted scarce more than a glimpse of its grey peaked roof; it was in reality, however, situated in the midst of a park, or rather *green* — for it did not aspire to the name of park — which opened at its margin into little wooded and grassy dells, upon whose sides the cattle grazed, and along which more than one clear and gurgling brook found a passage. The manse itself was a tall rambling place, with a gable here and a gable there, and a number of windows looking in different directions, without the slightest regard to the adjustment of their optical axes. Yet a dear old place it was, that same manse of Glenmore. There was a sweet fragrant air about it, a compound of all country things and occupations, and *peculiarly flavoured*, so to speak, from the quantities of pine-wood and heathery peat which were used in the house as fuel. And wide hospitable-looking chimneys there were in kitchen and parlour, up which the flame of that peat and fir-wood used cheerfully to blaze. Something *piquant* and delightful, too, there was, in the old-fashionedness and peculiar style of the furniture. The chairs upon which one sat were of black oak, carved in such a style as would seem to send their date back for several generations. Dr. Blair had been chaplain to a regiment in India before he came to settle in Glenmore, and up stairs and down stairs were many quaint Indian things to send the fancy pleasantly wandering from home, just to bring it as pleasantly back again. Even in the long roomy garrets, besides the usual sleeping-places, there were Indian-made berths or hammocks of cane, with drawers underneath, which might make the sleeper fancy in his dreams that he was sailing in some stately India-bound vessel, with the wide ocean gliding from beneath him.

But the manse garden! — what a delightfully primitive garden it was! at the distance of only a short walk from the house — just across the green, and a little further. It was quite full of fruit-trees and fruit-bushes, surrounded by a low wall, over which a grown-up person might see all around. For the sake of protection it needed no wall at all. No one in the parish would have stolen from Dr. Blair, and few vagrants found their way to that retired spot. The walks were not gravelled; they were of bright green sward, dappled all over in summer with *gowans* and buttercups. There were garden flowers in abundance; not many fine flowers, but such as childhood delights in — roses and lilies, and sweet heart's-ease, and long rows of daisies, crimson, pink, and white. Above all, there was a stream; but that is not the word — there was a *burn*, which ran through it gushing and clear, with the luxuriant grass dipping into its sides, and many a wild flower trying to get a peep at itself in the restless surface. What a garden for children to run wild in, and to luxuriate in the recollection of all their days!

But to return to the manse. The only room it contained of a modernized appearance was the drawing-room, which was on the ground-floor, opposite to the sitting-parlour. In it there were instruments of music — Dr. Blair's family were all musical; and in the windows were myrtles and geraniums, and many fine exotics, through whose green scented leaves the cheerful light streamed in, while the jessamine and roses, clustering outside, peeped gaily at their aristocratic neighbours within. Between this room and the parlour, from the extremity of the one to the extremity of the other, was Dr. Blair's daily walk. Here, with his staff in his hand, and a large cloak around his shoulders, he used to meditate and to study his Sabbath discourses, often stopping to address a word of kindness or advice to the members of the household who happened to cross his path. The sphere of his good lady was at the other end of the dwelling. The parlour communicated, at its extremity, with the kitchen, by means of a long passage, with sundry pantries and closets by the way; and there the worthy woman was continually perambulating on her errands of housewifery, or it might be of charity; for she had always some poor sick persons in the parish for whom to send inquiries, and to whose wants she administered in her own quiet, homely way. In appearance she resembled much the tidy mistress of an old English farm-house. She wore, in the mornings, a little straw-bonnet over her cap, and never wanted, in her household occupations, a white apron over her gown, and a clear muslin handkerchief crossed on her bosom. But she was not an Englishwoman; she was born and bred on the banks of the Dee, where her father had been a small landed proprietor. Now that her family were grown up around her, she did not abate in the least of her activity; she liked to go on in her old way. And what a quiet, kind way that was! What a world of motherliness there was in it! She had, indeed, brought up a large family, though now it was scattered. Several sons were honourably settled in the learned professions; three daughters and one son remained at home. Her eldest, Barbara, was a lively, active girl, whose exuberant spirits her father found it sometimes necessary to restrain, but who made a sad blank, as persons of this description generally do, when circumstances required her absence from home. The household seemed half asleep without Barbara.

Mary, the second girl, was one of those rare creatures who are acknowledged, by persons of all sorts of character, to be a blessing in whatever circle they may take up their abode. It mattered not how ill-natured people were, or how little disposed to think well of their neighbours — every one loved, every one praised Mary, There was scarcely an individual in the parish who would not have intrusted her with the secret of his heart — sure of sound practical advice, and of the gentlest and most charitable judgment of his own personal conduct. Sedate, cheerful, not brilliant, noways beautiful — an habitual self-sacrifice, an abounding charity, and a good sense, adapting itself to all occasions; above all, a deep and most humble piety, formed the basis of Mary's estimable character. *Dear Mary* was the appellation universally applied to her by her acquaintances. Dear *Miss* Mary she was called throughout the parish. The youngest and loveliest sister was a girl of a very delicate constitution, who was liable to violent attacks of asthma, which distressed, while it excited the kind sympathies of the family. It remains to notice only Dr. Blair's youngest son Charles, who took his place between Mary and the young Emily He had scarcely yet reached his twentieth summer, yet he was already a licentiate of the Church. Nor did his appearance and manner leave upon the mind the impression that his studies had been hastily carried on, or prematurely concluded. The sweet, serious expression of his countenance, spoke more of experience than of years. It had been his delight from an early age, to sit at his father's knee, and ask him questions in divinity, which at once pleased and startled, from their depth and acuteness. The father had never known a greater pleasure than to instruct this young son, with whose mind he fondly hoped that God himself had undertaken a course of effectual instruction. Nor was he disappointed, as Charles advanced to manhood.

In every mind of promise there is a transition period, between youth and maturity, when the mental consciousness is quickened, and the soul enters upon a higher state of existence. Nor is this an intellectual process merely. The sentiments then first find their tone; they become acquainted with their own *musical scale*, if we may so speak. From matters of fact they transmute themselves into matters of feeling. Good or evil is no longer good or evil merely. It is pleasing or harsh; beautiful or deformed. And who does not know that to the refinement of this mental ear, as well as to the power of the more mechanical processes of the mind, is owing much of what men term Genius! — Thrice blessed are they with whom this happy transition is made under the auspices of DIVINE TEACHING! Then, indeed, the mental vision is enlarged; for it embraces the things of the spiritual as well as of the natural world. The first note of the soul's awakening music is attuned in harmony with that Nature, from which all beauty and goodness emanate; the first act of the new-born consciousness is, the unselfish prostration of will before a perfection wholly without, and superior to itself And, ah! there are few youthful minds that do not prostrate themselves before some ideal monarch — love, ambition, or it may be the poetry and perfectibility of the human soul, unaided by any higher nature than its own! If such are not discovered by the more practised eye to be skeletons robed in *regal attire*, they are found to be at best but visions of mist, shadowy and beautiful, which must, sooner or later, dissolve into their native element. God alone is a KING in youth, in age, and amid the failing of heart and flesh, in the dissolution of nature itself.

Of the happy number whose first affections are given to spiritual things, was young Charles Blair. One of the leading topics which God blessed for the opening of his mind, was the consideration of the sacred influences of the Holy Spirit. He conversed often and long with his father upon this subject; and he loved, too, to develop the views which were opened to him by intercourse with the pious poor of the parish. He compared their thorough sympathy with the divine mysteries of God's Word, with the stolidity which is manifested when these things are conveyed by human agency alone. In vain he tried to account for this on merely natural principles. It was by no means invariably those of the quickest natural apprehension who understood divine things best, although these latter did seem to have a wonderful effect in training the mind to thought, after they had been received. Charles applied many theories with the ardour of a discriminating and energetic mind; but he became daily more convinced that the phenomena which came under his observation were wrought by other than human agency. Else, how that perfect clearness, that entire sameness of apprehension among people destitute of other intellectual culture, on subjects which, when viewed from the *outside*, and not as matters of experience, appear so abstract, so unmanageable even to philosophic intellects, but which, when put to the test of the highest philosophy, by an order of men such as Newton, Milton, and Bacon, are found to lie in the fundamental principles of things? Charles' mind was deeply impressed with the *fact*, that the Spirit of God does operate on the heart of man. "Oh, my father," he sometimes exclaimed, "surely that Spirit is the noblest gift of God to men! Does it not seem amazing, that, upon the very supposition of its *possibility*, all men do not long for it, mourn for it, and bless its approach ten thousand times more than the husbandman blesses the first shower after a time of parched and arid barrenness?" "It would be so, Charles," his father replied, "were it not for the natural depravity which that Spirit alone can overcome, and which seeks an *ideal* of any kind rather than one of perfect holiness."

The Spirit of God did descend upon the soul of Dr. Blair's young son, like "dew upon the tender herb." His mind was saturated with divine truth. He was, besides, gentle and affectionate in his disposition; and in his preaching, divine love breathed with a warm and gentle influence. The power of love was even more apparent in his manner than in that of his father, whose tone was oftener that of the high *morale*, which ought to constitute the difference between *Christian* perfection and that of the world. Dr. Blair's character did indeed well accord in this respect with his public ministrations, and an instance of it occurred in his conduct at this time with regard to his favourite son. Charles had been licensed much about the time that his own illness commenced, which from the beginning he foresaw must prove fatal.

His ideas of the standards of his Church were very high, as well as of the high-toned and exalted purity of motive which these required. He had, therefore, never allowed his son to preach in his own pulpit, lest it might appear a courting of the suffrages of the people in case it were necessary to appoint an assistant and successor. The parishioners had been much disappointed, especially on the late sacramental occasion, at not hearing "*their own Mr. Charles,*" and had even thought it unkind of their pastor to deprive them of that to which they thought they had a kind of hereditary title. Charles had purposely made an engagement in a distant parish,, where similar services were carried on. Many people, and those of known piety, had thought Dr. Blair unnecessarily punctilious in this matter; but he was very jealous — he had always been so — of keeping what he called his *Christian honour* untarnished. It was only a few, whose sentiments had been refined by a long course of Christian experience, who thoroughly understood him.

Upon the afternoon of the Monday succeeding the dispensation of the sacrament — upon which day the delivery of two sermons is customary in the Highlands — Barbara stayed at home during the latter discourse, to superintend the preparation of dinner. Scarcely any hot meat had been cooked for the four days previous, although the clergymen who assisted on the occasion, and some members of their families, were staying in the manse. Dr. Blair, being unable to go out, was taking his accustomed walk along the ground floor; but on this occasion he prolonged it to a pantry which lay on the way to the kitchen; in which pantry Barbara was busied with her preparations. There was an anxiety approaching to restlessness in his manner. "Where is Mary?" said he to his eldest daughter. "At church, papa," was the reply. Dr. Blair shook his head. "Ah, Martha, Martha — you know the rest, my child." He said no more, but resumed his walk, sometimes addressing a word to his sweet Emily, a poor invalid, who was seated in a large chair by the parlour fire. In a few minutes he was again at the pantry door. Barbara was at that moment carrying out a dish of pastry. Her father stepped up to her, and laid his hand on her shoulder. "Barbara," he said, in a quiet but authoritative tone, "put that away. You ought to know my wish, that such things should not appear on my table, especially at such a time as this. Nothing that is not perfectly simple becomes the household of a humble minister of Christ, like me. Let my table be full and hospitable, but it must be plain. I scarcely thought to have again to reprove you for this fault." Barbara blushed, and looked somewhat mortified, but instantly put away the pastry without remonstrance or reply. Dr. Blair then withdrew, not intending to repeat his visit in the same quarter; but in a few minutes his step was again heard approaching as hastily as his infirmity permitted. "Barbara, come to your sister — she is ill. Haste, child, haste." Barbara flew to the parlour, where she found Emily in the beginning of one of her terrible attacks of asthma. She instantly threw up the windows, ordered some strong coffee to be prepared, and took such other measures as the medical attendant had prescribed. At a time of sickness, no one was more prompt and valuable than Barbara. The poor invalid was in great distress. It seemed as if at every breath suffocation was about to ensue. There could be nothing more harrowing than to witness such an attack, especially in one so young and fragile. The lines of agony were drawn on her sweet face, and large drops stood upon her brow. Her father's mental anguish equalled her sufferings. He walked backwards and forwards with hurried step and clasped hands, as if in prayer, and now and then stopped beside his daughter's chair, and at every momentary interruption in her laboured breathing, inquired, with a kind of abrupt tenderness, "how she felt." Her answers were necessarily limited to a single word. At one time the paroxysm became so violent, that, to one not experienced in the complaint, death would have seemed inevitable. The venerable old man stood looking at her with indescribable distress. He wrung his hands; his prayers were expressed in an audible whisper, and, as if unconscious of being heard, he gave vent to a half-suppressed exclamation, "Would God I could suffer for thee, my child!" No sooner was an interval of relief apparent than he took the sufferer's hand in his, and in tones which that poor sufferer would in all likelihood never forget, pronounced these sustaining words: "When thou passest through the fire, I will be with thee; and through the waters, they shall not overflow thee." There was no commentary — only those words — but they spoke volumes. Emily turned upon her father a look of inexpressible gratitude — a look tearful from the emotion of the moment, but full of sweetness and love. It spoke of a father on earth and a Father in heaven.

  The violence of the attack began to subside, and the young girl was able to request that she might be carried to her own room, in order not to give uneasiness to the coming guests, who were now every moment expected. .When at length these assembled in the drawing-room after sermon, it was with an air of cheerfulness, induced by the expectation of spending an agreeable evening. They all knew how to prize the society of Dr. Blair; and they knew, alas! that the evenings they might pass with him would not in all probability be many. It happened that Mary Blair had not yet quitted her own room when the sound of an approaching two-wheeled carriage attracted her attention, and looking out she discovered a vehicle of the gig description just turning an angle of the road, and containing two individuals whom she knew but too well. The sight produced a most unwonted effect upon her usually placid tamper; she hastily flew down stairs, and, entering the drawing-room, exclaimed, in a tone of dismay, "What *shall* we do? here are Mr. and Mrs. M'Lean arriving in their gig!" The intelligence gave rise to a universal consternation. Even Dr. Blair uttered a short impatient "Pshaw!" "And Mrs. M'Lean has brought her band-box," cried Barbara mournfully, as the rather unwelcome couple alighted at the door.

It is necessary to explain who these persons were whose approach to the hospitable manse of Glenmore was so much the reverse of agreeable. Mr M'Lean was the minister of a parish at some seven miles distance, whose services or society were seldom or never solicited by any of his brethren in the vicinity. The first he never offered; the second he was not at all scrupulous in obtruding when he thought that he himself might be benefited thereby; and such, he was of opinion, could not fail to be the case, when better fare than usual was going in the dwellings of his neighbours. Luckily, his helpmate and he were of the same mind; they had been created for each other. M'Lean's settlement, some ten years before, was the most obnoxious to the popular feeling, except perhaps that of Donaldson, which had ever taken place in that district. The parish of Dalry had been long famous, even in times of persecution, for the pure and enlightened preaching of God's truth; and, consequently, the settlement of a man who was as defective in religion as in intellect, seemed to the pious and right-minded people a peculiar outrage on their dearest rights. Perhaps nowhere throughout Scotland had the committal been more rare than in this locality of any breach of those laws of the country which are founded upon the moral nature of man, and enforced by the law of God. And even to the law which gave to individuals a right to commit such an outrage — a sacrilege on the soul of man — a law founded neither on his moral nature nor on the Word of God — they gave implicit obedience for the time.

"To suppress its own indignation against vice," says a philosophic historian, "is the last effort of a virtuous mind." That which is attained only by the few, it must be a manifest absurdity to expect in the many. Yet even to this height of virtue, by a singularly high religious training, had the people of this district been brought. They gave to an unrighteous law, which they knew and felt to be unrighteous, an unresisting, passive obedience. Such an obedience can, however, in its very nature, be but of a temporary kind. The moral sense may for a time be restrained, but it has in itself a fearfully accumulative power; and as surely as the natural elements of air and water become irresistible by compulsion, so surely does the moral sense become irresistible by compulsion likewise. And to this natural necessity of our being the necessities of duty and providence run parallel. To submit to unrighteousness, personally or locally, may be virtue; to submit to it *nationally*, is either insensibility or cowardice. We say that national submission to evil never arises from aught but insensibility to good, or a fear to vindicate the right; — in the book of God's providence, in the history of nations, it will be so found. But it is otherwise when the heart of a strong people is in the right place. The consciousness of aggression may have smouldered long in this spot and in that, and the strong man may have yet bowed his neck to the yoke; tales of oppression from the storehouse of past generations may have been rife at the peasant's fireside, and have gone no farther; but when the *nation's* cry against iniquity arises, the "*power that is*," is the awakened strength and integrity of a great people, the enlightened, determined conscience of a nation — in which is the voice of God. Nowhere had the people suffered better throughout Scotland than in the poor parish of Dalry; nowhere, therefore, were they better prepared to contend when the time should come. There had been no demonstration of opposition made to the settlement of M'Lean — the church remained empty, that was all. The lands, too, in the vicinity could not be let, and became lowered in value, and thus the patron, who was also chief proprietor, came to suffer where most he could feel.

To return, however, to the manse of Glenmore. We cannot say that Dr Blair gave his uninvited a *kind* reception, but politeness his

Christianity required of him, and he practised it. M'Lean was not however, very nice in his feelings; — he was fully satisfied. Good humour was the habitual expression of his plump round face. One would even have thought him benevolent, if the contrary had not been well known. Not a wrinkle disturbed the smoothness of his narrow forehead. He was now bordering on fifty, but care could never have made the most distant acquaintanceship with him. Within his short squat person his mind seemed to repose as on a bed of down. Perfectly content was he with his empty church every Sabbath, and his good dinner, with a nap after it when he came home. Truly, despite of contempt, one could not help envying the perfection of this man's heart's ease. His wife, who appeared shortly after him in a cap covered with red ribbons and roses (the cap which the ominous band-box had carried), resembled him in a marvellous degree, only she was larger, and still fatter. Her complexion was not so fresh, however, nor did she rejoice in quite the same redolent expression of complacency as her better-half.

When dinner was served, the behaviour of this worthy couple at table furnished excellent entertainment for the younger portion of the guests. Notwithstanding her father's injunctions, Barbara had prepared rather a better repast than was altogether in conformity with his severe taste. In the dessert she had endeavoured to compensate for the want of pastry, by an abundance of fruit and creams, variously prepared. Who does not know that one lively temper may considerably alter the domestic economy of a household? However this may be, the good dinner in no way displeased Mr. M'Lean and his spouse, who placed themselves at opposite sides of the table, in such a position as to command as much as possible the whole of its contents. Their attentions were confined exclusively to each other. No sooner were soup and fish discussed in the ordinary way, than they applied themselves to the business of eating in downright earnest. Nor would this have signified, if they had eaten in silence. But their hospitable appeals to each other were incessant. "Let me lend you a bit of this fine fowl, my dear," cried Mr. M'Lean, at the top of his voice, to his partner on the other side. "If you please; but I would recommend a bit of this veal to you — it is uncommonly nice." "If you have finished your fowl, my dear, I'll send you some of these sweet-breads; they are really very good." "This moment — I am not quite ready yet" And Mrs. M'Lean began to despatch the plateful before her with renewed zeal. These little conjugal attentions at length became so very frequent, especially when the third course made its appearance, that the gravity of the young folks was completely upset. Barbara, who was seated beside a young man with a waggish expression of eye, burst into an uncontrollable fit of laughter. Mary, indeed, gave to this couple a reproving look, but it was with an air which showed her fully alive to the drollery of the scene. At length Mrs. M'Lean, who had indulged herself to such an extent as must have suggested rather squeamish ideas to every one present, pushed back her chair, placed a hand on each knee, and looked around, as if to announce her meal fully completed. "When will you learn to sit so genteelly?" whispered Barbara's companion. Poor Barbara hastily rose from the table to conceal the mirth which she could no longer keep within due bounds, while her companion, who had more command of countenance, instantly assumed an extraordinary gravity of demeanour.

There was one advantage attendant on the society of Mr. and Mrs. M'Lean, viz., that it was in no way necessary to abstain from the discussion of any topic which might be supposed to glance indirectly at their position. Their presence, except in the matter of eating and drinking, might at all times be safely considered a mere accident, which need not in the least trench on the free will of other individuals as to the choice of their topics of conversation. When the table-cloth was removed, they both relapsed into a nearly inanimate state, appearing conscious of the existence of the wine-decanters and the punch, and insensible to all other phenomena of the external world whatever. The conversation now, therefore, reverted to the channel in which it would have flowed before, had not an inclination to the risible prevented anything like an attempt at serious discussion The younger clergymen were naturally anxious to hear Dr. Blair's opinion fully expressed upon the position of affairs in the Church. Such was the veneration entertained by them for the wisdom and high-toned Christianity of his character, that they regarded him with feelings not unlike those which Elisha may be supposed to have cherished for the older prophet just before he was taken up to heaven.

At this precise period negotiations were pending between the most celebrated individual in the Scottish Church and a well-known member of the House of Lords.

"These will come to nothing," said the Doctor, "and it would be ill with Scotland if they did not. The Church of Christ in every age, by whatever name it has been called, has never gained anything by a temporizing course of policy. What would Luther or Knox have gained by such a course? It is common for us to speak of these men, in our littleness, as if *we* could have improved them by softening an asperity here, and planting a conciliatory grace there; but we must remember that God himself fitted them to lay the axe to the root of the tree; and had they been other than they were, no reformation had been ever effected. On the ground of uncompromising truth alone will the Church of Christ ever win a victory. On that ground alone can any attempt at a further reformation in our own Church be successful. Truth, and Bible truth above every other, has an entireness and integrity which suffers no curtailment without the most decided consequences. Therefore, I say to you, who will remain to fight the battle, when God will probably have withdrawn me from it — fight it on the ground of the apostles and prophets, and of those Reformers who were their meet successors in later years. Let it be your aim to make the Church on earth after the pattern of the Jerusalem above. "Cast out of it everything that defileth, and whatsoever *loveth and maketh a lie.*"

"But the *liberum arbitrium*" said one of his brethren, "which, for my own part, I utterly detest and abhor" — "Sir," said the Doctor, interrupting him, "I like you all the better for detesting and abhorring it — it is a detestable thing. They speak of leaving the Church free to work out her own principles; they would leave her free, likewise, to work out her own destruction, which would be the more probable issue of the two. No, sir; whatever are the evils of lay patronage, and they are great, they leave, with part of us at least, the sympathies of the people — and these sympathies we can work for their own highest interests; but let *clerical* patronage take its place, and the best men amongst us would not escape without jealousy and suspicion."

"It would, likewise," said Mr. Campbell, one of the older clergymen, "appear to justify the suspicions of our enemies, and expose us to all the odium of having agitated for our own sakes, and not in the cause of God, and the people."

"Assuredly," replied Dr. Blair; "but that odium we might

bear, as it has at all times been more or less the portion of the followers of Christ, were it incurred for the honour of our great Head, and to promote his cause. But the consequences would be exactly the reverse. Christ would be dishonoured in the jealousies and divisions which would ensue, nor do I deny that many might give just cause for them. It was a sentiment of the Infidel Hume's, but not the less founded on that profound wisdom which he displayed in political affairs, that *no government can be good which trusts much to human virtue.* Now, the most ample experience demonstrates that this axiom applies to the government of the Church as well as of the State. Our Scottish Reformers, sir, who were but too well acquainted with the signal failure of clerical virtue in the Church of Rome, although they left not the axiom on record, put it into practical operation in their admirable code of Church government. The system of checks they provided in the number of our Church courts; in the infusion of lay — no, not lay, I love not to deal in such Popish coin — in the great proportion of men not set apart to the ministerial office, though ordained to the eldership, whom they admitted into the administration of our spiritual affairs; and in the *call* given by a congregation to their future pastor, which was necessary to the validity of the relationship to be formed between them — all told that they believed, what they had the most irrefragable reasons for believing, that supernatural influence was confined in its operation to the hearts of individuals, and did not operate in the way of infallibility upon any public body of men whatever. Now, have we a right to derange this system, by subjecting the free call to the absolute arbitration of Church courts, and thus throwing the great balance of power into their hands? Can we take it upon us to answer for the virtue of presbyteries in our own day, in all possible circumstances? If not, how can we answer for that of our successors and of generations yet unborn? Sir, we have no right to commit the religious liberties of our people to such a precarious safeguard; the highest virtue which any body of men can manifest, is to place themselves beyond the reach of temptation."

"But, Doctor, do you not think," asked a young man, who seemed to be listening with some anxiety to Dr. Blair's opinion, "do you not think that in the present state of Evangelism in the country, we could afford effectual protection to the people?"

"If the spiritual independence of the Church were fully

acknowledged," replied Dr Blair, "we might do so as far as the civil power is concerned; but we could not protect them from ourselves. There is much sincerity and true piety amongst us; but in a time of rest and ease there would be, likewise, much of the weakness of a one-sided charity, which, out of a dislike to injure the worldly interests of a brother, would introduce other elements than the purely spiritual one into the deliberations of our Church courts. This is an obvious source of corruption."

"But," said the same young man, "do you think there is no danger of corrupting influences among the people themselves?"

"To an infinitely less degree," said Dr. Blair. "I conceive that the risk of the people's choosing a pastor from similar motives is always exceedingly small. A man who wishes to procure a living for a friend, is among them but a unit among hundreds, and it is more than probable that he will have all the hundreds against him. A minister in a presbytery is but one among a few, and he and his brethren (always supposing a declining state of things) might accommodate one another. The quarter from which the greatest danger ought to be apprehended from the free choice of the people, might apparently be error of judgment in choosing men of unsound doctrine; this, however, we ought not to forget, we ourselves have the means of *altogether* obviating. The people in our communion can only choose among the *licentiates of the Church* — those who have already passed the ordeal of examination by the office-bearers in all that ought properly to come within their cognizance, which is soundness of doctrine, and propriety of conduct. Perhaps it is one of the greatest advantages of a sound religious establishment, that the people within its pale *can* choose only from this class. The voluntary system has no such check. It becomes of less consequence to a congregation which pays its own minister, whether they remain in connection with any particular section or not. Then, our *electors* pass through the same examination in being admitted members of the visible Church; and it is unquestionably only they — I mean Church communicants — who have any right to a share in Church government, just as it is only the *subjects* of any government who have a right to a share in its representation. Thus we possess the full power of the keys; of all that Christ has given us we lose nothing, and ours is the blame if we suffer any unclean thing to enter in."

"Do not the same arguments apply to patronage?" remarked some one at the table. "The patron, too, can only choose from the licensed class."

"Ah!" remarked the Doctor, "patronage is an evil for which such a check is totally ineffectual, because it corrupts the administration of justice in spiritual matters at its very source. We shall suppose patronage to have its beginning in a very pure and efficient state of the Church — as indeed was actually the case in the year 1711. Patrons, we shall assume, present for a course of years men of good information and irreproachable morality, who cannot be rejected by any Church court, and who yet, nevertheless, are not religious in heart — that is, their motives of action are only such as belong to worldly men, and the people have no power of refusing them. Such men are bound to the patron by double ties. They are indebted to him for their own livings; they are dependent on him for those of their sons and relatives. We can thus easily perceive how the character of those who are admitted to license shall be in a short time fearfully deteriorated. A great proportion of them will be always found, in the like circumstances, to consist of the relatives of the clergy, and the dependants of the patrons. Such, I believe, has been the actual process of deterioration in our Church till within the last fifteen years, when God, who had always preserved for himself a remnant, arrested the downward progress of evil, and commenced a work, by his Spirit, in the hearts of many of us, which has inclined us to break the ties of interest and to prefer our duty to God to every worldly motive. Therefore it is that we are anxious to remove the source of corruption, and to restore the people to that just influence, which enables them to *demand* purity in those who are to care for their souls."

"How then, sir," said a young stranger, who had carried a letter of introduction to the manse of Glenmore two days before, colouring as he spoke, from the consciousness that his sentiments ran contrary to the general current of opinion in the company of which he was one — "How then, sir, do you find it consistent to be a minister of a Church established in a manner different from what you deem satisfactory?"

"Because," replied the Doctor, "the standards of my Church, which received the fullest sanction of the State, are conformable to the days of her purity, and to that condition to which we would again restore her, and have never been conformed to those innovations which the State has in later times introduced. When admitted to the ministry, I was required to swear obedience to the courts of the Church, and to Christ Jesus as its only Head; but I was required to swear neither to patronage nor to State control in spiritual affairs. Because, my conscience being thus left free, I hold the great principle of a righteous establishment, and think that, as long as there is a promise of vigour in the Church to shake herself free from her impurities, it is my duty to strengthen her hands in the struggle, and not to weaken them by dissent."

"Well, Doctor," said the clergyman who had preached the forenoon sermon on the previous day, and who was a man as estimable for piety as he was beloved in the country; "in case of the *liberum arbitrium* being offered us *bona fide* by the Government — I mean a power given to our courts to reject a presentee, simply in respect of the dissent of the people — what course of conduct would you pursue? would you separate yourself from the Establishment, rather than accept such a settlement?"

"I freely confess to you, my dear sir," said Dr. Blair, "that the subject is one encompassed with difficulty. It is probable that God in his providence will not see meet to subject me to the trial in my own person, therefore it ill becomes me to use language either boasting or peremptory; but I think that, by his grace, I would be found in that minority, if it were such, however small, which would reject the settlement of the *liberum arbitrium*. I cannot deny that I should be predisposed to this step as a point of honour — a vindication of my own purity of motive in the side I have chosen; but mere *points of punctilio* a Christian must always hold himself ready to sacrifice to his Master's cause. This, therefore, I should hold far from a *sufficient* motive to determine my conduct; but I have the fullest conviction that, from the causes I have already alluded to — the extreme detestation of the people to such a measure, which would alienate their sympathies from us — with this on the one hand, and with the necessity for an improbable virtue on the other, the l*iberum arbitrium* would be most detrimental, if not fatal, to the cause of Christ in this land. My earnest prayer will continue to be, that, in the spirit of the prayer, '*Lead us not into temptation*', a majority will be found who, when the day of trial comes, will, in the strength of God, steadily refuse this specious and dangerous bribe. I could not dare to judge men harshly, who, when the pressure upon their consciences was removed, would refuse to sacrifice the public benefits of an establishment to what they might deem too ultra an adherence to principle ; but such an adherence is, I am convinced, our wisest, as well as our noblest path. It would place our beloved Church in one of the finest attitudes which was ever assumed by any Church on earth. Would to God that England too would join us in the cry for purity in her religious establishment! If such a cry arose in that earnest voice which can only proceed from a true appreciation of spiritual benefits, we might look with an assured hope for the approach of those days when the knowledge of the Lord shall cover the earth as waters cover the sea".

During this discussion the female part of the audience had withdrawn, and when the gentlemen rose to rejoin them, Dr Blair, exhausted by the part he had taken in the conversation, retired to his own apartment. Mr. and Mrs. M'Lean took leave immediately after tea, and the circle of intimate friends who remained spent the evening in delightful and animated discourse. Dr. Blair's character — the commanding moral position he had always maintained — was unreservedly spoken of. The various parts of his history, in every stage of which his unremitting labours in his Master's cause had been equally blessed of God, were called to remembrance with a warm and circumstantial interest. In this discourse his daughters freely joined. With them the estimable traits of their father's public and private character had formed the theme of many an hour's familiar conversation. Why should they conceal how highly they valued him? Few men, alas! are heroes by their own fire-sides; and when they are so regarded, we may rest assured that the tribute paid to them is at least genuine. Of all the party Mrs. Blair only was silent. She seldom spoke much; and she felt as if, on an occasion like the present, to praise her husband would be to praise herself. The beaming expression of her countenance alone told that her heart was not uninterested. She joined in the conversation but once, and that was to relate a little anecdote of recent occurrence, which told in some measure to her own disadvantage. It was as follows:—

A period of temporary distress had existed among the small farmers of the neighbourhood, and, under the pressure of a demand for money, they had endeavoured to dispose of a part of the crop of the previous year at a very low rate. An honest poor man had come to the manse two or three weeks before, with a sack of meal in his little cart, offering it for sale at a price much below the average rate of the day. Mrs Blair unthinkingly, or, it might be, as she said, from the habit of a prudent housewife, accustomed to lay in her provisions to the best advantage, accepted the meal at the offered price. Her husband happened to observe the man as he was leaving the door in his empty cart, and making some hasty inquiries as to the nature of his business, he discovered the disadvantageous rate at which his bargain had been made. He instantly despatched a messenger with an additional payment for the meal, bestowing, at the same time, a more severe rebuke on his partner than she had ever before received from him.

CHAPTER VII

The clerks tak' benefices with brawls,
Sum of Saint Peter, Sum of Saint Paul's,
Tak' he the rent, nae cair has he
In taking suld discration be.
DUNBAR

  The regiment in which young Harry M'Leod had obtained his commission was ordered to India in the course of a few weeks, and Harry was to join it a week before its departure. In the meantime, he was determined, as he said, "to have some fun before he left old Scotland;" and with this object in view he rode to Fort-George, where an English regiment was stationed, in order to obtain leave for a few of the young officers to spend some time with him at Rosemount. The leave was granted, and the invitation joyfully accepted. Fort-George, although interesting to the stranger, as the most complete fortification in Britain, makes but a dull place of residence. It is situated on the margin of the Moray Frith, in a barren tract of country, about a mile from the village of Campbelton, and at the distance of ten or twelve from the nearest town. The officers are thus thrown in great measure on their own resources, which, with some of them at least, are not very many, and so leave of absence on invitation is for them a great affair. At Rosemount they enjoyed themselves to the full They boated, fished, danced, made pic-nics, raced a couple of horses to death, and within doors turned everything upside down. Sir Duncan placed no restraint on their frolics, so long as his cherished pictures were not made the subjects of any mischievous fancy. Indeed, in his own indolent, good-natured way, he enjoyed himself with the youngest of them.

  So much boisterous mirth could scarce, however, be quite agreeable to his niece, who if she had had less dignity of mind and manner, would have been exposed, not to rudeness perhaps, but at least to too great familiarity of address from young men without restraint, and in the hey-day of youth and spirits. But she, too, was at perfect liberty. She could keep her own drawing-room, which no one presumed to intrude upon, or she could walk to any distance with May for an attendant; — and of this liberty she made ample use. She joined in the excursions made for the general amusement only when she felt disposed, and when they were of a character which she could fully enjoy. On one such occasion it happened that a pic-nic was planned to one of the most lovely spots in the parish of Aird, and, by way of diversifying the entertainment, it was proposed to pay a visit to Donaldson — a kind of lion in his way — whose manse would lie quite in the neighbourhood It was the latter accompaniment which induced Miss Legh, who had often before visited the spot in question, to make one of the party.

To put this plan in execution, therefore, they set out one magnificent day, canopied by "the summer heaven's delicious blue;" — Sir Duncan and three of the officers in a carriage, Miss Legh and her cousin Harry on ponies, and accompanied by a certain Lieutenant Brown, who was, when occasion offered, the lady's most devoted attendant. He was, indeed, the most rational of all the young men, and soon learned to regard his countrywoman as something more than merely a beautiful girl. His heart was evidently touched by the nobility of her character and the attractive elegance of her manners. It was no difficult matter to discern that, when he addressed her, his eye beamed more brightly, and his voice became more musical. But he, too, had some nobility of heart. He remembered that a poor lieutenant was not a suitable match for a wealthy heiress, and determined, if he received no unequivocal marks of favour, to keep his secret attachment to himself. Such favours were never bestowed, and he was silent — for ever.

Now, however, many sweet influences combined to give enchantment to this ride. Love in the young officer's breast was not yet a passion; the presence of her to whom his heart began to pay its homage was all that was necessary for his happiness. Their way lay through an open valley, green with the tender braird of early summer, and skirted by noble hills of so gorgeous a blue as seemed but the tint of the sky deepened into a summer midnight. The river, upon whose banks lay the scene they were about to visit, wandered as yet comparatively bare and open through the landscape, its silvery mazes glittering beneath the bright sunlight. The young people, easily made happy by the aspect of nature, set off at a hard gallop, scarcely allowing themselves a breathing time, to enjoy at leisure the scenery which so exhilarated their spirits. In this manner less than an hour's riding brought them near the residence of Donaldson, where they had agreed with the party in the carriage to await their more tardy arrival. Not till then did they begin to consult together upon some mode of *entrée*, a difficulty which had never before occurred to them; and, accordingly, with this in view, they began to inspect minutely the minister's premises. The manse, a white-washed unenclosed place, in appearance like a second or third-rate farmhouse, was situated on the top of a rising hillock, bare and solitary, with no cottage in its vicinity where they might find a person to carry an introductory message. In this little dilemma Lieutenant Brown volunteered to ride forward and break the ice, when they became aware that an old man was walking leisurely down the bank, whom they all with one accord took to be the gardener. To him, therefore, they addressed themselves.

"Is the clergyman of this place at home, my good friend?" inquired Brown.

"Oo yes, the minister's at home," was the reply, in a drawling accent, which was neither Highland nor Lowland, but partook rather of the more disagreeable peculiarities of both. At the same time the old man set himself, with an air of great *non-chalance*, to inspect the appearance and accoutrements of those who wished to ascertain a fact of such importance, and in so doing he took a leisurely pinch of snuff.

" Do you think it will be convenient for him to receive strangers to-day?" asked Miss Legh.

"I'm no sure but it micht," again drawled out the man, as he directed his sunken eyes with a scrutinizing gaze towards the beautiful face of the speaker.

"Go away, old chap," said Harry, striking in, "and tell the minister that some of Sir Duncan Ross' friends want to see himself and his house. There's a half-crown for you," continued he, handing down the said sum.

"*I'm the minister mysel*" said the supposed gardener, with a certain expression of humour which certainly was not out of place; "nevertheless", continued he, depositing the money in his breeches' pocket, "I'll no refuse the half-crown. Come away, come away, the gude wife 'll be glad to see you." So saying, he walked or rather shuffled on before, leaving his guests to follow in not a little astonishment.

"I've heard," whispered Lieutenant Brown, "that this clergyman was an original, but I could not have conceived of this. Just look at him as he trundles himself up there." And look at him as a kind of natural curiosity, they well might. The coat he wore was exactly such as the minister might be supposed to have worn in his study till it was no longer wearable, and then to have handed over to his gardener, who might have exposed it to wind and weather for nearly a twelvemonth longer. His hat, a mis-shapen article, bare and cracked in the crown, an old clothes-man would not have bought for a penny. His shoes were whole certainly, but of the coarsest manufacture; and neither they nor any of the other habiliments seemed to have known a brush since the time of their first unpolluted innocence. Even the minister himself seemed to think that his appearance needed some apology; which mark of his partaking of the frailties of humanity in respect of any care for his outward man was probably elicited by the peculiarly noble aspect of the female rider of the party. When near the door of his house, he turned round and thus addressed his approaching guests:—

" We heard that ye micht be coming the way the day, and the gude wife was bothering me in the morning to put on my Sabbath clothes — but I just couldna be fashed. 'Gudewife,' says I, 'if I was to put on my Sabbath clothes for a' the gentry that comes, ye ken weel enough it would be Sabbath every day.' The truth is, I canna go out to take a dander about my bit farm, but I must meet some gentry or another; I dinna ask them a' into the house though or trouth it would he little better than a public."

His visitors looked at each other. "If it is in the slightest degree inconvenient," said Lieutenant Brown, "we shall return, and go down by the river. We wanted nothing but the pleasure of seeing you."

" No, no; ye'll no do that — ye'll no do that," said the old man hastily; "ye're respected neighbours — that's altogether different. Come down offa your beasts, and I'll take them into the stable mysel!" They alighted accordingly, but of the arrangement proposed the young men would not hear. They insisted upon themselves seeing their horses lodged, and led them away to the stable under the leadership of Donaldson. Miss Legh, being thus left alone, made her way in by the first open door. The shabby parlour in which she found herself, contained no furniture but a table and some chairs. The windows were uncurtained, and the carpet worn and dirty; but a set of tea-things were arranged upon the table for a party of apparently much the same number as their own. Were there other guests expected, or was this tea apparatus placed for them? If the latter, as Donaldson hinted, how could notice have been given of their intended visit? Miss Legh had scarcely time to think over this, when the minister and her young friends entered. "I must see noo who I have," said the former, as he drew near the lady. " Ye're a bonny lass — ye'll be Sir Duncan's niece that we have heerd o'?" Miss Legh bowed. "What's your name, if ye please, mem ? I have heard it, but I dinna mind."

Miss Legh gave a glance half-shy and half-haughty towards Lieutenant Brown, which he interpreted rightly, as a request to answer for her.

"You are very particular in your inquiries, sir"" said that young gentleman; "however, to satisfy you, this lady's name is Miss Hamilton Legh. She is a native of England."

"Oo ay," continued Donaldson, just as if his question had been answered by the person to whom it was addressed — "Oo ay; ye'll be connected wi' Sir Duncan by the mother's side. Is your father alive?" The tears sprung to Miss Legh's eyes, while Lieutenant Brown looked at the old man very much as if he wished he had been a young one, that he might knock him down. "If you will condescend," he said, "to address your examination to me, I shall be most happy to answer any questions you may choose to put regarding myself. I must beg you, however, to spare that lady."

"Oo, just so; I see — I see," said Donaldson, nodding his head gravely; "she's an orphan." And then turning towards the Lieutenant, as if his invitation had been given with all the good faith in the world, he went on.

"Ye'll be a gallant from the Fort, I'se warrant — a lieutenant, by the epaulet on your one shoulder!" Brown smiled. and bowed. "An Englisher, too, I fancy by your tongue!" "Quite right," was the reply.

"What was your father ?" continued Donaldson, without the least surmise that he might be touching on a delicate subject, especially in presence of the lady. Brown however, took it with great *bon hommie.*

"My father," said he, "was an officer, like myself, and so was my grandfather, which is all I know of my pedigree. You are certainly a most minute querist" continued he, smiling.

"Oo ay," replied Donaldson;" I like to ken my company. And what is he, yon braw chiel' that's standing at the door yonder, looking for the carriage? He's a strapping lad. 'Deed, ye're a' weel-faured for gentry; for I dinna think much o' the looks o' the gentry commonly."

This remark fairly restored Miss Legh to her accustomed cheerfulness. Brown and she laughed outright.

" That young gentleman," said the former, " is Sir Duncan Ross' nephew. I think I have heard him mention that he was a college companion of your son."

Donaldson contracted his mouth, and gave a long loud whistle. "Whe-e-e-e-ew!" said he. "Young Harry M'Leod! the wild laddie that stappit the fork in Geordie's ee ! Come in, come in," said he, calling aloud; " ye needna be feart for me. I ken yon was an accident, and besides, ye have promised him a parish. A body," continued he, nodding sagaciously, "may think himself very weel off now-a-days that gets a parish for one o' his een." Harry, who ludicrously enough had made his escape to the door, as soon as he heard the questioning begin, from some awkwardness of feeling similar to what the old man had guessed at, and which, indeed, had prevented him from making himself sooner acquainted at the manse of Aird, now came frankly forward and shook Donaldson by the hand. "And a parish he shall have," said he, "if it ever lies within the compass of my power. I can tell you I would have given my own two eyes for his one, but — "

" I ken that — I ken that," said Donaldson, interrupting him. "But what made you *slink* away to the door yon way, man, like a thief?"

Harry reddened. Any imputation on his manliness was what he could least brook; however, he merely replied by asking for the health of his friend.

"He's away fishing, or something that way," said Donaldson. "He's a grand hand at the trout. I'll maybe no see him for days thegither. I dinna think he cares much about the book. 'Deed, *naaturally*, as one may say, I dinna think he has so much in him o' the minister as mysel'; and neither has he my great powers o' memory. But we dinna cast our own lot," he continued, shaking his head with an attempt at devoutness.

The carriage was by this time heard approaching, and ere Donaldson had time to bustle out to the door to make an obeisance, Sir Duncan and his companions dashed into the room. The former was received by the minister with all the obsequiousness which his rather defective organ of veneration could command. There was a certain definite rank and place in the county which possessed a strong influence over his mind. It always suggested to him ideas of patronage. Nevertheless, after the first salutations were over, he would have proceeded to put the "loons" as he called them, to the question, with the same frank ingenuity which he had exercised towards their predecessors, had not Sir Duncan, with an instinctive horror of bores, cut him short in the commencement. "' We must not lose the day," said he; "we wish to explore the beautiful scenery in your neighbourhood."

"Ye'll stop and see Mrs. Donaldson, sir?" said the minister. "She'll be glad to see you; indeed, she was led to expect you the day."

"By all means," replied Sir Duncan, "if she will favour us with her presence speedily." Donaldson rung a little hand-bell which lay on the table, and a slip-shod maid, with hair in papers, presently opened the door. The message requesting Mrs. Donaldson's presence was despatched, and that lady herself appeared with a rapidity which looked rather as if she had been waiting somewhere not far off, on purpose to be sent for. She was a red-cheeked servant-maid-looking person, of an astonishing youth considering the age of her partner, and, holding a tray with glasses in one hand, and a bottle in the other, she stopped at the door to make a rustic courtesy, then advancing to the table, proceeded straightway to fill the glasses. "Drink to the company," said her husband laconically. Mrs. Donaldson, obeying the word of command, accordingly took up a glass of wine, turned to Sir Duncan, and, courtesying, pronounced the words, "Your health I wish, sir;" which ceremony having repeated towards each member of the party, she touched the wine with her lips, and set it down again on the table. Her husband took it up, and, with many bows, reiterated the same good wishes. After which the wine was handed round, Wickedly enough, one of the young officers, who was somewhat of a wag, set the example of imitating the courtesies of Mr. and Mrs. Donaldson. The humour caught; and an infinity of bows and wishes for health ensued — all executed with utmost gravity.

"I better show you my bit garden noo," said Donaldson. "There's a bonny view from the summer-house, that the gentry's a' fond to see; but I dinna show it to every ane o' them." So saying, he was about to take precedence of his guests, when Mrs. Donaldson, making a great effort at speech, struck in. "Ye'll come back to your tea, my lady and gentlemen," said she; "ye see I was expecting you. I have everything ready, and it would be a great disappointment."

"O by all means," cried out several of the young men at once; " we *shall* come back; sha'nt we, Sir Duncan? We shan't disappoint the lady!" Sir Duncan gave a careless assent, and after making a grave obeisance to Mrs. Donaldson, they all walked out in the wake of her husband. They were led into a small and ill-cultivated garden, which sloped down towards the river, whose sullen rush could now be heard, although the depth of the ravine through which it had cut its way prevented it from being as yet seen.

There was a picturesque-looking summer-house built upon a projecting crag, which it covered so entirely as not even to leave a foot-path around; and into this little place, no sooner had the foremost of the party entered, than he uttered an exclamation of surprise and delight. The windows commanded a prospect of the romantic scenery below in all directions, which now all at once burst upon the view. The river was not wide — perhaps not more in this place than twenty yards across — but deep, sullen, and dark; except that when opposed in its progress by some huge boulder or some mass of earth and stones, bound together by the roots of the still adhering bushes and trees, it raved and reared its whitened crest of foam, as if maddened by opposition or impatient of delay. The character of the scene would have been altogether wild and savage, had it not been for the profusion of birch trees which, with their small foliage and beautiful tracery of silver stems and branches, formed a tapestry of unrivalled elegance. Here and there the rock was bare, showing nothing but scars of wind and weather, and the sheer descent of the precipice; anon a birch would spring up, striving to throw its light mantle over the nakedness of the parent cliff, and bending till trunk and branches were nearly inverted. In every more favourable spot, a garden of such trees ensconced itself, whose colour of mother-of-pearl and green now shone softly in the still mellowing rays of the afternoon sun. "This," said Sir Duncan, " is after the manner of Salvator Rosa's finest pieces; only those graceful birches don't grow in Italy — a pity they don't. Come now, my young friends, what do you liken those same *innamoratas* to?" "To tresses on the cheek of beauty," replied one of the young men. This comparison was somewhat demurred to, on the score that, although the light streamers of the birch did resemble a lady's tresses, there was nothing in the stern masses on which they grew which could with any propriety be compared to her cheek.

"They remind me," said Miss Legh, "of a young beauty clinging with dishevelled tresses to the steel-clad form of an ancient warrior — her father, who is going forth to battle." A murmur of applause greeted this idea; but two or three of the officers thought that a lover would have been more appropriate, in the circumstances, than a father. Miss Legh, on the other hand, justified her fancy, as having in it more of poetical truth — the tree and the soil on which it grew holding the relation of parent and child. "But is not a lover the most likely to be in the situation you describe, fair niece?" asked Sir Duncan. "By no means," Miss Legh replied, "with deference to you, uncle. You know the fine old ballad,

'Stateley stept he east the wa', and stately stept he west,' "

and she repeated, with much animation, a few verses of the splendid ballad of Hardiknute, descriptive of the leave-taking of Fairly Fair with her noble father and his seven bold sons.

"Weel, weel, I dare say it's very gran'," remarked Donaldson, who had been showing some signs of impatience during this discussion; "I dare say it's a' very gran'; but for my own part, I would rather see a bonny kail-yard. I'll be going up to the house — ye can make out the way down to the river yoursel's. Go down by yon bit roadie that ye see turning the foot o' the scaur, and take care ye dinna break your necks. Ye'll be in to your tea; and as it's getting late o' the day, maybe ye can eat what ye have in the baskets as weel in the house as out on the grass." This was said in somewhat of a peevish tone, and the old man shuffled off with such an air as plainly indicated that his complacency had come to an end. No sooner was he gone than a volley of abuse was sent after him.

To the froth of fashion vulgarity is incomparably more revolting than vice. With them the manner of the sin is everything; if the surface be pleasing, they care little to examine farther. "The ugly beast!" exclaimed one, looking after Donaldson with set teeth. "Did his breath come across you?" asked another; "it smelt like a piggery." "The carbuncles on the swine's nose tell of a rather intimate acquaintance with the whisky-trough," remarked Sir Duncan cynically. Miss Legh alone was silent. She disliked Donaldson more than any of them, and *her* dislike was usually an instinct of moral aversion; but she had a strong feeling of the sacredness of the *salt*, and she recoiled from partaking of a man's hospitality for no other purpose than that of abusing and ridiculing him. She therefore merely expressed a wish that they might not return to the manse. This proposal was, however, received with noise and clamour. "No, no, cousin," said Harry, with little ceremony; no squeamishness. Let's have all the fun out of the old chap that we can." "And in the meantime," said Sir Duncan, let us linger here no longer. The sun is hastening down. We shall see him set upon the waterfall in yonder dell."

The scene by the side of the waterfall was one of exquisite beauty. The dark rocky masses towering overhead; the picturesque and motionless outline of the foliage which enveloped their sides, now seeming as if fixed in the calm against the cloudless heaven; the gloomy volume of the river, with its unceasing rush, whitening into a snow-fall, as it descended in its entire breadth a precipice thirty feet in height, the cloud of pearly spray hovering above, which reflected the oblique sunshine in a fading rainbow; — all spoke the language of nature's own majestic solitudes. The spirits of the most volatile were softened for the time; and little was spoken during a walk of half a mile along the water's edge, until, upon retracing their steps, they found themselves once more in the neighbourhood of the manse.

A fire had by this time been lighted in the unlovely parlour, which made it look somewhat less uninviting. The tea things still stood upon the table, accompanied by some eatables, in the form of pots of preserves, butter, oaten cakes, &c. The kettle was singing by the fire-side, and the tea-pot stood on the hearth; so the lads, in high glee, seated themselves around the table, although neither host nor hostess had yet appeared. Donaldson entered first, with spirits excited and temper considerably improved. His guests afterwards alleged that he had mollified himself by applications to the dram-bottle. However that may be, his lady had no sooner, appeared, and applied herself to the business of tea-making, which she did without any preface, than he became extremely loquacious, and he now seemed inclined to turn the conversation upon himself rather than on his guests; which disposition they gladly encouraged. He was soon deep in the mysteries of his own life, and especially of his various courtships.

"Mrs. Donaldson there," he said, with a wink, "is my third wife no less. It's a ticklish thing, ye understand, lads, to have to deal wi' the female sex; and as I always liked to ken weel wha I had to do wi' in the way of marriage, I just married my ain servant lass. I mind weel my worthy neighbour Dr. Blair was greatly astonished when I went to ask him to perform the ceremony between me and *her* there. The honest man began to comfort me for the loss of my former partner, who had been about six weeks buried. 'It's very true, Doctor,' says I, 'it's an inconvenient thing to want a wife, more especially when there's a hoose and a family to be taken care o'; and for that reason, I just came to ask you the favour that ye would buckle me to another ane.' If the Doctor had seen horns growin' out on me, he couldna hae lookit mair astonished. 'And who are you going to marry, Mr. Donaldson?' says he. ' Oo, just Jenny, my own servant lass,' says I. 'But is she a fit wife for you?' says he. 'What can she do?'. 'Do!' says I, 'she can bake, and she can shew, and she can keep the hoose red, and the bairns red, and she can work wi' the wires this way (making the motion of stocking-working with his fingers), and that's more nor ye'll get ane o' your fine ladies to do!' Weel, the Doctor declined to perform the ceremony. Although I have had no cause to complain o' unkindness from himsel' or his lady in any other thing, I thocht that a very unneighbour-like action."

The gentlemen expressed their great sympathy with Mr.

Donaldson, and vied with each other in condemning Dr. Blair's unfeeling conduct. "But how was it that you first thought of turning your attention to the ministry?" inquired Lieutenant Brown. "Your life would form a most interesting subject for an autobiography." "I'll tell you that, my good sir," said Donaldson. "My father was factor to the Laird of — , who, I dare say, ye ken to be a Roman, or a Papist, as we say in this part. My father and him were aye very chief; and when the laird was in want of company, he used just to send for my father, that they micht have a crack and a glass thegither. When they were very crouse one nicht — maybe a wee into their cups — at which time my father was always maist sensible, he began to speak something concerning his family. 'Noo, laird,' says he, 'I have gotten all my sons respectably provided for excepting Jock. I dinna ken what'll be done wi' Jock; reely, though I say't that shouldna, it's no an easy matter to see what way he can turn his hand.' 'Oo,' says the laird, 'I'll tell you what ye'll do; just make him a minister, and I'll find the parish.' Weel, wi' that I was sent to the college, and the factor took good care to keep the laird to his word — as ye see." "And how did you get on?" inquired one of the officers. " How did you contrive to make sermons, which, I understand, the people here expect their clergymen to do? I don't see, now, how I myself, for instance, should ever be able to make a sermon!" "Oo, fine," replied Donaldson, " 'deed I make little *makin'* serve me; there's more sermons made already than ever folks 'll make use o'. Every man has his gift, as I told the presbytery the day I was licensed — he! he! he!" — and the minister, tickled by the remembrance, broke out into a hoarse laugh; "every man has his gift, and the *memory* is mine. I read two good sermons every Saturday nicht, and I preach them, word for word, on the Sabbath; and if the people winna come to the church it's their own fault. It's been weighty on my mind this some time back, though, that my memory is not what it has been. I have been obliged this twelvemonth now, to read my sermons twice before I can repeat them altogether correctly."

An exclamation of distress, which here burst from the lips of Mrs. Donaldson, attracted the attention of her guests, who were all engaged either in discussing their own viands, which their footman, who waited, helped them to, with a very intelligent sneer on his countenance — or in laying up food of a different kind from the conversation of their host. Mrs. Donaldson, in the absence of politeness on the part of any one, had been making an effort to add to the contents of the tea-pot out of the kettle; but some unfortunate impediment in the spout prevented her from getting her purpose accomplished. First one person and then another, in this dilemma, offered his services, but nothing in the shape of water would consent to make its egress. Donaldson insisted on trying his own hand at it. He failed like the others, in the ordinary mode; but then, with an ingenuity peculiar to himself, he applied his mouth to the spout, and blew a blast so strong and sonorous as might have sufficed to clear a smith's bellows of its ashes. Tea, brown and translucent, directly issued from the kettle, the leaves of which had been evidently the cause of the unfortunate obstruction. Something very like a titter ran round the table; and poor Mrs. Donaldson, with her face scarlet with bashfulness, thought it necessary to apologize, though she evidently knew not exactly to which circumstance the apology should be applied. "It was Mrs. Blair that heard ye was coming this way the day, my lady and gentlemen," said she. "She sent white sugar and half-a-pound o' tea, thinking I mightna be prepared; and I thocht I couldna do better than put the maist o' the tea into the kettle."

One of the officers took it upon himself to assure her that she *couldn't* have done better; at the same time, they all professed their entire satisfaction with the tea they had already got, and declined taking any more.

The carriage and horses were immediately ordered, and poor Mrs. Donaldson was relieved of the intolerable burden of her fashionable guests.

CHAPTER VIII

Artist, attend — your brushes and your paint;
Produce them, take a chair — now draw a saint
                                    COWPER

A summer replete with "the joys of sunshine" passed away; and during its progress Miss Legh, under the guidance of her uncle, had visited all the more interesting scenery of the northern and western Highlands. Autumn came on, to robe the majestic hills in colours of less depth and intensity, beneath the driving cloud and the mottled sky. The streamlets swelled into torrents; the rivers rushed more tumultuously onwards in their channels; and the spirit of the blast began to pass fitfully across the horizon, casting his grey shadow over the earth. Autumn, in its turn, was darkening into winter, when Sir Duncan, too, began to look gloomy, and to talk of Italy. His niece. who refused to go with him abroad, looked forward with impatience to the time of his departure, when she expected him to accompany her as far as Edinburgh; at which place she meant to pass the winter with some not very distant relatives, ere she returned to settle finally among her own tenantry at Chesterlee. Dr. Blair had been lately called to enter his everlasting rest; and his death had thrown a gloom over the parishes both of Glenmore and of Aird. Various rumours had gone abroad respecting his successor, and although nothing definite had yet transpired, enough was said to excite the people's aversion towards the son of the neighbouring minister. The choice of their hearts and hopes was the son of their late beloved pastor — their own Mr. Charles, who, both in the pulpit and out of it, was indeed as great a contrast to George Donaldson as could well be imagined. The fishing and shooting, the boisterous mirth and careless manners of poor George, had passed well enough so long as he was merely a lad at college; but now that he had assumed the character of an "ambassador from God to man," the case was entirely altered. When, in returning from one of his hill expeditions with his rod or his gun in his hand, he met by chance any of the graver parishioners, they either avoided him with averted looks, or their cold greeting was such as even he felt to imply a censure. Such was the high idea entertained by this simple people of the consecrated character of him who was to speak to their immortal spirits the words of life, that they thought he should be wholly, in soul, body, and spirit, devoted to the work of studying how to elevate morally and religiously those who were committed to his spiritual charge. They, therefore, regarded amusements which were innocent in themselves as no longer such when they formed the occupation of one who had set himself apart for holier thoughts and employments. They had all met in the church of Glenmore, and had petitioned Sir Duncan, whom they conceived still to be the patron of the parish, to grant to them the pastor of their choice. Sir Duncan, for more than one reason, took no notice of the petition. Of all things, he disliked to be thought in want of money; and the transfer of this patronage had been made very secretly indeed, with an express understanding that it should be concealed as long as possible.

Things were in this position, when one day — a wet gusty day as it happened to be — the first hail-shower of the season having just rattled against the window-panes — a footman announced at Miss Legh's drawing-room door, that some friends of May's, who was with her mistress at the time, were then in the housekeeper's room, and wished to speak with her. A few minutes sufficed to bring May back again breathless with haste, saying that her old friend Samuel and some other men were below — that they hardly knew how to make the request, but if Miss Legh would favour them with her presence for a few moments, they would esteem it an unspeakable kindness. Miss Legh carried her reply in person, and assured old Samuel how very happy she was to see him. He, on his part, lost no time in explaining the object of his visit. "His companions," who had all saluted the lady, and now stood respectfully with bonnet in hand, "formed," as he said, "a deputation from the parishioners of Glenmore to Sir Duncan Ross — authorized to make known their united wishes respecting their choice of a successor to Dr. Blair. He had been requested to accompany them, as it was known that he already possessed some acquaintance with the young lady, through whom they hoped to influence Sir Duncan in their favour." The anxiety depicted on the men's faces, while Samuel thus addressed Miss Legh, was extreme; they watched her countenance intently; and as she, who knew how matters stood, shook her head despondingly, one would have thought that a dark shadow had flitted before them. "My friends," said she, in her gentlest tones, "do not, I pray you, be over sanguine. I much fear that matters are not in a good train for your wishes. I have very little in my power. For your sakes I wish I had more; but what I can do for you, be assured I will." She then begged them to wait till she herself announced to her uncle their wish to be admitted to speak with him.

Sir Duncan, as it happened, was at that moment deeply engaged with a foreign artist, whom he had lately imported to Rosemount for the purpose of making sketches in that part of the country. He was, therefore, extremely unwilling to be intruded upon in such a manner. "My dear Jane," he said impatiently, "you know I hate deputations of clowns; besides, you are aware I can do nothing for them." "Well, uncle," said Jane, "if disappointment must come, do let it come with as little harshness as may be. But can you do nothing in the way of writing? could your influence in no way prevail?" "Pshaw! not I; but you may employ your own pretty hand in the matter, if you please. Well, to satisfy you, you may bring in that *Samuel* — what is his name? — not the others, though. It is a wet day, and we should suffocate with the steam of their garments."

Kindly, and even respectfully, Miss Legh led the venerable old man into the room, and invited him to a seat by the fire; but he, with a humility not entirely devoid of dignity, stood near the door, waiting to be invited to a more advanced station by the proprietor himself. Sir Duncan looked at him, in silence, with an air of careless indifference; then, as if a sudden idea had crossed his mind, he whispered something to the little foreign-looking artist, who was peering up from his easel through a pair of spectacles, rose from his seat, and politely begged the catechist to come forward. He then rang the bell, ordered wine to be brought, and presented a glass to the old man with his own hand. The latter accepted it with easy simplicity, thanked Sir Duncan with a smile, but added, "You must give me leave, sir, to ask the blessing of the God of all mercies, without which I cannot find enjoyment in any of his gifts." "Assuredly, my good friend." was the reply; "place yourself under no restraint." The old man, in grave, earnest accent, implored a blessing upon the gifts of God's providence; to which he added a prayer, of which Miss Legh alone felt the value, for the well-being of that house and family. This was precisely what Sir Duncan wanted. He made a signal to the artist, who began a rapid sketch of a saint's head and face, upon the canvass which he had before prepared, at the suggestion of his patron. "Superbe! Superbe!" exclaimed the man of art in a suppressed tone, as he glanced at the fine antique cast, and the kindling devotional expression of the catechist's features. "Continue," whispered Sir Duncan, when the "blessing" was ended, "while I encourage the old man to talk. — My friend," cried he aloud, "what have you got to say to me now?"

The catechist paused for a moment, as if considering how best to make himself understood, then, pointing to the salver which stood on the table, he thus spoke: "There is food for the body; there is likewise food for the soul. It is a miserable thing to be deprived of the temporal mercies, but it is far worse to be starved of the spiritual. The people of Glenmore, sir, have sent me here, humbly to set before you that they are more anxious regarding the food which is to be provided for their immortal souls than they are about the wants of their perishing bodies. They desire me to represent that, while they will thankfully accept at your hands, *any* minister who truly preaches the Gospel of our Lord Jesus Christ, they feel an exceeding love for the son of him who ministered among them for the last forty years; and they conscientiously say, that they think themselves and their children will benefit more by his ministry than by that of any one else. If it please you, honoured sir, to grant their humble petition, that he may be placed over them in spiritual things, they will pray evermore from the heart for your prosperity. You are aware, sir, that the neighbouring parish is but ill supplied with the preaching of the Word, and if it should be dried up likewise in Glenmore, this would be a very destitute district."

Sir Duncan, who saw by a glance that the desired outline was finished, now started as if from a reverie, and exclaimed, in a tone altogether different from that which he had before assumed,

"What did you say, my good friend?" at the same time he fixed his eyes on the catechist, in a manner which was evidently meant to put him out of countenance. Seeing, however, that the latter stood silent and without losing his self-possession, he continued: "Ah! something about the minister of Glenmore. I never take any trouble about those things; you must speak to my factor; yes, speak to Dawson — Dawson will attend to you I am sure."

The blood, for an instant, rushed to the old man's brow. He drew himself up erect, as if about to frame a reply; but, changing his purpose, he bowed in silence, and with a countenance clouded and sorrowful, immediately withdrew. Miss Legh walked after him, with that firm and almost haughty step which showed that her generous feelings had been thoroughly aroused. In passing Sir Duncan, she sent him a glance of such scornful meaning, as brought a transient blush even to *his* cheek, and made him feel for a moment humiliated. And as the door closed behind her, she laid her hand on the catechist's arm. "My friend," said she, I am grieved — ashamed — that your simple and truthful appeal should have been so received." Samuel looked at her humbly and gratefully, yet without losing his native superiority, and a tear filled his eye. "I am grieved, dear lady," said he, "for the heavy tidings I must bear to those who sent me. I am grieved for the hiding of God's countenance, in that he seems about to withdraw the light of his public ministry from this quarter. Distress and poverty are making many of us look to a foreign land, and myself among the rest; but so long as the preaching of the Gospel was continued to us, we could not bring ourselves to leave the place of our fathers; now, everything is pointing that way."

"Not so, Samuel," said the lady firmly; "let not your trust in the Most High forsake you. You and such as you, are *the salt of your country*. I see it — I feel it. Would God that the owners of the land — they who owe to it most, and pay to it least — were but aware of half your value. The day may not be far distant, when I shall rank among their number, and that, too, in the immediate neighbourhood. If, therefore, it is any comfort for you to know that my money and influence shall be employed solely for your benefit, and that I consider it to be for this end that God has given them to me, take that comfort for yourself, and give it to your friends. Farewell, now! I shall probably not see you again for a length of time, but I shall not forget you. Let not your heart fail."

"And may the Almighty never fail you in the hour of trial!" replied Samuel, in a voice by no means so self-possessed as it had been in presence of the proprietor. And thus they parted.

While this scene was enacting within the walls of Rosemount, it happened that May was engaged in one of a very different description elsewhere. She had gone, in the meantime, on some embassy to the nearest village, and, in crossing a field, had espied George Donaldson approaching with his usual attendant — a dog, of the terrier breed — and a gun. For reasons known to herself, she diverged from her straight path rather than encounter him; but with his active, muscular stride, she stood no chance of escape, so that she was obliged, at length, to pause, with heightened colour and a beating heart. "Well, May," he exclaimed, as he overtook her, "you have got very saucy of late. You are going to leave us, I hear; I fancy you look down upon your old friends now." "I think, sir," said May coldly, "that a minister should be such a one as no one could look down on." "Humph!" said George with an ironical grunt, "you're of the preaching sort; but I would rather hear a sermon from you than from any other body; that's sure." "The more is the pity." replied May, "since it but shows your great need." "You have got a tongue since you went up to the big house!" said George. "Would ye not like to have a house of your own, May? I'm going to get a kirk some o' these days; what would ye say to be the lady of the manse?" "I would *set* the manse as ill as ye would set the kirk, Mr George — though maybe not altogether," she added, with a toss of her pretty head. "You saucy gipsy!" said George. "I must get the kiss that ye promised me yon night though — the night mind that ye were in such distress about your grandfather." May looked this way and that, to see how she might fly. No way of escape appeared; and George snatched her by the waist, and succeeded in obtaining a kiss, while she, poor child, in the innocence of her offended dignity, burst into a passionate flood of tears. But at this moment George himself was embraced from behind in a pair of most powerful arms, and dashed to the ground, at the distance of several yards, before he had any ability to help himself. "The *scoundrel*!" exclaimed Kenneth Ore, a tall, athletic, and remarkably fine-looking young Highlander, as he stood over the fallen youth, with sparkling eyes and a flushed brow. "*He* a minister! Go home , sir," he added addressing his fallen foe, who was noways remarkable for courage, and who slowly rose with a look of considerable humiliation — "go home, and keep to your dog and your gun; dinna meddle wi' the lasses again, or else worse may come out of it yet." The minister made no reply, but muttering something to himself, and with a glance of sullen resentment, he turned and strode away.

"And so you're going to leave us, May?" said young Kenneth, whose blue eye had considerably altered its expression, as he walked by the damsel's side to protect her from farther annoyance. The poor girl was not yet of an age to disguise her feelings, nor, indeed, had she any to disguise. She knew what love was only from songs and stories; but she well knew what strong affection meant; and upon Kenneth's knee she had often and often sat in her grandfather's cottage, when several years younger, and played with the pretty brown locks that encircled his head. The tears of affright were scarcely yet dried upon her face — others now came to her eyes from a different cause; but she tried to smile, although the blood forsook her cheek. "You'll not forget your old friends May?" said Kenneth again. "No, never, never in my life," replied May eagerly. "Do you know, Kenneth," continued she, "I would *far, far* rather stay in a cottage than in a grand house." "Oh, but you'll change your mind," returned he; "you'll get accustomed to grand houses, and then you can't put up with things as you used." "No, indeed, I don't think it," was the girl's reply; "for there's no *goodness* in a big house. I don't think there's anybody the least good in our hose but my own dear mistress. Among the servants, it's all lies, and swearing, and quarrelling. I would rather live on bread and water, and love with it, than have all their grand things." "Ah! May, if ye would but keep to that opinion," said Kenneth; "but it's not easy," added he with a sigh, "to get a cottage, and bread and water itself, in these days. There's nothing now but corn and cattle where there should be men and their wives and children. I'm sure it would be better for the landlords to have those that would work for them, ay, and spill their heart's blood for them too, if there was need for it, than to be spending their money upon brute beasts. But they use us *worse* than the brutes now. Maybe, May, I may never see you again. If the worst comes to the worst, my old father says we must just cross the ocean." "Don't speak that way," said May. "I don't know," replied he; "there's a great many of the hill-folks turned off, and they say our turn is coming. He's a black rascal that Dawson, that factor of Sir Duncan's. There's little good to be looked for from his hand. But good-bye, May; ye're near home. *Dinna* forget me, and I'll no forget you. I wish I had anything to gi'e you for a keep-sake. I have no breast-pins or braw things. Will you take this ribbon off my bonnet?" added he, taking his bonnet off and pulling out a smart blue ribbon, with which it had been newly decorated." "That I will," said the girl; "I will put it at the bottom of my chest, and you will see if anything ever parts me from it. I have nothing to give to you — except," she added, after a moment's consideration, this silk handkerchief;" and she took the handkerchief from her artless bosom, and gave it to Kenneth, who deposited it carefully in his own. He looked at her speaking face and glowing cheek, as if he would have taken from thence a still dearer token; but a feeling of the girl's extreme youth, and of the rudeness to which she had been so lately subjected, came over him; and so, pressing her hand between both his, he turned away, and with elastic step quickly disappeared.

CHAPTER IX

What dreadful pleasure there to stand, sublime,
Like shipwreck'd mariner on desert coast,
And view th' enormous waste of vapour, tost
In billows, lengthening to th' horizon round
Now scooped to gulfs, with mountains now embossed!
BEATTIE

Upon a day which was like a resurrection-glimpse of the past summer, Miss Legh thought of revisiting a spot where she had spent many delightful hours. Nature to her, during the last year, had been every thing — friendship, society, happiness. She lived only in the beautiful and true; and to her they were nearly convertible terms. Truth she found to be full of beauty; and in the beautiful she failed not to discover the reflected image of truth. Poetry of the higher kind was thus peculiarly congenial to her mind; and she felt it always most full of meaning, with its living materials — its sights and sounds around her. She had thus formed the habit of taking a favourite author to some unfrequented spot, and there imbuing her imagination at once with poetry and with nature. There was one spot in particular to which she had often directed her steps. It was a moory hillock, from which — though less commanding than the great chain of mountains rising behind it — the eye could still embrace a rich prospect for many miles of the varied scenery in the great valley below. Upon the day in question, only two or three before that fixed for her departure from Rosemount, she took, without much selection, a volume of Mrs. Hemans, and proceeded, ere the sun had yet reached his meridian, to spend a few hours at her most cherished place of resort. Having arrived at the well-known eminence, and full of enthusiasm for the romantic scenery around, enhanced by the idea that she was now to bid it farewell for a time, the thought struck her, that if she could but attain to a certain point on the neighbouring mountain, she should obtain a view of the country beyond the continuous ridge which formed the southern boundary of the valley at her feet. With buoyant step and eager fancy she climbed steep after steep until she found herself within such a practicable distance of the summit of what was by no means the highest mountain in the chain, that to that point she determined to persevere. The way was perfectly solitary. She had met with no one, except, in the lower regions of the steep, a plaided shepherd, followed by his dog, who deferentially touched his bonnet as she passed. It was with a feeling of exultation, such as she had never before experienced, that she at length reached the top, and saw the wide landscape with features diminished by distance, and bounded only by the horizon, spread itself out like the pattern of a rich Eastern carpet at her feet. But that which was most novel to her in the prospect, was the tumultuous sea of heathy mountains, which stretched on interminably, as it appeared, towards the north. Over their vast barrenness, their brown and naked sterility, silence and solitude reigned undisturbed. Ridge within ridge heaved themselves upwards, as if the long rolling waves of an ocean of molten land had been transfixed in their gigantic swell by the hand of Omnipotence. A single tarn or mountain lake, upon a neighbouring height, alone gave some relief to the mind oppressed with sterile magnificence. It seemed, with its beaming eye for ever glancing upwards, and mirroring only the heavens, like the spirit of contemplation dwelling in the desert, or like the pure in heart amid the wilderness of this world.

Miss Legh had not long looked upon this scene when she was aware that a light mist was gathering in the hollows, and had begun to creep up the bases of the hills. At first, thin as the web of the gossamer, it reflected the rays of the sun, and served merely to add softness to the landscape. Almost insensibly, like the change in a diorama, it rolled itself, as it stole upwards, into fantastic wreaths, and transformed the rugged features of the mountain scenery into those of varied gracefulness and beauty. Then, deepening in volume and gathering into dark clouds, with edges of silver, it came rapidly and more rapidly onwards, until the tops of the mountains, still shining clear in the sun-light, looked like islands in the midst of an ocean of clouds. Not till then did our young heroine — charmed with the novelty of this magnificent picture, and inexperienced in mountain travel — think of swiftly retracing her steps. But the descent was a different matter from her easy and buoyant progress of the morning. At first, indeed, it was pleasant and romantic, as the mist thickened, so as to conceal even the large grey stones at a few yards' distance, to call to her remembrance the various wild legends she had delighted to hear since her residence in the Highlands, and to fancy that the grey spirits of Fingal and Ossian, and the heroes of Celtic song, were hovering around; till, as she looked upwards, she almost expected to see the faces of "the warriors of other days looking from their clouds." She remembered, too, a persecuted clan who, from their residence in wilder heights than these, were termed "the children of the mist;" but as the twilight began to aid the thickening gloom, she felt that the reality of her situation was becoming serious, while fast losing all sense of direction, she found that sheer descent was all she had to serve as a guide. The habit of dependence, too — insensibly acquired by those accustomed to have their wants anticipated, and every difficulty removed as soon as encountered, though it may be scarce suspected, until some circumstance renders self-help absolutely necessary — made her feel her adventure become more and more unpleasant. And, sooth to say, the most experienced shepherd of the hills not acquainted with every stone and heather-tuft in that particular locality, could not have made much progress in the thickening gloom. Nor could our wanderer proceed straight downwards. She was obliged to keep to the right or left, as the nature of the ground — more difficult than that she had passed over in her ascent — compelled her.

At length, fatigued with unwonted toil she sat down, almost resolving to remain in that spot until the morning sun should dispel the darkness. She ran over in her mind the chances of assistance, but found them exceedingly few. As night drew on, Sir Duncan might probably be informed of her absence — would become alarmed, and despatch the servants in quest of her; but how should they dream that she had taken such a direction? It was then, with a thrill of indescribable joy, that, after some time spent in this perplexity, she heard the cheerful sound of a whistle at no great distance. She was about instantly to call aloud, when again the extreme solitude of the place where she was came to her recollection. Would it not be preferable still to pass the night in the open air, than to trust herself to the protection of a person totally unknown? Had she been in more southern districts, she would certainly have chosen the former alternative; but when she thought of the unoffending manners of the people among whom she had lived — who seldom heard of wrong or outrage but as echoes from the distant towns — she determined, fearlessly, to put herself under the protection of the stranger, whoever he might be. She called in a low voice, but distinctly enough, it would seem, to be heard, for a whistle, louder than the former one, immediately greeted her. She called again in a more assured tone, and proceeded in the direction of the answering sound. Nor had she gone far, when the son of the village store-keeper and farmer, Evan Munro, stood before her. At the unexpected sight of the lady of the *Castle* (as great mansion-houses are often termed in the country), Evan started back in unfeigned astonishment, and his very handsome features became suffused with the deepest crimson. Had a goddess emerged from the mist, as Venus rose from the waves of the sea, he could not have been more awestruck and abashed. He retained presence of mind enough to touch his cap with the most profound respect; but when he attempted to articulate, voice failed him, and he waited till the Lady —or her apparition, as he almost believed — should speak, as he would have waited for the first words of an oracle. Miss Legh, with her accustomed simplicity and sweetness, explained the predicament in which she was placed, and begged that he would kindly either point out the path she ought to take, or, if he were going in the same direction, would guide her towards her home. Evan's voice, in reply, was not distinctly audible, but he took the precedence, and beckoned her to follow. The ground was rough, and in many places even dangerous, and had the young man followed the dictates of his heart, he would have assisted his fair companion with the utmost assiduity of kindness; but although not unaccustomed, during his college life, to mix in good society in a large town, such was the sentiment with which the near vicinity of the high-born beauty inspired him, that he felt as if it would be a kind of profanity to aspire to the touch of her hand. Once only, when Miss Legh struck her foot against the stump of a tree, and uttered an involuntary exclamation of pain, did he turn quickly round to inquire if she were hurt; he then continued his walk in advance, as before.

    It was not without a sensation of great relief, physical as

well as mental, that Jane found herself once more upon level ground, and saw the moon shining full in a clear heaven — the obscurity being entirely confined to the hilly region she had left. Such was her pleasure that she could not help pointing to the mist-clouds hanging over the sides of the mountains, and now shining with the softest radiance to the moon-beams, as she said to her guide, "Those silvery clouds are more pleasant without than within. I scarce know how I should have passed the night in yonder spot. I feel already sufficiently, chilled with the penetrating vapour of the hill." Evan, giving way to an irresistible impulse, threw off the plaid which he wore around him, and inquired if the lady would *condescend* (he faltered as he pronounced the word) to wrap it around her, to protect her from the night air.

"Oh, no!" she replied, "I have already taxed your kindness enough. I shall presently have the comfort of a fire and of supper too — though," she added, with a smile, "heroines so foolish as I have been, seldom think of so common-place a matter." Changing the conversation, she then made inquiry respecting the time of the young man's return to his studies, induced him by degrees to speak of them, and of his hopes and prospects, till, on their arrival at the gate of the mansion-house grounds, where she bade her conductor adieu, Evan found, to his surprise, that the spell which he had at first found it impossible to break, had been insensibly charmed away, and he took his way to his humble home, with the music of that lady's voice ringing on his ear and in his heart. Miss Legh, on her part, reached her own apartments unobserved, and in changing her dress, heavy with night-dew and the mountain-vapour, only remarked that she had lost the book which had been her morning companion — a circumstance by no means to be greatly wondered at.

CHAPTER X

*"This question, Sir, has been right well disputed;
And meikle weel-a-wat's been said about it."*
ALEX WILSON

Once established in Edinburgh, in the habitation of her friends, Lord and Lady Lentraethen, Jane found herself in an atmosphere of genial and attractive kindliness, very cheering to her orphan heart. Most susceptible of unartificial enjoyment of every kind, it was yet an orphan heart which she bore in her bosom after all. Nor could her sense of solitude be perhaps dispelled, except — all unconscious as she was of it herself — by the formation of dearer domestic ties than those she had ever known. The names of *wife* and *mother* always vibrated sweetly on her ear, but she had never *loved*; and of the foolery of mimic passion, with which girls of her age entertain themselves, she was entirely incapable. The interchange of domestic affection, in the amiable family where she now was, infused its own sweetness into her spirit. Father, mother, brother, sister! — of these names she had known only the first, but that to her was so holy and beloved, that it seemed to concentrate within itself the endearment of all the others. It was true that the father of this family was very different from him who had been so much to her; but he *was* a father, and a kind one, and that was a great deal. Possessed of those attributes which the vulgar fancy, at least, connects with the aristocracy, in a well-formed person, and a noble cast of features, animated, however, by neither intellect nor soul, but simply expressive of good-nature, Lord Lentraethen spoke but little, and loved those best who amused him with a well-told story or a smart repartee. He was a man of no vicious propensity. What moral principles he had, no one could well say; they were probably but ill-defined to his own consciousness. Certain it was, that his good nature, not based upon any thing very high, made large allowances for those vices in others which he did not practise. His wife was a person of rather a higher order. The amiable and good were to her not so much indolent instincts, as objects of sensibility. She felt them keenly, and keenly felt their reverse; but she drew from her own bosom alone, and wanted fixed and stable principles whereon to rest from any other source, either religious or educational. Consequently, with judgment less strong than her feelings, she was often led into error. Their two daughters, Lady Grace and Lady Emily Maitland, resembled each other in character, which they drew both from father and mother. Highly accomplished in externals, they were too indolent, mentally, to give themselves any trouble as to the grounds of either their beliefs or habits of acting, right or wrong; yet, decidedly amiable, they disliked all that was obtrusively offensive in temper or disposition, as they would have disliked an unpleasant taste or smell. There were thus many points of cohesion, so to speak, between Miss Legh and the family of the Lentraethens; but there was this difference, not discernible to every eye — at first not even to themselves — that with them, good was a surface thing, a matter of little more than mere taste; with their cousin, it was earnest, serious — her chief end of living.

Once more, then, we introduce our young friend to the reader, seated at her work-table of a morning, in a very handsome drawing-room in Ainslie Place. The front windows of the house look into a retired and elegant crescent at the fashionable west end of the New Town of Edinburgh, which no squalid abode of wretchedness is permitted to contaminate; the back windows command a prospect most uncommon for a city — that of a noble frith, extending from east to west as far as the eye can reach, with the little rocky islands which stud its waters, and the blue line of hills on the opposite shore.

Lady Lentraethan had not yet come downstairs. Lady Emily was entertaining two or three morning loungers in the perspective of the back drawing-room; and Lady Grace had just left the piano, where she had been practising a German song, and was standing before the fire talking to Jane.

"We are to dine at Sir Charles Murray's to-day," said the latter; "you will go—won't you, dear? We accepted for you as well as for ourselves a fortnight ago, knowing you were to be here. The party is to be small, I believe, but select." "I shall be extremely happy," replied Jane. "Don't you think," added she, "that there is something very pleasant in the first *flavour* of new society before it begins to pall upon one's taste!" "Yes," said Lady Grace, laughing;

"like that of early strawberries or peaches, which are worth all that come after." "I fancy," continued Jane, "I should like to mix a little — just enough to know it — in the society of all the large towns of Europe, and leave it — for I care very little for gaiety for its own sake — just before it begins to get common-place." "You fickle girl!" exclaimed Lady Grace. "Not fickle," said Jane, "I should have but one *home*." "And where should *it* be?" inquired her cousin slyly. "Alas!" replied Jane with a sigh, "*my* home is very desolate — I almost dread returning to it." "Well, dear," said Lady Grace, sitting on the couch, and putting her arm affectionately round the orphan's waist, "don't think of that. You must have another home, and I know," said she, "it will be a delightful one. But I want, this forenoon, to go and pay a visit to that poor creature, Miss Matheson. She likes one of us to go and see her, and take her for a drive sometimes. Will you go with me, or will it be a bore?" "Who is Miss Matheson?" inquired Jane. "Oh! I forgot," said Lady Grace, "that you didn't know. She is an old governess of ours — a good creature whom papa supports. She is a dreadful sufferer from a very terrible complaint; indeed, it is not always pleasant to be near her. But we cannot keep away from her on that account; you know she has all the more need of kindness." "How sweetly you speak, dear Lady Grace; I shall be delighted to go with you," said Jane, looking at her cousin affectionately. "Don't *Lady* me," said the latter, who still sat with her arm coaxingly round Jane's waist, as if anxious to efface the little pain she had caused unintentionally. "I think," continued she, "I have heard that you ride beautifully; shall I order my horse for you? He has the slightest touch of blood in the world, but is quite manageable by a *good* rider; and I think you will like him all the better for it. Our old friend lives, for the sake of the country air, two or three miles out of town." "Thank you, love," replied Jane, "I do like riding, but for the present I will go with you in the carriage. Will you think me very peculiar," added she, "when I say that I am averse to horsemanship in the streets of a large town. I fancy that it savours too much of exhibition." "How very humble you are!" exclaimed Lady Grace. "We heard that you were such a beauty, and such a piece of perfection, that we fancied you would want to throw us all into the shade." "I believe I ceased to be very *vain*," replied Jane, "when I had no longer any one to gratify; but I am not *humble,*" added she, smiling, "notwithstanding. Yet I have been trying to learn humility from a better source. Does not that book teach it to us?" she asked, pointing to a small New Testament which always lay in her work-box. "Oh, to be sure," said Lady Grace, at the same time withdrawing her arm from Jane's waist. "Well, I can tell you," she continued, "your humility will be sufficiently tried; for everyone says you will create a greater sensation than anyone who has appeared here for I can't tell how long. Come now, dear," said she, resuming her affectionate manner, "come and put on your things."

When they reached the cottage of the invalid, which was pleasantly situated at no great distance from the frith, they found her not prepared to give them quite such a reception as Miss Legh had anticipated She was seated upon a sofa, propped up by pillows, in a very neat parlour, surrounded, indeed, with every comfort; but she was suffering, and somewhat peevish. "You have quite forgotten me," she said to Lady Grace; "how long since any of you have been to see me!" "Only last week, dear Matheson," said Lady Grace; "how have you been?" "Oh, very ill, very ill," was the reply; "but nobody minds a useless creature like me." "Don't say so," said Lady Grace; "you know we all love you. Do you feel able to take a ride with us to-day? It is very pleasant out of doors. I am sure you would be the better for it." "No, I don't think so," returned Miss Matheson; "I had a terrible night — I never shut my eyes; but you don't know what suffering is, and therefore you can't feel for it in others." "Indeed I do," replied the amiable girl; "but you will sleep better to-night after having had the fresh air. Do let the maid bring your bonnet and shawl, and let us assist you to the carriage." By dint of such entreaty, the old lady was at length prevailed upon; and Lady Grace offering her arm for support, nodded to Jane to do likewise. Miss Matheson would have been highly offended if a servant had been permitted to offer such services, when there were persons of higher rank present.

Through the reviving influence of the air, the unceasing attention of the young people, and the various offerings of grapes &c, which they had brought to tempt her appetite, poor Miss Matheson was, by degrees, soothed into a more comfortable frame of mind. She began to converse on other topics than her own troubles, and Miss Legh perceived that she had been a person of a superior and well-cultivated mind. Her conversation, however, turned entirely upon light and entertaining subjects — the state of the drama, with which she showed a thorough acquaintance — the last novel — above all, the prospects of her young friends for the coming season. There was something in this strain which, in connection with the situation of the individual, pained Miss Legh's feelings, though she scarce knew why, in its full extent. While she delighted to see even a short interval of enjoyment in the midst of an existence of suffering, she felt that it was to vanish like the transient flush on a winter evening sky, to leave nothing but dreariness behind. The disease was incurable; its torment almost incessant. Forgetfulness was impossible; it was *support* which was needed. And how derive support from the recollection of pleasures which could no longer be enjoyed? These ideas forced themselves upon our young friend's mind with a painful vividness; and, with a like force, a sense of ETERNITY became present to her. In eternity alone could the mind of one who was related to time by nothing other than its pains and penalties, be said to be any more capable of *living*. Death to the powers of the soul had already begun, as mortification takes place in a living body. But one class of interests, Miss Legh felt, was capable of preserving them undecayed; that its *faith* should become alive to the divine promises which spring up as life beacons when death casts his dark shadow over the soul; that its *hope* should cease to flutter around the littlenesses of time, and should spring forward to embrace the greatness of eternity. The words of the Saviour of mankind came into her memory: "Come unto *me* that ye may have *life.*" They seemed full of heavenly light; they were a revelation to her own inner soul. Nevertheless, she became absent and sad, for *there* sat the poor sufferer whose circumstances had given rise to these thoughts, all unconscious of them, and no ways the better. She herself was aware that light upon this greatest of all subjects was but struggling into her mind; and she felt as if she never should be able to communicate it to another. She thought of the cottagers of Glenmore. How lucid were their views of Scripture truth! With what delighted earnestness could they converse upon them as of a congenial theme! She felt acutely that *she,* with all her accomplishments and trained intellect, was, in this department, immeasurably inferior to them.

After replacing Miss Matheson upon her sofa, with a book of plays, with which she said she should now be able to amuse herself, on a work-table by her side, they took leave; Lady Grace, with a good-humoured complacency, at having procured for the invalid a momentary cheerfulness — Miss Legh, with a new emotion, which gave her a ten-fold interest in the dying stranger.

At eight o'clock in the evening of the same day, she found herself at Sir Charles Murray's, where there was a select dinner-party. She had spent the winter before her father's death in London, and although she had not passed through the regular routine of a *season* there, she had seen enough of its best society to be able to draw a comparison between it and that of the Scottish metropolis. Her first impressions she did not afterwards find reason to change. The style of the dinner, for example, was considerably less elaborated than she had been accustomed to see; but there was a plain unpretending elegance about it which better pleased her taste. The style of the guests, on the other hand, struck her somewhat differently. Well-bred people are, to a certain extent, everywhere alike; still there are national peculiarities, which are smoothed over by education and society, rather than effaced. The manners of the ladies seemed less soft and polished than those of Miss Legh's country-women; which effect was probably aided by their harsher language. There is, indeed, an exquisite harmony in the tones and movements of a highly educated English woman unequalled, perhaps, throughout the world. Miss Legh imagined that the Scottish ladies, on the other hand, possessed the advantage of a more unconstrained frankness, and a more unsuspecting utterance of their sentiments and opinions. Had she come but a single degree lower in the scale of society, she would have found that they could boast of a very much higher degree of that kind of intelligence which is called *thinking for one's self*; but this is an excellence for which the aristocracy are nowhere the most remarkable class. One proof of good breeding she remarked, *en passant*, viz., that the *eatables* were a subordinate matter, and never on any occasion formed a subject of conversation — a vulgarity which she had not found so entirely abolished in the sister kingdom.

Talking was at first carried on only by the individuals who sat next to each other, and did not for some time become general, as in small parties it has a tendency to do. Miss Legh was seated beside Lord Moir, a young man who had travelled a good deal, and who liked to talk as if he had. He would have been agreeable were it not for the habit which he, like many young men of fashion, had contracted of hesitating in his speech to such a degree as to make it appear a matter of extreme difficulty for him to find words to express himself withal; and the more rational the subject, the more painful the defect. Whether it be that such young gentlemen are really unaccustomed to give expression to their ideas, or whether they wish to make it appear that they have hitherto been above the necessity of thinking, is uncertain. But it is true that, after one has patiently waited the forthcoming of the new-born thought, expecting that it is to be worthy the exercise of patience, it often happens that there comes out at length, with a jerk, some piece of desperate common-place.

Sir Charles Murray was remarkable for being a great Tory and aristocrat; and Lady Murray, on the contrary, was remarkable for nothing, except that she made no pretensions to being remarkable at all. There was, besides, a Lady Clementina Edgar, who was a single lady in middle life, of a tall robust figure. *She* was remarkable for wearing feathers and diamonds on every occasion, and for being always in the van of her party, whatever it chanced to be. There was a Colonel Campbell, who was remarkable for a very red face, and for being always on the eve of going into a passion; and there was an advocate of the Edinburgh bar, a great assertor of the majesty of the law. He was a large man, with a very pompous manner, and had a habit of putting his hand frequently to his head, as if he fancied he ought to have a wig to adjust. Lastly, besides the family of the Lentraethens, there was a clergyman, who has been once before mentioned. He had spent part of his life in the north, though not now settled there — his name was Dr. Bremner, and his manners were bland, mild, and dignified. He belonged to the gentlemanly section of the Moderate party in the Church, who, although not very strong in numbers, occupy rather a conspicuous place in the public eye. Dr. Bremner was now in Edinburgh, for the purpose of consulting on public affairs with some of the leaders of his party. He was not a man of high birth; but there was no other mark of his origin visible in his breeding than that, perhaps, it was too sedulously refined. His wife had been a distant connection of Sir Charles Murray's; which connection the clergyman had carefully cultivated.

It was by means of the advocate that the conversation at last took a more lively and general turn. "So," cried he from the top of the table to Sir Charles, "these *nonintrusion agitators* are still flying about the country. There have been no less than three fresh interdicts broken during the last week." "They will get themselves hung," said Lady Clement, "and there is no doubt they deserve it." Dr. Bremner bowed and smiled, and the young ladies laughed. "It is disgraceful," continued the advocate, "that the law does not assert its supremacy, and vindicate its insulted dignity." "And that of our insulted aristocracy," added Sir Charles Murray. "These men ought, every one of them, to be clapped into prison. I would soon put an end to this disturbance of the public peace." "It is conceived," said the lawyer, "that they would have no objections to a few of their leaders being imprisoned. It would help to increase that notoriety which is their chief aim" (Dr. Bremner shook his head, as if to say, it was too true); "and besides, they would thus have leisure to deluge the world with effusions which would no doubt be eagerly read." "Put a guard over them — place them under martial law," said the Colonel; "that is *my* advice." "Ahem!" replied the advocate, "that would scarcely be constitutional, as *yet*," he added with emphasis. "The worst feature of this case," said Lord Lentraethen, in a manner which betokened unwonted excitement in him, "is the way in which tenants are roused against their — landlords. I have some claim to be regarded as an indulgent landlord" (he spoke truly), "but on this subject I find my tenants wholly impracticable. You know they refused to hear my tutor — a very excellent fellow." "Ah, yes! poor Jacko!" interjected Lady Emily, in a half careless, half whining tone. "And they got a chapel erected," continued the Earl, "with a canting preacher for it, under my very nose, whom they thought, forsooth, to support with their Sunday pence and halfpence. I seized the collections, as I had a legal right to do, for the benefit of the poor." "It was nobly done," said Sir Charles.

Miss Legh did not feel so satisfied of the nobility of such a mode of procedure. The subject under discussion had presented itself to *her* in its simplest and most natural aspect — that of a people, poor, yet anxious, as their chief good, to hear the Word of God preached in truth and purity. Besides, the ethical axiom upon which her own education had been founded — that of producing the greatest good to the greatest number — had been presented to her in a forcible point of view, as connected with pure religious instruction. The benefit, the cause of the people, was with her the most sacred of things; and how the assertors of such a course, under such a peculiarly sacred aspect, should be men of the character now ascribed to them, was a problem which she could not explain. Even by name she was almost totally unacquainted with them. "Who is the leader of that party?" asked she. "Oh it is — it is," replied Lord Moir, "it is one Dr. Candlish." "No; *Dr. Chalmers*" cried several other voices. "Indeed!" exclaimed Miss Legh, "is he not a great and good man? I have been accustomed to respect his name from my childhood." "Ye-e-e-es," drawled the young Lord, with somewhat more than usual of a lisp and a stammer, "ye-e-e-es, in the-the-the-*abstract*." "He is very violent — very violent, exclaimed the Colonel. "He has quite lost himself on this occasion. They say it is alarming to hear him. He has written books, indeed, which I believe some people admire, but which I, for my part, could never read." "Ah, indeed!" said Miss Legh, with the slightest possible admixture of contempt. The Colonel turned round quickly. He did not know whether to go into a passion or not, but the countenance of his beautiful neighbour was perfectly placid, so he resumed his knife and fork. "I must have your mind informed on the law of the case, ma'am," said the advocate, bowing towards Miss Legh; "it is of importance that *you* should be rightly informed on the subject." "I shall not venture so far as law," answered Jane, smiling, "in my present ignorance of the *facts* upon which your law has been brought to bear, but content myself with names, as a kind of prelude. May I ask who are those of your judges opposed to the claims of the people of Scotland?" The lawyer ran over the names of several law lords; and Miss Legh smilingly shook her head — they were all strangers to her. "And who are those who give their opinions on the other side?" asked she again. Her informant enumerated six, placing Lords Moncreiff, Cockburn, and Jeffrey last on the list, and speaking with evident reluctance. "Ah! Lord Cockburn! an old ornament of your bar; is he not? I know him from 'Peter's Letters to his Kinsfolk.' And Lord JEFFREY! *he* is known over Europe! And have *you* no celebrated names to boast of?" The advocate looked somewhat discomfited, but pleaded that he had numbers on his side. "Very strange!" repeated Miss Legh, "Dr. Chalmers and Lord Jeffrey!" "Dr. Chalmers," exclaimed the high-complexioned Colonel, "is deluded by his passions!" "And Jeffrey," added the advocate, "is entirely a party man." "I should argue differently," said Jane, again smiling. "I should infer that the superiority of my Lord Jeffrey's genius has raised him above the *esprit de corps* by which it is perhaps natural that the lawyer should be influenced in a case of collision with another court; while I should certainly imagine the cause espoused by the greatest Christian patriot of his day to be that of Christian patriotism."

This was a very simple piece of inference on the part of our young friend, who had no idea of not discussing independently any subject that lay in her way; yet it was very strange that the advocate began to adjust his wig in a state of agitation, while he looked warm, as if he had just been foiled in a piece of special pleading; the Colonel became more florid than ever; Lady Clementina shook her feathers, while almost every one at table appeared displeased. "Good heavens, Jane," exclaimed Lady Emily Maitland, "don't become a *Non-intrusionist*; it is bad enough to be a Whig!" Miss Legh, on her part, as she glanced around the table, felt an uncontrollable disposition to be amused. The merriment danced in her eyes, and at her cousin's exclamation could no longer be repressed, but gave itself vent in that kind of laugh which can scarcely be resisted by any one within hearing. Every one laughed with her. "No," said Dr. Bremner, bowing and speaking with extreme blandness, "I am sure *that* lady has nothing of the *Non-intrusionist* about her." "Believe me, ma'am" said the lawyer, recovering his good-humour, "they are a mean set although they have one or two respectable names." "Yes," said the Colonel, "there is — has been *convicted* of lying; and what do you think of the mean wretch? he has actually been going the round of his congregation, begging money to buy him a great-coat!" "You have picked up that piece of calumny at second-hand" said a gentleman who had not spoken hitherto, conveying a severe and contemptuous glance towards the vender of it. "Calumny, sir!" said the Colonel, who would now have made a respectable lamp-post in a dark night, and who, moreover, trembled all over. "Not yours," said the person he addressed, speaking with the same significant coolness, "I said you were obliged to some one else for it." "I am not sure," said the Colonel, "that *that* is a sufficient explanation; but in presence of the ladies we shall defer — ." "*I* am not sure," said Sir Charles Murray, with the politeness of a thorough gentleman; "*I* am not sure that we do not owe General Maitland an apology for introducing this subject in his presence; he is an avowed advocate of the Non-intrusionist party." General Maitland bowed, and Lady Murray took the opportunity of the pause which ensued to withdraw with the other ladies.

No sooner had the latter section of the company reached the drawing-room, and clustered around the fire, than they fell, one and all, upon Miss Legh, for the views she seemed to entertain. "What *could* have made you speak so, dear?" cried Lady Emily. "My dear love," said Lady Lentraethen, "you really should not give an opinion on a subject of which you must be ignorant." "I am sorry if I have done wrong," replied Jane; "but do you think it wrong to ask for information? I do really wish to be informed, because my own dearest father taught me, that whenever I may have a duty to perform in connection with any subject, ignorance is a crime. You must recommend me some books to read on both sides of the question," added she, seeing that no reply was made to her remark. "What shall I begin with, cousin Grace?" "Indeed," said Lady Grace, laughing, as if she were tickled with the proposal, "I don't believe there is any one here who has ever read a word about the matter. For our part, we *see* enough of it. The ingratitude of our tenantry at Barnwood is really shocking; people whose rents papa has remitted time after time, and whom, I am sure, we — I mean mama and we two — have been very kind to, and yet they will *not* go to hear *Jacko* preach." "Why do you call the man *Jacko*?" asked Jane. "O, because he *was* very like a monkey, especially when he bit his nails, which he did shockingly." "Well, dear," said Jane, "don't you think *the people* might have been seized with a sense of the ridiculous, instead of being able to derive benefit from the preaching of Monsieur Jacko?" "Oh, but he *must* have been very superior to them," argued Lady Emily. "I am not at all certain of that," replied Jane. "Well, but you know," said Lady Grace, somewhat chagrined, "they might go, to oblige us." "Suppose you were to ask them to murder some of their children to oblige you?" said Jane. "Oh Jane, what an idea." "Well, my love," said Jane, taking her cousin's hand in hers, and speaking with affectionate earnestness, "they may solemnly *believe*, that by obliging you in a concern of such moment, they might run the risk of murdering their children's souls and their own." "That is really too shocking!" said Lady Grace; "you ought not to have your head filled with such things. Come," said she, skipping to the piano, "help me to sing this glee; or else, when the gentlemen come in, we shall all look like so many death's heads, to frighten them." So saying, and accompanied by Jane and her sister, she began a strain which soon brought the music lovers among the party below to her side.

CHAPTER XI

Behold them take a last look at that roof
From whence no smoke ascends, and onward move
In silence; whilst each passing object wakes
Remembrance of scenes that never more
Will glad their hearts.
GRAHAM

THE uninviting light of a coarse December morning rose sluggishly over the valley of Glenmore, and a bitter blast, accompanied by a shower of small rain, came scudding across the cottage roofs, as if to give warning to the sleepers within that they need be in no hurry to break their repose, and that when they did, they had best light up a cheerful fire, and keep their doors fast closed. Strangely enough, however, not so did the cottagers of Glenmore. There was an unusual stir among them on that December morning, yet it was a spiritless, joyless stir, like that in the weather outside, without any life or heart in it. Breakfast was set down before the day was more than a dark twilight on many a small table by many a homely fireside; but it was breakfast set down rather than eaten. There was an uneasy restlessness about the men as they rose and sat down, rose and sat down again; the women looked as if they had been weeping, and the corner of the apron was often employed to wipe away their still starting tears. A strange love of open doors, too, prevailed, in spite of the blast and shower that occasionally came tearing by, as if there was a choking and stifling feeling among the inmates, to which fresh air brought some relief. As the day wore on a little, men, women, and children, might be seen ascending now and then the highest points in the neighbourhood of their cottages, and looking long and wistfully all in one direction. It was in the direction of the manse.

There stood before the manse door, on that December day, two large waggons, heavily laden with furniture, which was covered atop with matting, to preserve it from the wet. Time-worn enough the greater part of it was. The high-backed curiously-carved chairs, which had stood in the parlour for forty years, might be seen peeping, with their clumsy angles, from out of the covering; and the round oaken table, at which the rich and poor stranger had often sat, was close beside them, to keep them company in their unwonted elevation. There was the venerable passage clock, whose ancient site in the lobby had never once been altered, and where had echoed to its contented chime the pattering of childish feet, the merry bound of boyhood, and the grave, deliberative step of old age; and, like a thrifty yet bountiful housekeeper, it had measured out time to young and old, by its minutes, days. and years. Ay, the eye of childhood had rested on its grave face, and yet had not discovered that time was moving on; youth had thought it stood there just to measure out happiness; and age had pondered on the staid dial-plate, as its few remaining years were passing rapidly away into that eternity where the sense of time should be once more lost in the ever-gushing spring of new-born life. Many other things there were which looked as if they ought to have mouldered and decayed each in its own familiar spot, now brought out once more to taste the bleak air of the world. Never mind; — they were all dead things, and had no feeling. Nevertheless, it had cost bitter pangs to some loving hearts to remove them out of their places. There was an apparition of servants, with faces swollen with weeping, who glided backwards and forwards from the doors to the waggons, and felt and felt again if everything was tight and in no danger of falling, and whose weeping was renewed every time they heard the sound of their own footsteps in the empty rooms, and saw but the bare walls and naked floors.

Upon the parlour hearth the fire still blazed, and around it, clad in deep mourning, sat the family of Dr. Blair, ready for their departure. A few chairs and a table had been borrowed for the occasion from a neighbouring cottage. Mrs. Blair, in her widow's cap and bonnet, sat, looking sadly, almost stupidly, at the fire, and spoke nothing. Poor Barbara, quite unable to restrain her feelings, lay half across the table, her face upon her arms; loud sobs bursting from her bosom, and her frame almost convulsed with weeping. Her young sister Emily, who had evidently suffered much during the last few months, sat quite motionless, a painful flush upon her cheek, over which silent tears coursed large and fast. Her eyes were seldom withdrawn from a single spot: it was that which her father used so often to traverse. Mary alone, who stood behind looking upon the group, was perfectly calm. Her face was of an ashy paleness, and her eye was dim; but what right had *she*, as she thought, to add to the general distress by her sobs and tears? She should be content to watch when and where she could be of the least use. At length the chaise was heard approaching, in which Mrs. Blair, accompanied by Charles and Emily, were to proceed to the nearest town — while it had been arranged that Barbara and Mary should follow in an open cart. Certainly the day was not such as would have been chosen for journeyings or removals of any kind, but the conveyances had been ordered a week before; the weather from that time had been clear and open until this same morning, so that there had been no time to give counter-orders, as the chaise came from a town fully twelve miles distant.

And now Charles entered to convey his mother away. Study and anxiety had of late reduced him even to emaciation, and his worn appearance was heightened by the contrast which the crape he wore made with his pale face. He had been shut up in his father's study, where he had spent an hour or two in devotion, and he was calm and even cheerful. "Are you ready, dearest mother?" said he; "the chaise is at the door." The dear woman rose up quickly. "Mary, Mary," she said, speaking with a great effort, "put out that fire; and there is fire in the kitchen — I'll go and take that off myself." "No, dear mother," said Mary, "I'll do all these things; just go at once into the chaise." "Well," said Mrs. Blair, "see that there will be no danger of fire. Lock the doors, and you know where *he* desired the keys to be left. Let him find everything right." A slight involuntary shudder passed through the group; but Mary answered quietly, "Yes, dear mother." "Forty years ! forty years!" ejaculated the good woman, as she passed over the threshold which she was never again to call her own. As for poor Emily, the necessary effort was for her fearfully trying. Charles and Mary, each with an arm round her waist, supported her almost sinking frame; but when she came to the spot which, in her eye, was occupied by the beloved figure of her father, passing to and fro in those walks where he had so often stopped to give his invalid a word of kindness or comfort, she could no longer restrain herself. With a convulsive burst of weeping, she laid her head on her brother's shoulder, saying, with a bitter cry which she could not suppress,

"My father — oh, my father!" In that momentary pang, she felt, poor thing! as if she alone had lost a father, or suffered from leaving the scenes which he had made so dear.

Mary, with a composed air, but hearing all the while the beating of her own heart, attended to her mother's wishes. She saw the fires extinguished; the borrowed articles restored to their owners, who came to take them away; and she herself went to a house at no great distance, where George Donaldson had intimated his desire that the keys of the manse should be left in custody. She then, with her weeping sister, whose cheerful activity had entirely forsaken her, seated herself in the open cart, at the lower end of which two servants likewise took their places. The day was still wet and chill, although the wind and rain had moderated in some degree; but the kind hands of the neighbours arranged the wrappings and coverings with as much attention to comfort as the nature of the conveyance could possibly permit. And many a prayer and blessing were poured forth, and many an affectionate shake of the hand was given, when at length all was in readiness for departure. As the cart jolted slowly and heavily away, Mary buried her face in her mantle. She dared not look upon the receding walls of the beloved abode she was leaving. But there was a painful distinctness in every familiar sound, which, in their very familiarity, seemed strange and unusual. The gates creaked on their hinges. The house-dog, which they were obliged to leave confined in an out-house, for a friend to fetch away, filled the air with his howlings. The stream that flowed through the garden, now swollen with the rain, brawled noisily along, as they crossed it outside the garden wall; and as these sounds grew fainter, the wind, passing through the belfry of the church, made the bell give one mournful toll. This was nothing unusual — the wind had often done so before; but how like a knell it now struck upon the hearts of the sisters!

They had very soon to pass by a group of cottages — not a village — but a cluster that lay thickly scattered by twos and threes, in this particular spot. It was a slow progress which they made in this part of their journey. Men, women, and children, came out — many of them had been long watching — and pressed forward to give a parting shake of the hand and a blessing. The children hung back by the way-side; but Mary once more rallied her spirits, sand called some of the older ones forward to bid them farewell. "May the blessing of your father's God go with you!" was the prayer that came from many a full heart. "And oh! Miss Mary," said a woman of a group that stood at one time around the cart, and came forward, one by one, to receive the much-valued shake of the hand — "oh, Miss Mary, and *what* are they going to do about the *kirk*? Although we dinna get the man of our choice, are we not to have the liberty to refuse one that we *canna* like?" "You remember what my father used to say, Annie," replied Mary; "THE LORD REIGNS." "Ay, Miss Mary," said the querist, "that's a great truth; but your father saw dark days coming, and och! och!" said the poor woman, weeping, "*this is* a dark day!" "God is purifying his Church," said Mary, "and he never purifies his Church without trying his people." "Oh, but Miss Mary," pleaded the speaker, who anxiously desired some glimpse of information, in which desire it was plain that those around her fully participated; "Oh, but they'll no *let doon* our cause?" "God has raised up men to testify on your behalf," said Mary; "and as this is His doing, we may hope that He will carry it through to His own glory and your good; but, remember, dear friends," said she, in a subdued and earnest voice, "remember what my dear father often said to you — If God should see meet to try you farther, let not your good be evil spoken of. 'The wrath of man worketh not the righteousness of God.'" "I dare say," said two or three of the others, speaking in the Gaelic tongue, and looking wistfully into Mary's face; "I dare say we have much need of grace?" "Much, much," replied Mary; "and oh, do not forget *us* before the throne of grace!" "Could we forget the children of our hearts?" was the reply. And with many tears they parted — the two sisters, with what breaking hearts *He* only knew who made them; and the cottagers still continued to gaze after them so long as they could be seen, and then disappearing, with a void in their bosoms which language has but feeble power to describe.

CHAPTER XII

*"Concerning the bonds of unity in the Church,
the true placing of them
importeth exceedingly."*
                    BACON

It may be conjectured, that after the coincidence of sentiment which had been accidentally elicited between Miss Legh and General Maitland, the brother of Lord Lentraethen, upon the subject which occupied the public mind at the time in Scotland, they would converse together frequently in the course of the ensuing months upon the same topic. The reader will pardon us for throwing, for the sake of continuity, the substance of several such conversations into *two*, bringing out as much as possible the questions in their more general and world-wide application, and leaving the intricacies of Scottish law so far as may be behind us, as being now somewhat out of date. "And so," said the General, on the morning after Sir Charles Murray's dinner-party, as he sat on a couch opposite our young friend in the drawing-room, in Ainslie Place — "so you made the discovery for yourself last night, that the weight of intellect lay on the unfashionable side of our Scottish Church question, and the weight of bone and muscle in the Court of Session at least, on the other?" "I thought so," replied Jane; "but there is a vast deal of mystery hanging over this *question* of yours, as you call it; not so much in its principles, it seems to me, as in its effects." "How so?" inquired General Maitland. "Why, in the first place, the common people in general seem to understand it, while many well-educated persons profess to find it quite incomprehensible." "Well, mystery the first," said the General, smiling. "What then?" "Many very amiable people," continued Jane, "have their sympathies enlisted *against* what I would suppose they ought naturally to be favourable to." "True," said General Maitland; "and what next?" "There is an immense deal of violence, and a disposition to personal aspersion, among your opponents; yet when they are a little pressed on the subject, they almost invariably profess to be perfectly ignorant of it." "I must allow," said the General, "all that to be somewhat marvellous. But as for your first anomaly," continued he, "perhaps a little reflection will make it intelligible. The fact is, that the educated classes are apt to lose original ideas in the technicalities which express them; while with the common people the ideas are everything, for they have derived them solely from their own experience. Thus the *veto* suggests to us some notion akin to the power exercised by the Roman tribunes, and its application in society at present seems incongruous and unintelligible. But with the humbler classes, especially in the country, the remembrance is vivid within their breasts of an inability to relish some one man or other in the pastoral relation, and it simply suggests to them the power of giving expression to that inability. *Non-intrusion* with the fashionable, and I am afraid I must add the superficial world, is a half-barbarous technicality of the Presbyterian courts; with the peasantry it means that the pastoral tie, to them of such importance, shall not be founded on constraint and violence."

"Is it not natural to think," inquired Miss Legh, "that the pastoral relation should be formed from affection?" "Quite as much so," replied the General, again smiling, "as that the marriage-tie should be so formed; and I am persuaded that, in either case, the holier, the more sacred the relation appears in the eyes of those contracting it, the more this ingredient of affection will be deemed a *sine qua non*. In England, as you know, where the relation is often so grossly venal, the feelings of the people are blunted, their moral sense on the point is corrupted; and just as the carelessness of the slave as to his fetters indicates his degradation, so the state of the English mind on this subject indicates *nationally* a low degree of religious sensibility." "I love 'the cottage homes of England,'" said Miss Legh, colouring slightly, "and our tenantry at Chesterlee were very favourable specimens of the English peasantry; but I must admit, after all," continued she after a pause. "that their wants are more of a physical than of a religious and intellectual character. I have certainly found a very high kind of intelligence among the poor in Scotland." "Ah, believe me," replied the General, "that the intelligence which begins at the heart is always the soundest; our people have been accustomed to a *pulpit* education, and they love it." "Do you think, then, that, after all," said our friend, "the power of electing pastors, which they so highly value, would be a very great sacrifice for the aristocracy to yield to them?" "Far from it," said

General Maitland, "and very much less in the Scottish Establishment than in that of England, where the livings are so much better, and the aristocracy, in consequence, so much more incorporated, in their younger branches, with the clerical body. *Here the sacrifice would be merely nominal, and the gain immense; because influence founded on affection is at once the most powerful and the most permanent,*" "That was one of my dear father's maxims" said Jane. "I fear, I fear," continued the General, "that what we of our class have for a long time wanted, especially in Scotland, is *enlightened patriotism*, not to speak of that highest description of it which is called *Christian* patriotism. Fain would I hope that we are on the eve of an awakening. But as a leaf before the eye will shut out the beauties of a whole universe, so do the small personal and party interests of my Lord *this* and my Lord *that*, too often take precedence of those grand and beneficial laws which ought to regulate social order. I believe that if the world's government were placed in the hands of some of our nobility, they would let it jar on as it might, so that their own temporary ease were secured; or, if the eternal interests of all mankind were theirs, to dispose of as much as their own estates, they would just place them in the hands of a factor, and never inquire into his character."

"Is not that a strong mode of expression?" said Miss Legh, smiling. "Of course," replied the General. "You must understand that I do not speak sweepingly; for with noblemen of a most fully awakened intellect and philanthropy, I am on terms of intimate personal friendship; but is there no truth whatever in what I assert?" "I much fear there is," replied Jane. "Then," said General Maitland, "it is *truth* which is severe, and not I; or rather, it is they who create the truth who are the severest censors upon themselves." "You seem to think," said Miss Legh, anxious to pursue the original subject, "that the aim of your Reformers, and those whom you deem their representatives of the present day, was one and the same. How would you characterize that unity of purpose, since the external aspect of the nation is in many respects dissimilar?" "My dear Miss Legh," said General Maitland, speaking in an earnest voice, "what was the great purpose of the Founder of Christianity, and what the impulse communicated by him to his apostles?" "It surely was," replied Jane, "the moral regeneration of the world." "Yes," replied the General, "through the grand and simple medium of *faith* in the Son of God. Then what ought to be the aim of his true Church?" "I should imagine it," replied Miss Legh, "to be the same." "Well," said the General; "and carrying this idea of *unity of purpose* along with you, which would you apprehend to be the *purest Church*?" "That," replied our friend, after musing for a few moments, "which should *in the same spirit, and by the same means*, labour most strenuously to carry out the same great end." "Assuredly," said the General; "and," added he, with a grave smile, "all wrangling about inferior marks of the true Church — such, for instance, as the laying claim to a pedigree by laying on of hands, which no man can trace — reminds me of the quarrelling which might take place among the foolish virgins of our Lord's parable on the eve of his coming; regardless of the *oil*, they might dispute about the manufacture and beauty of their lamps, till they were brought to the sad knowledge that an *empty* lamp is equally useless, howsoever constructed. What then," he continued, "in connection with that primary idea which we agree upon as a first principle — what would be the *beau ideal* of the best *national* Christian Church?" "That which should," said Miss Legh, "best accomplish the moral regeneration of the *nation*" "Then how," said the General, "would you set about the establishment of such a Church?" "You are better able to reply than I," said our friend; "for my ideas cannot be other than obscure on the subject."

"To begin with the simplest proposition, then, the number of pastors must be equal to the wants of the population," said the General, pausing, that the young inquirer might fully comprehend the idea. "Certainly," said Miss Legh, as if her reason perfectly embraced the truth of the proposition, for notions of ethics and economics were sufficiently familiar to her mind. "Whatever part of the population did not partake of the benefits of an Establishment must be beyond its pale, and in so far that Church is incomplete in its internal economy." "Quite so," said the General; "I see you comprehend me. Well, then, another point of strength in the position of our pure and efficient Church must relate to the position of each individual pastor with regard to his flock." "Ah, I see," said Miss Legh, "according to your first axiom, he must be a man whose whole efforts shall be directed to the moral regeneration of the people under his charge" "Yes," said the General, "but that is a high aim. He who would address himself to it effectually must be devoid of the selfish and the secular, as the chief ends of his being; indeed, they must not occupy a prominent place in his scheme of existence at all. Now the great question comes to be, how secure, so far as the defects inseparable from human agency can, a large body of men, composed of some thousand individuals, where the aims of all shall be equally pure and great? thus originating a unity which I take to be the *true* unity laid claim to, as one mark of the genuine Church of Christ, by Churches, or rather *corporations of clergy*, which possess nothing of it in the real intelligible sense." "I should suppose that a problem," said our young friend, "exceedingly difficult to solve."

"First, then, the true Church must be founded, in its creed and constitution, on the Word of God?" "Assuredly," said our friend. "Then, as the very apple of the eye of the Church's purity, the sacred rite of ordination must be kept holy, unworldly, and pure. How think you stands it in the greatest danger?" "If he who receives it," said Jane, "shall receive it merely as an instalment into a temporal benefice, and not for high spiritual ends." "And if there be *many* such in a Church," continued the General. "do you not perceive that they who bestow it must of necessity come to a level with those who receive it, seeing that the difference between them is only a difference of time, and that only through the hands of those who receive it can it ever be bestowed." "True," said Jane: "but is there not an invisible grace attending the rite of ordination?" "With that I do not meddle," replied the General; "I speak of the practical effects which shall ensue to the Church and the nation. When irreligious men bestow the rite of ordination upon irreligious men, we do not see the *invisible grace* carry with it many practical fruits." "Rome herself sufficiently testifies to that point," said Miss Legh. "Well, then," said the General, "seeing that they who receive and they who bestow ordination are one and the same, how would you most successfully corrupt the whole body of the clergy, supposing you made the attempt?" "A strange question," said Miss Legh; "perhaps, however, it might be done without difficulty by placing the allocation of benefices at their own disposal, seeing that their own families alone would benefit by the arrangement, with but little regard to moral fitness." "Take heed," said the General; "if you make that admission, you admit the important principle that *a check* upon the clerical body in the allocation of benefices is absolutely necessary." "We have in England lay patronage to answer that end," replied Miss Legh. "Well, then, we have only to inquire," continued the General, "whether lay patronage secures or controverts the great object of piety and spiritual-mindedness in a body of men who ostensibly have in their hands the spiritual regeneration of the nation, seeing that its distribution is in fact in the hands of rich men, who may be of any religion or of no religion at all." "*Secure* it, it certainly does not," replied Miss Legh; "for though our family has generally taken care to place its livings in the hands of men of good conduct, we know six or seven clergymen in the neighbourhood who were, some of them, mere men of pleasure; others profligates, whom no gentleman would ask to sit at his table. My father often expressed so much disgust at this, that I believe I was predisposed to sympathize with popular feeling in this country, seeing it had a similar basis, without knowing the intricacies of your *question*."

"And how could it be otherwise, my dear young friend," said General Maitland, "seeing that the only question with regard to a living is whether a man be influential enough to have it purchased for him? Secular-minded men must of necessity make of all that belongs to them a secular use. We must, then, of necessity, find our patrons *within the Church*; for, to constitute the common mob such, as it is erroneously said we do in Scotland, would be the greatest sacrilege of all. *Within the Church* alone can we hope to find the high spiritual motives we desiderate." "Did we not agree," said Miss Legh, somewhat surprised, "that to place the allocation of benefices in the hands of the clergy, would be the speediest way to effect their ruin?" "Doubtless," said General Maitland, smiling; "but you are falling into the common error of making the Church consist of the clergy, and none else. It consists in reality of all who, as Christians, are *members* of the Church, which is Christ's body. By being admitted into Christian communion, such are already pre-supposed to be possessed of enlightened consciences, of matured capacities, which have fully compared the standards and doctrines of the communion they have joined with the revelation they profess to believe. These surely are invested with most sacred interests, peculiar to them as members of a most sacred commonwealth. Who, then, can be actuated by such motives as they, for keeping safe the integrity of their spiritual privileges? If we place any class of interests whatever exclusively under the guardianship of men possessing a *different* class of interests, we shall not fail to bring these two classes into collision with each other."

"I understand you," said Miss Legh. "The interest of the patron is to get as much for his living as he can; the interest of the clergyman is to get as good a living as he can; but the interest of the people is to get as good a clergyman as they can. But has not patronage its vested *monied* interest? Is it not a right of property?" "Undoubtedly," answered the General; "so has slavery; but *monied* interests cannot prevent us from discussing questions of abstract right; they cannot blind us to the evils either of slavery or of patronage. Whether, on the other hand, men's bodily and spiritual freedom can ever *become* property —i e., whether money *ever can be an equivalent* for that which has no price — I do not stop to inquire; I shall continue our line of argument. Once admit the axiom, that where interests do exist, there alone exist the motives proper for their guardianship, and everything adjusts itself — all comes into harmony. In the case in question, Scripture authority is invested with its full weight as addressed to the *hearers* of Christian doctrine — to the taught as well as to the teachers: 'Beware of false prophets, which come to you in sheep's clothing, but inwardly they are ravening wolves. *Ye shall know them by their fruits'* — 'If I, or an angel from heaven, preach any other gospel unto you, let him be anathema maranatha.' The responsibility which God has laid on every man, and which no one man can lay on any other man, since all have to answer for themselves at the bar of judgment, regains its true place. The sentiments and affections have scope for action; in a word, the vital functions of the spiritual body once more begin to play — the compressed lungs begin to breathe."

"But," said Miss Legh, "in the Church of England the people do not *know* their pastor until after he is ordained by the bishop to his cure; how, then, can they have any share in his choice?" "Not," replied the General, "unless different regulations in this respect were adopted, which would by no means *un*-church the Church of England. In Scotland, it is different, for the Church has been constituted especially with a view to the giving effect to this great principle. Young ministers are licensed after having undergone a due examination by a Church court, just in order that the people may exercise their right of choice; and by our standards, not till the free call has been given, can there be any ordination to a special charge." "If your Church is thus constituted," said Miss Legh, "how then can there be any controversy on the subject? why is it not all clear?" "The origin and intricacies of the controversy would weary your patience, my dear young friend," replied the General, "which has continued so exemplary throughout this discussion. How patronage was introduced by Queen Anne's Tory ministry in 1711, as a stroke of policy to alienate the people from their pastors (introduced surreptitiously, too, without the consent of Scotland itself); how it operated too surely in introducing a set of worldly-minded men; how the free call degenerated in most cases into a form and a mockery; how the people, mindful of their ancient rights, still clung to them, and in many instances resisted the arbitrary intrusion of an ungodly man; how, of late years, the right-minded of the clergy, anxious to stem the flood of iniquity entering by the door of patronage into the Church, wished to give practical effect to their anxiety to protect the Christian people; how the patron called in the aid of the Court of Session, a court not legally constituted the superior of the Scottish Church courts, to help him to perpetrate intrusion on the people, while their *free call* on the other hand had never been disannulled; — for all this, and for the whole statistics of the case, I must refer you to books and pamphlets, with which, if you please, I can supply you in abundance. You will thus see explained that which you discovered the other night, how it happens that the six clearest heads on the bench of the Court of Session itself are opposed, on the law of the case, to seven other heads — some dull unit thus, as it has often done before, swaying the fate of Churches and of nations."

CHAPTER XIII

"Let not human quillets keep back divine authority."
MILTON

When our young friend had sufficiently perused and pondered the pamphlets and papers put into her hands by General Maitland, she sought the first opportunity of renewing a conversation with him on the subjects to which they related. For although her feelings had from many causes taken a decided bias towards the popular side, there were many points which appeared still dark to her understanding, especially where the controversy had become complicated with the claim of independent jurisdiction invariably put forth by the Church of Scotland. Here, as an English woman, her feelings had a decided leaning towards the other side. She therefore appealed to her friend and cousin at the breakfast table of a morning, where they two generally appeared first, and had thus frequent opportunities of a quiet *tête-a-tête*.

"Are you not," said she, "rather hard, after all, upon our statesmen; for I fancy that what they fear most is that claim of independent jurisdiction put forth by your Church? They consider it subversive of the principles upon which the other Establishments of the United Kingdom are founded." "If that independence," said General Maitland, "was made the basis of union by a free people, it is surely entitled to some attention." "Then," said Miss Legh, "you think the claim a just one?" "Our ancestors certainly thought so at the time of the Union," replied the General; "so that it comes to rest just upon the foundation of treaty and international faith. Allow me to read a part of the Treaty of Union to you. I believe many talk of it, and few know what it is. It is perhaps necessary to premise that the Act of Security for the Church at the Revolution 'allows and declares that the Church government be established in the hands of, and exercised by, those Presbyterian ministers who were outed since the 1st of January, 1661, for nonconformity to Prelacy, or not complying with the courses of the times, and are now restored by the late *Act of Parliament*, and such ministers and elders only as they have admitted and received, or shall hereafter admit or receive.' It is variously asserted in this act that the Church *government* shall be *only* established in the Church courts, and in the ministers and elders then being, and authorized by them and their successors. Here is not a word either of civil review or of state review of the sentences of Church courts, which would, indeed, have rendered this solemn investiture of supremacy in the Church herself over her own affairs a mere mockery. And now for the Treaty of Union, of which the last clause perhaps is sufficient, as it is an epitome of the whole: 'And lastly, that after the decease of her present majesty (whom God long preserve) the sovereign succeeding to her in the royal government of the kingdom of Great Britain, shall, *in all time coming*, at his or her accession to the crown, *swear* and *subscribe* that they shall inviolably maintain and preserve the foresaid settlement of the true Protestant religion, with the government, worship, discipline, rights, and privileges of this Church, as above established by the laws of this kingdom, in prosecution of the Claim of Right; and it is hereby statute and ordained that this act of Parliament, with the establishment therein contained, shall be held and observed in all time coming as a fundamental and essential condition of any treaty or union to be concluded betwixt the two kingdoms, without any alteration thereof, or derogation thereto, in any sort for ever.' Upon this broad and solid basis I think we have a right to maintain, that should our Church, or any portion of it, basely yield up its liberties to any foreign power, it would cease to be in truth or identity the ancient Established Church of Scotland."

"Indeed," said Miss Legh, "that wears a serious face, I grant; but as I have an interest in *another Church*, you will forgive me if I wish to hear the claim of independent Church jurisdiction discussed upon its intrinsic merits." "Let me then, my dear madam," said the General, "ask *you* a question to begin with. Do you believe the Scriptures to be of divine origin?" "I hope I do," replied our young friend. "Do you believe they were given as a law from God to *all* men, kings, statesmen, and judges?" "Without question," said Miss Legh. "Then," said the General, "there must be a divine law superior to human law; and if by subjecting the human to the divine we incur civil pains and penalties, by subjecting the divine to the human we must sin against the Majesty of heaven." "I suppose," said our friend, "that is what you mean in your national mode of expressing the thing by the HEADSHIP OF CHRIST — you mean the sovereignty of the divine Lawgiver." "Exactly," said the General; "and can there be any such noble principle for which to contend? One of the wise men of Greece anciently pronounced that to be the best government in which the laws were above the throne. Solon is said to have died voluntarily, that his laws might endure in Athens; the Son of God died, that his laws might reign everlastingly over his Church throughout the world. If you have thought seriously over the subject, has it never occurred to you that the endowment of Christianity is in itself an acknowledgment of its truth? Since it cannot be true unless of divine origin, does not its endowment by the state, and its subordination to the State, involve a very great contradiction?"

"You will allege that Mussulmans are more consistent," said Jane, smiling. "According to their belief they are," said the General. "We establish a religion which declares GOD the ETERNAL, the IMMUTABLE, and declares MAN to be of yesterday and to know nothing; and by the same act we subordinate God to man! Surely a monstrous contradiction! — such as only a creature comprehending little of God could be capable of!" "At the same time," said Miss Legh, "the extravagance of the Papal claims in past ages, which prostrated the world at the foot, not of God's throne, but at that of some ambitious or profligate priest, has led to great perplexity with regard to that principle."

"The fact is," said General Maitland, "that since the time of Constantine, the world has been governed in this respect by two extreme errors. Without deferring to the fundamental axioms and plain distinctions laid down by Christ as the moral legislator of the world, they made use of the grand truth of God's superiority to man, for the purpose of subordinating temporal interests to their spiritual claims. In a later stage of the world's history, after this error had sprung up and borne its poisonous fruit, that cycle was performed to which the human mind is so prone. It overleapt the intermediate truth, and adopted the opposing error. Since then, the bias of Protestant states has been to subordinate the spiritual to the civil; and as the first extreme operated *positively* in producing gross impurities, the second has operated in the main, except in its persecuting form, negatively as a drag upon the moral regeneration of the world.

Our Scottish Reformers seized the entire distinctive meaning of that statutory law of Christ, *'Render unto Caesar the things which are Caesar's, and unto God the things which are God's.'* The same two principles are distinguished in that other comprehensive sentence: 'My kingdom is not of this world.' In *his* kingdom he owns no superior; but he announces a full permission to the kings and rulers of the world to take that with which he has endowed them. How profound the wisdom is — I speak with reverence, it is the wisdom of the eternal God which dictated this enactment — may be fully perceived in the effects produced when it is disregarded by either of the parties to whom it is addressed. When the spiritual power assumes a temporal superiority, there is a foreign and impure element introduced — that of worldly ambition, which wholly falsifies its own sublime nature. Again, when the temporal attempts to subordinate the spiritual, being inferior in its essence, and unstable in its objects, it cannot do other than deprave and degrade it. Now the Reformers held the necessity of independence in each jurisdiction as indispensable to the maintenance of a pure faith. They repudiated the idea of spiritual supremacy over any temporal interest as absolutely as they did the converse. The principle was caught up and thoroughly understood by the Scottish mind in general; and for the maintenance of it, as the only right foundation for true faith and worship, our forefathers even yielded up their lives. At length triumphant, it was secured at the Union upon the firmest basis which national wisdom could devise, in making it a term of the compact of union; by any infringement of which, therefore, that union would come virtually to be dissolved. The act of Queen Anne, restoring patronage, against which the Scottish representatives voted two to one, attacked the principle indirectly, and rather went to undermine, than immediately to overthrow it. Your countrymen did certainly on that occasion take our national shrewdness at a disadvantage; for it never was suspected that a clause in an English statute, which was, that a presbytery should be bound to take the presentee of a patron on trials, should, in the course of time, come to be interpreted so as to prostrate that great principle which was an essential term of the Union, and which is, indeed, the very foundation of our national Church."

"How did it happen then," asked Miss Legh, "that that same clause did not give rise to collision between the ecclesiastical and civil courts sooner?" "Several causes combined," replied the General. "In process of time, as we said before, patronage worked out its natural effects, by introducing creatures of its own into the Church courts, who were willing to take the odium of forced settlements upon themselves, and so render them the act of the Church rather than of the State. It was all along taken for granted, that the Church courts might have done otherwise, if they had chosen. Then, when cases of collision did occur, our bench and our bar were adorned with truly great men — men capable of understanding the spirit of the laws, and who interpreted that *foreign* clause in accordance with the terms of the national treaty. They applied the very simple and efficient check which the law had provided, viz., that if a presbytery *refused* to take a presentee on trials, the living should, in the meantime, be separated from the pastoral charge."

"Might not such a check," inquired Miss Legh. "be found inconvenient in an established Church?" "Its very inconvenience," replied General Maitland, "constituted its efficiency. The people who refused to accept willingly of an individual, presented to the cure of their spiritual interests by a patron, in the event of the presbytery giving effect to their aversion, and refusing to resort to violence in the case, would of course need to resort to the *voluntary* system in the support of a pastor such as they wished. But they would not cease to be sensible of the advantages of a *free* Establishment, which is, indeed, the well-earned birthright of every Scotchman. After a term of years, when by death the parish became again vacant, it is probable that both people and patron would become more amenable to each other's wishes, and thus these people would be *preserved* to the national Church, instead of going off into dissent, as would have been infallibly the case under a more arbitrary state of things. Had this mild check, indeed, been put more frequently into operation, by the refusal of Church courts to settle an unacceptable presentee, the 500,000 Scottish Dissenters of our day would never have had an existence. This provision, instead of separating the people from the Established Church, as has been inconsiderately asserted, was a wise provision for preserving them to it."

"Then, if that check be the *legal* one," remarked Miss Legh, "the fines and imprisonment with which your clergymen are now threatened for refusing to settle unacceptable presentees in your parishes, cannot be legal also. Either the lawyers of the last century, or those of the present, must have erred; both cannot be in the right." "The statute stands on record," replied General Maitland, "and speaks for itself; and whether it is more probable that the majority on the bench in our days should err, or the large-minded men of the last age, let those who know something of both judge." "But," said Miss Legh, "I have heard a great deal from my infancy of the good effected, at small cost, by the Scottish Establishment — the fidelity of the pastors, the intelligence of the people, and so forth. How is it that, if the majority of its ministers were for so long a time the ready instruments of tyranny, the creatures of patronage, and men of worldly motive — how, in that case, did not your Church entirely lose affection at home, and respect abroad?"

"The constitution of our Church," replied the General, "framed and consolidated by the Reformers, is of that nature that it does not admit of venality to the same extent as that of the sister kingdom. The small emolument of the pastors, their equality, the number of schools which form a part of the Establishment, the eldership, who were intended to be the best and most enlightened of the non-clerical members of the Church, the number of courts, ascending by regular appeal, the introduction of a body of elders into these courts having equal votes with the clergy — all this excluded venality in its most repulsive forms; while every pastor, by being brought into immediate contact with his flock, expended upon them, at least in average cases, whatever amount of good he possessed. That constitution, the majority, entitled Moderates, would not have framed; but, being framed, they found it impossible essentially to alter it. Above all there was a minority, to whose zeal and piety our Church has been mostly indebted for her character. Notwithstanding the large numbers of Dissenters driven off by the tyranny of their stronger brethren, this minority preserved inviolable the attachment of the bulk of the nation. It is *their* names which are uniformly embalmed in the traditional remembrances of the people; and through them every public scheme of Christian philanthropy struggled into existence. This minority, always the representatives of the founders of our Church, through various influences, especially through that of the Reform Bill, which enhanced the efficiency of public opinion, have of late come to gain the ascendency in the country. They have, since that time, endeavoured to restore the Church to her ancient purity, to exercise discipline with more severity towards themselves, and more leniency towards the right feelings of the people. Hence, chiefly through the disappointed hopes of mercenary presentees, a collision with the civil courts; and the clause in the act of Queen Anne, which I have alluded to, serving as a pretext, the fetters of State control in spiritual affairs threaten again to be as completely rivetted on our Church as if no national struggle for its liberty, no Treaty of Union, and no independence of the Scottish nation, had ever existed. The men who uphold the ancient principles of our Church and country are denounced as rebels; and there may ensue, for aught we can see, ere our civil and religious faith be again acknowledged, a persecution as bitter as that of old."

"Is it not singular," continued General Maitland, "how an enlightened *faith*, simply and honestly acted upon, may supersede the necessity for a most lengthened and painful experience! Had the fact asserted by the Divine Lawgiver, that God and Caesar have their own independent provinces, been fully believed and never departed from both by Church and State — what centuries of painful experimental demonstration might have been spared! Must the ancient story of the fall be for ever repeated? God said, 'In the day thou eatest thereof thou shalt surely die,' and is not the history of the human race told in those words, '*Thou hast eaten, thou shalt die?*' Every form of evil has been followed by every form of death, moral, and physical, and spiritual."

"Alas!" said Jane, "that is most true. But as to the *fact* or foundation of belief and action stated by our Saviour, regarding the distinct sovereignties of God and the king, is it not said to be difficult at times to distinguish between those two provinces accurately?" "Ah!" said the General, "it is so *said to be* but it does not hence follow that it *is*. Depend upon on it, whichever party makes that assertion, does so for the express purpose of confounding the two jurisdictions. And to perplex and confound matters, in place of making them plain, is ever the interest of him who is the aggressor. Are there, in fact, any two provinces in nature more distinct than the *spiritual* and the *temporal*? If it is impossible to distinguish these, then all distinctions may be abolished."

"Is it not true, however," said Jane, "that in a Church established by law, where certain civil consequences are attached to the performance of certain religious duties, that which is otherwise clear becomes in some measure involved?" "Certain civil consequences," replied General Maitland, "follow certain religious duties and beliefs, although not established by law. We may take, for example, the case of a trader, who, in the midst of a highly Christian community, professes himself an Atheist, and refuses to comply with the religious forms of his fellow-citizens. In this manner he is not likely to increase his trade. It is possible that bankruptcy may follow what is in itself an abstract belief. Does this confound the spiritual and the temporal? Now what the public may lawfully confer or withdraw from the trader, viz., the patronage which it is at liberty to bestow where it pleases, the State may confer upon, or withdraw from, certain forms of religion. Does this imply *control* in the one case, any more than in the other? The public may withdraw the custom, which is its property; the State may withdraw the money, which is its property. *That* is competent to either. But did the public compel the trader, by physical force, to attend chapel or church, they would incur the guilt of persecution; so when the State goes one step beyond the withdrawal of what alone it has bestowed — that is, its money — it incurs the guilt of persecution, and of invasion into the province of Almighty God."

"I have frequently admired," said the General, "as I would admire a finished piece of mechanism, the complete accordance of the check I have mentioned to you before — the simple withdrawal of the benefice in *the individual case* where the State felt itself aggrieved — with the principle of the two jurisdictions. It involves a vast amount of great principle and legislative wisdom. In the first place, it is a thorough acknowledgment of the principles both of spiritual and of civil independence. Through this provision the State and the Church thus plainly express themselves: 'Act with your own in this instance,' the State says, 'as you please. I shall act with my own as *I* please. I did not *create*, I merely endowed you; and control other than over the endowment I may not exercise.' 'Right,' the Church replies: 'you acknowledge my independence; I do not question yours.' And here the matter takes end. There is no collision in fundamental principles. A trifling local breach takes place, which, in the course of a very few years, is healed, and then all things go on as smoothly as before. In truth, I hold that this check, simple as it may seem, and as all great things are, holds a position in law whose importance has not been adequately appreciated. It shows how an independent Church and an independent State may be allied, without the continual danger of a disruption between them. It constitutes, in an Established Church, the landmark between the two jurisdictions — the very point of separation; it sets well-defined bounds to the spiritual and to the civil authority, so that every step beyond its limits, is on the one hand *Popery*, and on the other *Erastianism*. Just bring your understanding to bear on this point, and you will see in this light, how grossly Erastian the proceedings of our civil courts of late years have been. Every interdict, every threat of imprisonment, every action for damages for the mere performance or non-performance of spiritual acts — to the use of all which instruments of coercion the legal check renounced all right — is in itself an assertion of civil supremacy over the spiritual, in the very face of the constitution."

"May I ask," said Miss Legh, "how you would define the *spiritual*?" "Thus," replied the General; "it means religious belief, or any act which embodies religious belief. Thus preaching is an act which embodies religious belief; so are baptism and the Lord's supper; so is the discipline of the Church over its members, which proceeds upon the supposition that they have fallen into religious error. This last must include doctrine, immorality, or any course of conduct greatly detrimental to the spiritual interests of the religious body. Any attempt upon the part of civil judicatories to follow such spiritual acts, *whatever their occasional causes may have been*, with penalties other than the simple withdrawal of the endowment, is Erastianism, and cannot be submitted to without a renouncement of the grand principle, that Christ is the only *Head* or *Lawgiver* of the Church, as he ought to be that of every believer."

"But," said Miss Legh, "must there not be, by some supposed terms of compact, a power in the State to judge whether the

Church keeps by the terms of her endowment — is, in fact, *the* Church which she has endowed?" "Unquestionably," replied the General; "but to what extent? Clearly to the withdrawal of her endowments, and no farther. The position which an individual benefice ought legally to assume, upon any supposed specific encroachment upon civil rights — that is, temporary separation from its emoluments — is no more than an epitome of the position which the whole Establishment ought to hold with regard to the State. It is indeed, the local application of the grand law which ought to regulate the two jurisdictions of these allies. But the State *cannot*, according to the intrinsic principles of justice and toleration, coerce the Church by any other penalties, or suffer her inferior courts so to do. By the just and enlightened law of Scotland, founded both on *faith* and reason, the Church is the *ally*, not the *vassal* of the State. It pretends to no power of making aggression, and it will endure none to be made upon it."

"And what do you think," said Miss Legh, "would be the consequences of submission on the part of your Church to the State, in the event of the latter making what you call Erastian pretensions?" "Before the consequences become apparent, it is necessary first to understand the exact position which our supreme spiritual court holds. We shall, then, again revert to the republics of Athens and Sparta, where, in the one, the laws of Solon were binding in its earlier times at least; in the other, the laws of Lycurgus till a later period. The supreme courts in these republics were merely the *interpreters* of the statutes of their deceased lawgivers. Their business was chiefly to see that a code which they did not enact was observed within their jurisdictions. But, like all supreme courts, they possessed a certain legislative power, which consisted in adapting the old laws to the present circumstances and necessities of the people. Now, suppose that a foreign power were to attempt the enforcement of pains and penalties against either of those States, merely for interpreting its own laws to the best of its own judgment — what would submission to this alien intermeddler involve? Would it not involve not merely a base and cowardly abandonment of their own independence, but likewise a change of *lawgivers?*" "Assuredly," replied our friend. "Well, then," said the General, "for the courts of Areopagus and Ephori substitute the General Assembly of a National Church; PUT THE LAWS OF THE SON OF

GOD ABOVE THE THRONE, instead of the laws of Lycurgus; and for the foreign power substitute the STATE, with all its shuffling objects and changing administrations — one only principle, that of temporary expediency, holding the helm of affairs. What would be the consequence of acquiescence in any penalties — other than the withdrawal of State alliance — for no other offence than the deliberate and conscientious interpretation of the law of Christ, as the great moral Legislator?"

"According to the analogy," answered Miss Legh, "it would be a change of lawgivers." "And he who consents," added the General, "to a change of *lawgivers*, has no right afterwards to complain of a change of *laws*. At all events, the least evil that can happen is, that ecclesiastical law shall be brought within the narrower limits of civil law. And what is the direct consequence? — That a man who has not offended against the laws of his country, who has but abstained from attempts on life and property, may be a member of the Church, or may feed the flock of Christ within the Church. He may have done what else he pleases.* How noble a spectacle, on the other hand, is that of a State guaranteeing the Church's independence as equally dear with her own — as being, in fact, the brightest jewel in the monarchy! The Church, on her part, holding as her only chart THE WORD OF GOD, points with unvarying finger, to the immutable laws of God, and the immortal destinies of man, and fixes upon them the wandering eye of the State, ever ready to bewilder itself in the shifting and turnings of a short-lived expediency. Each exists for the well-being of the other; like twin planets revolving together round the same sun, they feel each other's power — they shed upon one another a brilliant though reflected light; and yet, each maintains the independence of

---

Is it not thus that the Popish Church, with its impure hands, has been able to fling upon the Church of England such an upbraiding as this: " We assure you, we feel no more inclination to deny that there may be criminals in Sicily, than you do to deny the guilt of one of your own ministers, whose flagitious abominations were recently proved in a court of law, and who, by virtue of Parliament canon law, still remained as minister of your church, an example to his flock, the reprover of the impure, and the encourager and protector of the innocent." This occurs in a correspondence between the Catholic Institute of England, and Sir Culling Eardley Smith, Bart, in 1844.

its sphere. What a spectacle would a nation present blessed with a National Church, thus pure and efficient; and a State ruling on such enlightened principles of Christian philanthropy! Surely health should vibrate through every pulse of her material frame. Immortal Hope should make the sky above her ever serene, and she should sit a queen among the nations."

" Then, you hold," said Miss Legh, " that no pure Church can receive its laws from the State?" — "I lay it down as a first principle, that the Church, which is the first instrument for the moral regeneration of the world, can admit of *no* intervention between itself and the world's heaven-sent Regenerator. The *human*, whether in the form of State supremacy, or *the traditions of men*, must deteriorate or corrupt the *divine*. As Christ himself declares, it must make the Word of God of none effect. The Church, to be *pure*, must hold Christ's words as of immediate, paramount authority; to be *efficient*, it must be unfettered in deliberation and discipline, so that it may apply the moral remedy, which God has intrusted to it, in such form and manner as the circumstances of the country may require bound by nothing but conformity to the standard of God's Word."

CHAPTER XIV

"The admission of ministers to their offices must consist in the consent of the people and church whereunto they shall be appointed."
                                                                JOHN KNOX

The humble petition of the people of Glenmore had, as we have seen, been treated with neglect; — how their more direct application was received, we have seen likewise. The presentation to George Donaldson had been issued, and there was a large majority in the presbytery willing to give it effect. If it had not been so, George and his father were fully prepared to raise an action at law, in order to compel that which no law court in Scotland had ever before lent its authority to in opposition to the will both of *Church and people*. The parishioners had now, therefore, only to consider what course of conduct it was most advisable for them to pursue; for to give consent to the placing over them of an irreligious pastor — above all, of him whose want of religion was most obnoxious to them, from their ultimate acquaintance with his character — was what no man in the parish for a moment thought of. Yes, there *was* one man who thought of it — and that was the keeper of a small dirty public-house or dram-shop, which was situated at the foot of the hill where old John Morrison's cottage had stood, where George used often to stop on his way to or from his shooting expeditions, and with the host of which he was, consequently, on very intimate terms. The very last time he had been there, he had prevailed on this person to adhibit his name to his call. The man indeed scratched his head seriously, at the idea of setting himself in opposition to the whole parish; but an extra mutchkin settled the matter. He shook George vehemently by the hand, vowed he was the best young fellow in the whole country-side, and that the people of Glenmore were a set of pitiful fools, who might go where they pleased; — to all which George most heartily responded

These people, however, had interests too important at stake to be discussed over a mutchkin of whisky. They met, therefore — that is to say, the leading men both of Glenmore and Aird — to consult together as to their best mode of procedure. Two or three of the more fiery spirits were for renewing the old scenes of resistance even to bloodshed. "I'll tell you what, my friends," said our acquaintance, M'Gillivray, rising up in his place with sparkling eye and vehement gesture; "place around this church a wall of men ten deep; they may bring their military or their police; but if the hireling attempt by their means to come in at door or window, let it be over the mangled bodies of the flock."

"Right," responded an old soldier who had spent a great part of his life in foreign service, and who had returned to pass the remainder of his days in his native parish. He was a sober, quiet man, well-disposed to religion, as people thought, and in general deportment notable as a peace-maker; for he said, "When men had seen war in earnest, they came to like peace all the better afterwards." Now, however, the old soldierly blood was stirred again within him, and he responded heartily to the sentiment of M'Gillivray. "Right!" he re-echoed; "I have spent the best part of my life in fighting for my country; and I have heard, in Spain, in Egypt, and on the field of Waterloo, that there are no better soldiers than Highlanders. — If we didn't grudge our heart's blood to our king, shall we grudge it in defence of our dearest privileges? I say, if we could fill yon bloody trench at *Quatre-Bras* —ay, God above knows how it was filled with dead bodies, every one with its kilt and plaid — shall we suffer the military or police to invade the place of the ashes of our kindred? and shall we not lay our own bodies on their graves around the church of our fathers?"

This kind of military harangue produced its effect; — there were other men in the church, who, with kindling eyes and angry brows were ready to second the motion of M'Gillivray. But the catechist, who was seated hard by the old soldier, rose, and with steady countenance and dignified demeanour, spoke as follows: — "My friends, your anger is just; God forbid that I should say it was not an unrighteous thing to drive the flock after the hireling, when they knew the voice of the true shepherd. But, dear friends, we must bear our testimony as Christians, in such a way as not to cause the enemy to blaspheme; for *the wrath of man worketh not the righteousness of God.* Do not, I beseech you, let the words of the beloved pastor, who left us to this day of trouble, slip out of your mind: and for his sake, as well as that of our Heavenly Master, let us use forbearance. My advice is this: — Since the arm of the law is at work in the matter, let the law give admission, as it has power to do, to its own; that is, the stipend and stone walls. Let the parishioners attend here on the morning of the settlement in a quiet and orderly manner, and let them give their testimony against the profaning of the spiritual rite, by rising as one man, and leaving this church before the ordination begins — to return no more, until," he added, after a short pause, and with a slight tremor in his voice, "until the Lord be pleased again to light his candle here. And have we not abundant cause for thankfulness, that though we leave these walls, we do not leave the Church of our fathers, but that it will still provide us with the bread of life. Surely, surely, our trial is less than that of many in by-gone days, who have had to bear witness in sorrow and grief of heart against her who bore them, and to go out from her, scarce knowing whither they went." The catechist's address came home to the good-sense of all present — even M'Gillivray and the soldier at once gave in, and the people separated with the utmost harmony of feeling, to wait for the day when, in lieu of their rightful but dead-letter call, their Church, by a law intended at least as a kind protection from outrage, permitted their attendance, for the purpose of giving in the dissents of *communicants, heads of families*, from the settlement of an unwelcome presentee.

Upon the incidents of that day we shall not dwell at much length. The church was crowded with people — the people of Glenmore, who sat patient and unmoved during the lengthened proceedings by the hostile presbytery; and with people from the neighbouring parishes, among whom were some of the wilder and more untaught spirits, who were not equally desirous of suppressing all manifestation of their feelings. The call, which has always preserved to the Presbyterian people the *appearance* of a free voice in the election of their pastors when the reality had disappeared — that call, at present setting forth that George Donaldson was the free, and unconstrained, and unbiassed choice of the people of Glenmore, after the clerk had read it aloud in the hearing of that same people, lay on the table, that they might come forward and adhibit their names thereto. Old Donaldson and M'Lean vociferated loudly, inviting them to come forward for the purpose of signing. A dead and ominous silence on their part prevailed. The elder Donaldson at length intimated, that only five minutes additional would be granted, and then the voice of the dram-shop keeper, from a remote corner of the church, was heard, declaring that *he* was there, and that *he* was ready to put down his name. Way was immediately made for him to advance; which he did, wiping his brow several times during his progress, and amid whispers such as these from the people of Aird, upon the border of whose parish he lived, and some of whom stood in the passages: "How many glasses did he tak wi you, Jock, the last time he cam frae the hill?" — "How much did he gie you for the last mutchkin, Jock?" — "What do ye ken o' sermons, Jock? ye ken mair o' gill-stoups." Jock, however, succeeded in setting down his name in the very scrawl in which he set it to the curiously-spelt bills which he made out for his customers. The *call*, with the one signature appended to it, was then handed to the presentee, who signified his acceptance of it, though not without a lurking sneer, visible on his countenance.

The object of the Moderate majority was to wear out the patience of the congregation in such a manner as to induce them to separate before the time for tendering their dissents should arrive; and for this purpose they had interposed petty interruptions, at every step, too trifling and tedious to be recorded. With the same intent, they now proposed an adjournment, under pretence of taking some refreshment; which motion the minority, who were men of no great energy of character, although of good intentions, were not successful in opposing. But it was of no great importance. There patiently sat the people, although the sun, shining through the windows, showed, by his slant beams, that he was near his setting, and that it would probably be amid the darkness of night they would have to make their way to their homes. At weary length the time came when the dissents should be tendered. A roll of the names of three hundred communicants lay on the table. The *negative* form of dissent implied in the refusal to sign the call, had, as we have seen in the course of Moderate or patronate domination, been rendered of no effect as a protection to the people against intrusion. And this it was which induced the General Assembly of 1834, sensible of the abuses and outrages committed during the minority of the then dominant party, to frame a law which gave to the people's dissent a more positive form, which should induce a presentee of modesty and religious feeling to wait for a presentation to a place where he would be likely to prove more useful; or if he persevered, by forbidding the presbytery to proceed farther for the time being with his trials, to interpose an effectual barrier between those people who regarded him with aversion and his self-interested views. Only to communicants, however, was that privilege, as well as that of the call, accorded; because they alone, as members of the visible body of Christ, were presumed to have arrived at full maturity of religious judgment.

One by one these now came forward — the greater part of them elderly or middle-aged men — with deliberate step and clouded countenances, to set down their names to a solemn declaration, that they conscientiously believed this man — George Donaldson — not calculated to advance their own spiritual interests or those of their children. Again at every moment their forbearance was tried by higgling and questioning about the most trifling forms; and on one occasion a lone and serious interruption took place, when Evan Munro, the farmer and storekeeper, advanced, because it was suggested that he having a son of the same name, the person on the roll might possibly mean his son, instead of himself. But the long and tedious day did come to an end at length. The roll, with the names of three hundred men — all of them in full communion with the Church — all heads of families likewise — men grave, devout, reflective — from whose hearths the voice of prayer and praise arose every morning and every evening — that roll, no light or frivolous thing, was at length concluded, to be again opened before the bar where its moral weight will assuredly be appreciated by One who said, "Whoever offendeth one of these little ones, it were better for him that a mill-stone were hanged about his neck, and that he were cast into the depths of the sea." The last communicant set down his name and retired to his seat. Then it was that M'Lean — prompted by our former acquaintance, Davidson of Kilblair, who was the real executive in the Moderate party during the day's proceedings — moved, that as the veto law was *ultra vires* of the Church, the presbytery should proceed to the settlement, irrespective of the dissents. And a majority agreeing to this motion, it was declared,

"That as the dissent and complaint of the minority of the presbytery, and the agent for the dissentients, to receive and admit George Donaldson, are founded on the veto act, which has been declared *ultra vires* of the Church and illegal, such dissent and complaint is ineffectual and incompetent, and ought not to bar the execution of the presbytery's finding; that the presbytery, accordingly, proceed to the induction on Friday the 15th of January next, and that the record now be closed."

At an hour past midnight the presbytery adjourned. The people, too, separated for their homes, some of them several miles distant, to partake of food, which, since the previous morning, they had not tasted, and to lie down to rest for the short time which would elapse ere many of them were called to the early labours of the ensuing day.

A feeding storm set in, and moorland and upland lay under one deep compact covering of snow. The rivulets in the glens were covered in from side to side, the little pathways were effaced, and the hollows filled up in such a manner as to render the lesser inequalities of surface almost imperceptible. Around the Manse of Glenmore there was an air of peculiar desolation. No sound of voice or tread now broke in upon the cold wintry silence. The window-shutters were fast closed — the windows dingy and battered over with snow, and all around had already assumed a strange and neglected aspect. When, before, in the dreariest storm, had the well-known path-way to *the Manse* remained untrodden? When, before this sad winter, had a day passed that some poor man did not come there for comfort or aid? Yet why should the past be awakened from its long, long slumber? There was to be once more a noise of many voices, a crowding of many feet, a stirring of many hearts — and then all was to sink into the blankness of the deserted and forsaken spot! There was to be one solitary heartless man! — an unfrequented church! — an unfrequented manse!

Morn arose, the morn of the 15th, with the same leaden sky above, and the same unbroken winding-sheet below. The snow fell, but only in thin flakes, except when occasionally a heavier shower filled the atmosphere, and seemed to blend earth and heaven into one. The people were early astir, not only the people of Glenmore, but those of many neighbouring parishes, especially those of Aird and Dalry, who themselves groaned under the evil to be inflicted on their neighbours. There were among them angry spirits and burning words; but it was not so with the parishioners of Glenmore. They attired themselves quietly in their Sabbath suits — old men, young men, and maidens — one thought within their bosoms — the intruded pastor and deserted church — and this thought weighed down their spirits into silence.

Anon, groups were seen wending through the murky atmosphere, blackening here and there the white surface of the earth, or advancing toilsomely along the edges of the ravines, the strongest taking the lead, in order to break the snow in the more impassable spots. One by one these groups dropped into the church-yard of Glenmore, and stationed themselves partly on the tomb-stones and partly on the low stone wall which surrounded the church-yard. As they arrived thicker and faster, many of those sitting on the tomb-stones had to make good their positions by standing instead of sitting, especially as a *fresh* came on accompanied by some gleams of sunshine, and the hard gritty surface of the grass and stones began to be trampled into mud. Before the hour for opening the doors arrived, the crowd become extremely dense; and as new arrivals brought accessions to its outer edges, or endeavoured to make way into the centre, the mass around the doors became more and more closely locked together. Scarce a movement could be effected by those within the pressure; the noise of feet therefore ceased; but a sound of voices, now rising, now falling, maintained here in low earnest whispers, and there ascending into louder and more vehement declamation, kept bubbling over the surface of the mass and echoing within the church, over the empty pews and within the aisles and galleries, like the confused noise of living voices and the jabbering of unseen spirits falling on the ear of one whose soul is about to take its departure.

Some minutes passed after the clock within the church had tolled twelve, when a strong body of men armed with batons were seen taking the road towards the manse; and a few minutes more elapsed, when the sound of carriage wheels was heard in the same direction. Three carriages full of people drove up to the manse door. The first contained George Donaldson, the captain of police, the procurator-fiscal, and the Edinburgh lawyer, who had been employed as intrusion-agent in the business, and who had managed it very much to his own advantage and the satisfaction of his employers; the second carriage contained M'Lean, and sundry

Moderate members of presbytery; and the third held the person of Mr. Davidson, with certain of his protégés and follower, who came for the benevolent purpose of supporting the modest merit of the intruders against the persecutions of the oppressed. George and Mr. Davidson jumped first from their separate conveyances, both apparently in high spirits; and the latter, shaking hands with the former, told him "to keep up his heart" — which was manifestly an overflow of superfluous anxiety, seeing there was no present need for the exhortation. "There is the manse, my lad!" continued he; "it shall be yours in the face of Heaven; and as for those bulls of Bashan down at the church, I heartily wish we had some one to unchain upon them, who would do *their* business." A policeman was despatched without delay to the house where the keys of the manse lay; but the man, after an absence of some minutes, returned, saying "that the family were in the church-yard, and that it would be a matter of considerable difficulty to get at any of them, so as to let them know what was wanted." This was enough to light the easily kindled fuel of Davidson's ire. In the midst of no very minced oaths, he made a dash with his stick at the low window of the parlour, which he broke, forcing the shutter open by the same means; it indeed, being old, and secured only by a very feeble latch, gave way at the first pressure. The fastening of the window was then easily undone, and the sash thrown up: "In with you — in with you," cried Davidson to his protégé; and, with a hoarse laugh, George leapt into the room, whose echoes gave back the sound, as if the shades of the departed still lingered within the walls. One by one, the other occupants of the carriages entered in like manner, each casting a contemptuous glance around him. An empty room standing a good deal in need of refitting, with a blackened gaping fire-place, alone met their gaze; — yet how much would still have been in that room for the eyes of those who were gone from it for ever!

George and his party hastily formed a knot in the centre of the floor for consultation, and it was agreed that two or three of the policemen should be despatched forthwith to inspect the crowd, and discover, if possible, which was the least difficult mode of access. "If you please, sir," said the first policeman on his return, addressing his captain with hat in hand from outside the window, "there is no getting through yonder no more than through a stone wall." "Well," responded Davidson, with one of his usual oaths — "well, Atkins, I suppose we must put you at our head as the stoutest of us, and make good an entrance as we best can. By Jove, if a volley of musketry were discharged among these country fellows, it would soon send them yelling home." The man moved his head with something between a nod and a shake, as much as to say, "I am not so sure of that."

"Geordie, my good fellow," continued Davidson, "you ought to get down on your knees and ask a blessing on our endeavours, and on yourself as minister of the gospel in the parish of Glenmore." This joke was received by the Moderate presbytery with shouts of laughter, and in the highest good humour, they were about to sally forth to make an essay upon the human mass in the church-yard, when, lo! there arrived at the window, breathless with haste, a notary-public, bearing the protest of the minority of the presbytery, which he insisted on reading before the party should leave the house, notwithstanding all their remonstrances. The protesting minority consisted only of three; rather a singular thing in this stage of the Church's history, though not uncommon in the old days of Moderatism; which three, feeling the utter inutility of their presence, and likewise willing to avoid the pain to which the proceedings of the day would subject them, were content, instead of appearing in person, to send their protest, as we have said, by the hands of a notary-public. That protest was founded on the fact, that the majority were acting in defiance of the laws of the Church, which required them to respect the solemnly-expressed dislike of the people to the presentee, and required, from the most ancient times, a "call" signed in his favour to give at least the colour of their approbation to his settlement. But the notary-public had proceeded but a small way in his reading, when Davidson, who was not disposed to be kept there per force, snatched the paper impatiently from the man's hands, and having glanced over it with an angry eye, instead of handing it to the presbytery, threw it on the floor, and kicked it with his foot. "Pooh! pooh!" said he, "you may light your candle with that, George;" then addressing the notary, "My good fellow," said he, "pray get out of the way." He was again about to leap from the window, when one of the reverend gentlemen of the company suggested that they had almost forgotten the *calling of the edict*, and that it must needs be proclaimed at the most patent door of the church, which was the west. Davidson's patience now almost entirely failed. He threatened to go away home — raved at Church forms and all Churchmen whatever, saying, that they were made — without being particular in specifying which he meant — for the express purpose of driving people mad; however, when he had cooled a little, it was, notwithstanding, agreed that Captain Fleming should once more despatch Atkins for the church officer who should be instructed to call the edict forthwith.

Upon the arrival of this functionary, after a delay which served further to incense Mr. Davidson, one of the members of the presbytery placed the edict in his hands, instructing him to call it aloud at the west door, or as near it as he could manage to get. "That'll no be owre near, sir," said Peter, as he trudged away, accompanied by the policeman, "but I'll e'en do my best." Accordingly, honest Peter, seeing that it would cost him some little trouble to approach the door, was wisely contented to stop at the edge of the crowd, scrupulously taking care, however, that it should be directly facing the west; and there, at the top of his voice, he proclaimed aloud the edict, which bore "that all who had any competent objections to the presentee or his settlement in this parish," should immediately appear before the presbytery, or his settlement should be forthwith proceeded with. "Objections!" cried one of his auditors; "how dare you ask, Peter, if we have any objections?" "Hoot! no offence, no offence," cried Peter, shrinking back, however, a step or two; "ye ken its only a form." "Humph !" resumed the speaker, "a form without the spirit, like some ministers and their sermons that we ken o'." "As many objections as there's folk in this kirk-yard, I'm thinking," cried another. "I'm thinking mysel'," said a rather shrewd-looking man, "that the presbytery, such as it is, would easy get owre a' the objections that we could bring, which is may-be mair than ane; and as for the objection that we're no like to get guid o' his ministry, which is the likeliest, as well as the most ceevil, its been telt weel already." "None of your nonsense, Peter," cried several voices at once; "off with you, off with you;" and honest Peter, who had, notwithstanding the people's good humour, some idea that they would have no great objections to play at the game of breaking heads, took himself away accordingly, and trudged back to the manse, making his own jocular remarks, under the rose, to his companion on the document he held in his hand.

And now in earnest did the manse party, who had in the interim succeeded in opening the house door from the inside, sally down towards the church-yard — sheriff, proprietor, procurator-fiscal, presentee, presbytery, police, and all the crowd — meaning those who came from adjacent parishes, for the Glenmore people persisted in maintaining a moody silence — received them with shouts, and some of the wilder spirited lads began to throw snow-balls, which they aimed at George and his father, and at M'Lean — against the two latter of whom there were old scores to pay off. Davidson received one aimed from a distance at the party, which struck his hat and knocked it off. "Pick up my hat," he shouted, in accents of fury, to Kenneth Ore, who stood at a few paces distance from him. Kenneth folded his arms and stood erect. "Pick it up for yourself, Mr. Davidson," he replied quietly but haughtily, "or order your footman to do it. *I* am no man's footman." Davidson stepped up to him, almost beside himself. "If I had my pistols here," he vociferated, "by — , I would send a bullet through you!" The low and somewhat mean figure of Davidson, and his face purple as it was with rage, presented rather a curious contrast to the manly form, the handsome features, and contemptuous lip of the young Highlander. The latter certainly looked for that moment the aristocrat. Kenneth replied not a word, but several voices in the neighbourhood cried out derisively, "There may be some as good marksmen here, Mr. Davidson, as you." Davidson was not a man of courage. The very mention of a serious assault frightened him into coolness; and he, therefore, thought it his wisdom for the time being to join his friends, who were engaged in making fruitless efforts to gain a passage through the crowd. Nobody touched them; the snow-balling, owing to the remonstrances of some wiser individuals, had ceased; but as soon as any attempt was made to gain admittance, the crowd swayed their whole pressure in the same direction, so as to present an effectual barrier against all efforts from without. At length a magistrate, who was friendly to the cause of the people, but at the same time aware of the uselessness of such a procedure, succeeded in gaining an elevated position, and in a friendly spirit addressed the multitude, representing to them the fruitlessness of the mode of resistance they had adopted, and assuring them that, if they persevered in it, the settlement must instantly take place within the manse. It was perhaps the manner of the address which had its effect more than the force of the argument; for the magistrate, making his way to the spot where the baffled presbytery sulkily stood, took the church officer who carried the key under his protection, and gained access for him, as readily as the density of the crowd permitted, to the door of the church.

And now the opening of the door was the signal for a simultaneous rush to the galleries, which were in a few seconds crowded to suffocation; the parishioners, meanwhile, taking their places in a more orderly manner down below. The presentee and his party occupied a large seat in front of the pulpit, and the police stationed themselves here and there in the passages as they best could. No sooner had these arrangements been completed, than Mr. M'Lean ascended the pulpit stairs, and his round face began to shine out above the disc of the pulpit, as if it were about involuntarily to deliver a lecture on the science of good eating. The parishioners, poor people, held down their heads. They had never seen M'Lean in that pulpit before, and by the law of contrast the remembrance of the beloved pastor, who had so often, from the same spot, raised their thoughts from the work-day toils of earth to the hopes and enjoyments of heaven, came over their hearts with an irrepressible gush, of sorrow. But M'Lean, in proceeding with the services of the day, soon drew attention upon himself. He began to look behind him and before him, within the pulpit and around, at the same time fumbling in his pockets, as if in want of something he had forgotten; and at length, in some confusion, he beckoned to one of his brethren to approach. An anxious whispering ensued. The man who spoke with him returned to the seat where his other brethren were stationed, and again a whispering, which went along from one to another, commenced. The countenances of the various dignitaries fell. They seemed puzzled and a little dismayed. At last one of them rose up and whispered to a person in another seat. It was to ask a Bible to hand to the man in the pulpit. The BIBLE had been forgotten! Not one of the band had so much as one to lend to their brother in distress.

No sooner had the galleries, which kept a watchful eye on the proceedings below, perceived the cause of all this delay, and saw the Bible handed up, than a tumult began, which re-echoed from gallery to gallery — rose and fell, and swelled again. A snowball was aimed at M'Lean's head, who ducked down in order to avoid it, and in a few moments looked out again, as if to ascertain whether it was safe to venture forth. The ball had been aimed by one of the lads in his own parish — no doubt, with right good will — for what was this accident, but an epitome of the man's life? was that not altogether a negation of the Bible: Had it ever been in his heart, or even in his head? had *he* ever reached so much as the threshold of knowledge — which the lad who so improperly threw that ball had reached — that the Bible contained important truths, which to know, and preach, and urge, was the chief end of his office, as God's ambassador to men, and that he, putting his carcass, his empty name, in the room of those truths, to his people, was a forgery! — a lie!

The aiming of the snow-ball was the signal for renewed uproar in the galleries, cries, shouts, and groans; while small missiles, consisting of little bits of plaster picked out of the walls, half-pence, sleeve-buttons, and the like, were thrown at the terrified presbytery. The police looked about in vain for offenders. Around them, in the body of the church, all was as silent as the gathering thunder-cloud; while above, every one joined in the various noises alike, and the missiles flew, it was impossible to say from whence.

Again the mild magistrate arose, and ascending the pulpit stairs, commenced another address to the unruly auditory, who immediately ceased their tumult to listen, although still holding the riotous position of standing on the seats and the fronts of the pews. He represented to them that there was an impropriety in these proceedings in connection with services which wore the appearance of being religious, even though beneath that appearance there dwelt no reality; and he entreated them to remember the advantage over them which such conduct must infallibly afford to their enemies. By way of reply, the people sat down, and seemed to prepare themselves to listen, though in attitudes which said plainly, "Well, what has that man without the Bible got to say? — let him say on." The magistrate then turning to M'Lean, told him, in rather a stern voice, that he might proceed; and accordingly he, with unsteady hand and quivering voice, read out of the small pocket Bible what was evidently the first psalm which chance opened to him. The sermon had been intended — in order to flatter the feelings of the Glenmore people — as an eulogium on the late Dr. Blair, sliding into a meet introduction of his successor. The text was therefore chosen from 2d Samuel, 12th and 23d verses: "But now he is dead, wherefore should I fast? I shall go to him, but he shall not return to me." The latter clause was received with expressive coughs, though the guardian magistrate still held his place on the stairs ready to suppress, in its first manifestations, any renewal of popular outbreak. The sermon contained sundry remonstrances upon the folly of excessive grief for the departed, delivered in a low monotonous tone, varied only by the query pronounced in a more emphatic manner at the end of every few successive sentences — "And I, wherefore should I fast?"

When this discourse came to a close, George Donaldson stood forth to take upon him his ordination vows, which were to be administered to him by the individual who had just concluded the sermon.

Now, however, a movement was observable among that sober and staid portion of the audience which occupied the body of the church — the parishioners proper of Glenmore. An agent whom they had employed stood up, and asked leave, in their name, to read a protest which they had drawn up against this presbytery in proceeding to the ordination of George Donaldson, on the plea that it was in the face of the authority and constitution of that Church to which they adhered, and would be supported only by the civil courts. Much demur and altercation were thus given rise to; but the agent carried his point, and the protest was read. In the meanwhile the parishioners were occupied in gathering up the Bibles which lay in the pews, many of which had retained their places there, for three or four generations. What was to be done next? The men stood up, and by a simultaneous impulse, gave a momentary glance around them, as if to take farewell of the hallowed familiar place of their weekly sojourn and wonted communion. The women, on the other hand, bent their foreheads to the pews, while the sound of more than one sob was heard, and some of the older ones who wore the tartan plaid or screen, drew them down more closely, to cover their faces. The doors of the pews were opened, and the grey-haired men led the way out. They walked feebly, and covered their heads only as they reached the door of the church. Then the movement became more vigorous. Every man put on his bonnet as he left his seat, and pulling it down over his brow, strode hastily forth; while the females kept close by their fathers, husbands, and brothers. Seat by seat these parishioners pressed forward, and passed for the last time the threshold of the beloved church of their fathers. A scroll of witnesses, written in living characters, faithfully and mournfully refusing a lie for the truth — a hollow semblance for a vital reality! Alas! in this history the faithful people began, and the faithful pastors ended. But this revolution was then only in the perspective of the Church of Scotland's history — the cloud had but just cast its shadow above her horizon. Here, at this moment, in the church of Glenmore, were the faces of the people turned in the direction whence it arose.

    When the presentee found himself alone in the area of that place which was to be the future scene of his ministrations, except for the presence of the few strangers who kept him company, he wore a rather bewildered aspect. No soul was there to be spiritually tended, not even that of the public-house keeper. It was at its usual vocation of selling whisky. The reverend presbytery, on the other hand, were used to this kind of thing. They exchanged looks, winked, and smiled. Among the crowd above there had been breathless silence until the last parishioner disappeared, and the door closed behind him; but then an irrepressible cry of exultation burst forth long and loud. It was of that kind which completely took the mastery over the craven spirits below. Even Davidson felt humiliated, and poor George fumbled in his pockets, and thought longingly of the free hill-side with the deer a-head, and his dogs by his side.

    At length the sounds subsided, and M'Lean had presence of mind enough to seize the first moment of silence to proceed with the ordination, and in the usual manner to address the presentee on the duty he owed to his flock in the pastoral relation. It is customary next to address the parishioners on the relations subsisting between them and their new pastor, and the duties and regards which that relation involves. This ceremony on the present occasion was of necessity dispensed with. What matter? George Donaldson proceeded forthwith to take upon him his ordination vows. "Do you," said M'Lean, "believe the Scriptures of the Old and New Testament to be the word of God, and the only rule of faith and manners?" "Yes," was the unhesitating reply. George's faith was easy enough to fit anything; and as for his manners, they were conformed to no particular rule whatever. "Do you," continued M'Lean, "sincerely own and believe the whole doctrine contained in the *Confession of Faith*, approven by the General Assemblies of the Church, and ratified by law in the year 1690, to be founded upon the Word of God ; and do you acknowledge the same as the confession of your faith ; and will you firmly and constantly adhere thereto?" &c., &c. George had never read the Confession of Faith. The controversies of the times had informed him that there was something in it about *not giving to the civil magistrate the power of the keys*, by which he knew was meant admission to the ministry, and other privileges of a spiritual nature; and likewise, that intrusion into the pastoral charge was there expressly deprecated; but these were only vague notions, and he knew, besides, that somebody had written a clever work to disprove the confession of *his* faith in these particulars, with which, though he had never read it, he was quite satisfied; so he again confidently answered, "Yes." In like manner he went on to promise implicit obedience to the judicatories of his Church. He had, indeed, some idea that he was standing there in direct contravention of the judgment of the supreme judicatory of his Church; but for that he considered his presbytery to be responsible. "Are not," continued M'Lean, *"zeal for the honour of God, love to Jesus Christ, and desire of saving souls, your great motives and chief inducements* to enter into the function of the holy ministry, and not worldly designs and interests?"

What was it that here groped with its fingers darkly into George's conscience, and made his blood recoil for a moment towards his heart? The words just spoken were sacred words, although uttered in a careless and hurried manner, yet they went no farther than his ear; but by some strange mysterious associations there came to his recollection the sentence uttered by old John Morrison's dying breath, "He that entereth not into the sheep-fold by the door, but climbeth up some other way, the same is a *thief* and a *robber*." The midnight robber, who has crept into the precincts of peaceful life, and has used with success all the secret implements of his trade, feels, if he is not yet lost to humanity, that, with the last barrier which interposes between him and the life and property of his victim, he has still some remnant of conscience to overleap. But can he stop *there*? — he tramples on his conscience, and it is seared for ever!

George, internally irritated at the recollection which had obtruded upon him, entertained for the moment a sentiment of anger and bitterness against those who were implicated with the occasional cause of his uneasiness; and making an effort to subdue these unpleasant sensations, he uttered a loud and astounding " Yes." There was a momentary silence. The empty pews seemed to reverberate the monosyllable as if it had been a question instead of an answer. The man in the pulpit even was appalled by this bold knock-one-down kind of utterance. But the silence in the galleries gave place to a simultaneous shout of execration. It mattered not.

The remainder of the questions — "Have you used any undue methods, either by yourself or others, in procuring this *call*? Do you engage, in the strength and grace of Jesus Christ our Lord and Master, to rule well your own family, to live a holy and circumspect life, and faithfully, diligently, and cheerfully, to discharge all the parts of the ministerial work to the edification of the body of Christ? Do you accept of and close with *the call* to be pastor of this parish, and promise through grace to perform all the duties of a faithful minister of the gospel among this people?" — these questions were lost in tumult, but as a matter of course affirmative answers were returned to them all. In vain did the peaceable magistrate again attempt to be heard; — the feelings of the multitude had reached that pitch when they would not be repressed. Burst after burst of indignant clamour arose, till at length, after patiently standing for upwards of half an hour, he entreated, during a temporary lull, that they would grant but five minutes' peace for *his* sake — for the sake of the late pastor of that place — who, he well knew, if he were standing at that moment where he himself then was, would have his voice respected so far as to procure silence. A spell was at last raised — a chord touched — and there was a hush during which a pin might have been heard to fall; George Donaldson then again stood forth and knelt down, and the presbytery likewise standing up, and gathering around him, placed their hands on his head, M'Lean lifting up his voice to implore the blessing of the Holy Spirit upon this minister of Christ.

Any one who has seen a Scottish ordination service, must know that its impressiveness depends in a great measure on an unshaken confidence in the earnestness and sincerity of all the parties engaged in it. If the officiating clergy are insincere, they must act a lie; if the person admitted by them into the ministry be insincere, the whole affair is turned into a solemn farce. A man kneels in the presence of God and men, to receive that for which he cares nothing, in which he has no vital belief! Other men pray to receive for what they care not. Of all farces *this* is the most unbearable. And in the simple unadorned service of Scotland, there is nothing to call away the attention of the lookers-on from that faith which they must or must not feel in the earnestness of those who set themselves forth in such manner before them. And George Donaldson knelt, whose soul had never taken delight in aught higher than the pleasures of an untamed boy, united in some degree to the passions of the man — there he knelt, as if to do God service, by means of God's own blessed Spirit, had been the chief end of his life. And there stood, with hand placed upon his head, the man who prayed, and was a sottish sensualist; his aged father too, the gross and vulgar, and habitual tippler; and those other men whose habits of life had no relation to the God whom they addressed. High time it is that such solemn farces were done away from the earth, with men of whatever sect or creed. High time that a more universal faith were acted on our Saviour's words: "By their fruits ye shall know them" — *them*, the shepherds and guides of your souls. High time that all apologies for wickedness, or all that might serve as an apology for the worldly and the selfish, in such an office, be it what it may, were abolished by rational men! God himself condescended to appeal to the senses of the multitude in proof of the mission of his divine Son. And shall the disciple be above his Master? Shall we dare to reverse the process which God himself has instituted, and argue fitness for the most sacred of all offices from some unknown invisible spell, instead of reasoning from the visible substantive *effect* of the Bible-taught *fruits* of the Spirit, to the presence and influences of that HOLY Spirit!

Thank God that in Scotland, at least for the last two hundred years, the people have been fully aware of their right, established by divine precedent and authority, to demand from him who is to be their leader in the path to immortality, a pure faith and a holy life. Shall it not be the harbinger of a millennial time, when this sensibility extends itself over Christendom!

The words of mockery were now heard amid the silence, and it was not till they were concluded that the confused noise of voices again arose. It signified little. The ceremony was made all the shorter. The legal form accomplished, and the prayer having ended with a hurried Amen, George arose from his knees. The Edinburgh lawyer, the red-faced proprietor, and all the reverend men who were to celebrate their triumph that evening over the punch-bowl, came forward to shake him by the hand. But *people* to welcome the hireling there were none! The traditionary customs, even the legal forms of the Scottish ordination, are founded on the people's attachment to their minister; and so it is the practice to come forward and welcome him to the place which God intended him to fill in their hearts and regards. Their highest interests and his are *now one*. They are united in the most solemn sense. Has *he* not to answer at the bar of God's judgment for his guidance of them, of what sort soever it shall be? Have *they* not to answer at the same tribunal, for the use they have made of his ministry? Toward the same awful goal they go; and shall they *feel* nothing — the pastor on the one hand, his people on the other — when they have newly entered upon such a relation? In this case, aversion and coldness was met by a want of all sensibility to feel it. Not a thought or feeling of the PASTOR had ever awoke in poor George's bosom. He and his friends made their way arm-in-arm, with self-complacent smiles, to the carriages which waited for them at the manse, with the exception of M'Lean, whose horse had been brought to the church-yard gate, and who, to the astonishment of the spectators, had no sooner mounted it, than he set off at full gallop, and when within safe distance, took off his hat, waved it over his head, and with three cheers, which were intended to say, "We have gained the day !" he again set spurs to his horse and disappeared.

"If I had that fellow on a hill-side," said Kenneth Ore, as he stood near the church door, "I would make his bones rattle, if his heart can't feel." "Hush, hush," whispered Samuel, the old catechist, laying his hand on his shoulder, "you know not what spirit you are of."

CHAPTER XV

"Oh looks of love, devoid of guile
I prize you more than beauty's magic smile."
                              GRAHAM

"What very odd notions my uncle has!" said Lady Grace Maitland to her cousin, Miss Hamilton Legh, during a tête-a-tête drive in the neighbourhood of Edinburgh; "yet he is an interesting man notwithstanding — don't you think so?" "Yes," replied Jane, "I have gained a great deal from his conversation." "Possibly," said Lady Grace; "but he imbibed very singular ideas when abroad in command of a regiment of Highlanders. Such odd Presbyterian prejudices had these men, that they refused to hear of a Sunday the chaplain provided for them, and insisted on paying a clergyman for themselves. They all had a Bible, and used, positively, to read it morning and evening, with other things in the religious way, which I don't remember." "And did they make good soldiers?" asked Jane. "Yes," replied her cousin; "to do them justice, I have heard my uncle say they were the bravest men he ever knew; and that he would rather have ventured on a forlorn-hope with twenty of them, than with a hundred common men. He used to associate very much both with officers and privates, by whom he was literally adored; but the effect this intercourse had on his mind so changed him, that it quite grieved my poor father, as you know he has no son, and uncle Frederick being so very much younger, will in all human probability succeed to the title. By the way, dear, I wish you could manage to captivate my uncle. It would do delightfully, and I am sure would please papa. His title in prospect, and your acres and gold pieces — on my word, it is a charming idea!"

"The worst of it is," said Jane, laughing, "that *I* do not mean to marry for title, nor does your uncle, I fancy, mean to marry for the sake of his rent-roll." "There are more serious obstacles than these," said Lady Grace, musing. "He may be nearly ten years older than you: but that is nothing; — for he is really the handsomest man, and the most — what shall I say? — there is no word in our stupid English — the most *pleins de graces* I mean that one sees; *n'est ce pas ma chère?*" "Really!" replied Jane. "the ascending scale is so gradual between him and my own father, and my uncle, to whose society I have been so much accustomed, that I never thought of General Maitland, except as an old bachelor; no, not a bachelor; I think I have heard that he was married in India." "Ay," said Lady Grace, "and there's the rub! His wife has been long dead; but the connection was peculiarly unfortunate. He was drawn in at nineteen to marry one of those baby-wives that are so common in India; a very lovely toy I believe she was, some three or four years younger than himself. However, she proved an expensive toy to her husband. Uncle Frederick was not rich; but his beautiful wife having rejected the best offers in India, at the rate of some half dozen per day, thought she had gained a right to indulge in all manner of extravagance, so that I believe it was not till some years after her death that my uncle got rid of his embarrassments. The levity of her conduct, too, was excessive. Of domestic happiness she was incapable of forming an idea; so that my uncle himself, sufficiently thoughtless at the time of his marriage, was actually converted from giddiness into gravity. Indeed, we have always attributed the change to excessive seriousness, which afterwards took place, to the soreness of heart which this unfortunate marriage occasioned him. Now delicacy, of course, prevents him from ever hinting at the cause; but when any of us venture to allude to his second marriage, his countenance becomes almost gloomy; and he says, with emphasis, 'It is not probable that *I* shall marry again.' And he does keep at a very awful distance from all the marrying fair, so that we allege that the danger of coming too often in contact with a marketable young lady, is sufficient at any time to send him away out of town. But he does seem really to like conversation with you, though in too papa-like a way. Your reflective turn suits him, and I have observed — but you have looked so provokingly stoical during my narrative, that I shall not tell you what I have observed, till you do penance by showing some interest in my poor uncle." Jane laughed, and a transient blush passed over her countenance.

"Ah, now!" said Lady Grace, laughing in turn, "that blush has a touch of nature in it. So I will go on. Well, it is no great thing to hang expectation upon, I mean, supposing you were in love, which you are not; but I have certainly observed uncle Frederick watch your countenance, when he thought himself unobserved, and follow your movements with an interest that I have never seen him manifest in any one of our sex, with the exception of his own Julia. You have never seen Julia, have you?" "I did not so much as know of her existence," replied Jane. "Ah, indeed!" said Lady Grace; "did none of us ever mention her to you? Uncle keeps her almost always shut up in his old castle of Glenmiglo. He has odd notions, you know, and says he does not like too early intercourse with the world. Here again his unfortunate marriage peeps out. Perhaps, after all, however, Julia is none the worse for her retirement. She has an old *bonne* as much the reverse of a fashionable governess as you can suppose. She tells the poor child Bible stories, and makes her say her prayers; and she is certainly a very unsophisticated, and at the same time, intelligent child. You shall see her this afternoon. Her papa allows her a short visit now and then to us."

General Maitland was one of those characters who endeavour to hide great tenderness of heart, and a deeply wounded sensibility, under a slight appearance of external coldness and reserve. He said scarce anything of the expected arrival of his little daughter. But as the day wore on he became restless and anxious, and often returned to the front windows as if to reconnoitre for some one; yet conscious, perhaps, of a degree of weakness, in the importance which his heart attached to so trivial an event, he endeavoured to conceal his anxiety from observation. At length an approaching carriage stopped at the door. A stout, matronly, and plainly-dressed woman stepped leisurely down, and then the furred and mantled figure of a slender child, whose long fair hair the winter breeze scattered over her shoulders, hastily passed bonne and footmen, and all, and came bounding up the staircase. Jane involuntarily looked at General Maitland, who still kept his eye fixed on his book. The door flew open, and the bright eyes of one of the loveliest children Jane had ever seen looked eagerly around the room for her papa; and in a moment she was locked in his arms. The little external frost-work of the General's manner instantly gave way, as once and again the child hung on his neck, and hid her face in his bosom.

Lady Grace looked at Jane, as if she wished to exchange glances with her; but she saw with surprise that her eyes were full of heavy tears, which coursed one another down her cheeks. She turned therefore to the child: "And have you nothing to say to me, miss?" asked she "Yes, that I have, dear Gracy," said Julia, running up to her, and kissing her half a dozen times. "And how is Emily, and your papa, and your dear mama? Oh, I have longed so much to see you all." "And you shall see them all presently, dearest," said Lady Grace. "They have stayed at home to-night on purpose for you." " How kind that was! Wasn't it, Mrs. Lewis?" said Julia, appealing to her *bonne*, who replied to her in the affirmative with a good-natured smile. "But" said Julia, whispering, "who is that lady stooping over her drawing, or something, with her face hid in such pretty ringlets? Is she a *very* great lady? She does not notice me!" "She is your cousin, love — Miss Hamilton Legh; and I am sure will love you very much." "Then I will go and speak to her" said the frank and artless child; and going up to Jane, she placed her hand on her knee, and looked up with a half timid glance, as if she almost repented of her boldness. Jane was not one who could easily resist such an appeal. She put her arm round the little girl's waist, and kissed her affectionately, though in so doing one of her own still fast-starting tears dropped upon her face. "Come, Julia," said General Maitland, rising to lead her away; "you are troublesome." He had observed Miss Legh's reserve, and had felt perhaps somewhat mortified at her apparent indifference towards his only child. Now, however, he observed that her countenance was pale and agitated, and her eyes brimful of tears. "You must forgive me, General Maitland," said she, looking up and endeavouring to smile. "This child has reminded me irresistibly of — of twelve years ago; — and you know," she added, her expression changing into that of deep sorrow, "my dress is still mourning!"

  The dark and now softened eye of General Maitland became rivetted on the speaker's face with an expression as if it meant to read her soul. It was neither beauty nor accomplishments that could win his regard. He knew — ah! did he not? — how surface these things were; it was the pure and the true heart — that which he yearned to find, yet was afraid to seek. He had felt, and painfully too, that his own mind had become a touchstone to detect the artificial in its lightest degree. How often had he turned away from it in the gay saloon and in the house of sorrow — amid laughter and fascination, amid weeping and words of woe!

Miss Legh, although not unconscious of his gaze, was so absorbed in the recollections of the moment, that she failed at first, with her intuitive quickness, to detect its meaning. She stooped her face over the child whom she still held within her arms, and who was gazing on her with an expression of wonder, that seemed likewise to question her, and said in a low voice, as if to explain to the little one the cause of her emotion, "Dear child, you have still a father! God has taken mine away from me. When I was like you, he was all the world to me; for I had no other friend!" A shade passed over the child's open countenance. She perceived in a moment the similarity of her own circumstances to those of the person who addressed her, and she laid her head affectionately on the speaker's arm. Jane raised her eyes again, and found those of General Maitland still fixed on her, and now for the first time she perceived a peculiar meaning in the look. It was scrutiny — not curious, but most earnest and melancholy. It expressed that sensibility which could fervently love, rather than love itself. A flush rose to her cheek; but it was called up by a certain high-minded pride, which restored her composure, rather than by a conscious shrinking from General Maitland's gaze. She made a motion to resume her place at her desk, and the General drawing Julia away, bowed respectfully, and withdrew.

Jane's first emotion, in recurring to this perusal of her countenance, and, as she felt in an indefinite kind of way, of her character, was that of the *hauteur*, which in some aspects was the fault of her nature. Should *she*, who might wed with the proudest of England's nobles, not repel as impertinent even a look which implied a doubt of her sincerity? — *she*, who would not have stooped to pick up the world at her feet, were there a shadow of falsehood implicated in the action? But was there not, too, her consciousness told her, something in that deep heart-gaze, beyond the glitter of the richest coronet? And ever and anon its dark lustre, coming from a soul so conversant with lofty and serious thoughts, all touched and steeped in its own hidden sorrow, would penetrate and subdue her. But General Maitland did not repeat the offence. He resumed his kind and rational, and to her almost paternal, manner; but he did leave with her a secret uneasiness which, in spite of all her efforts, she could not altogether stifle.

It happened, before Julia left Ainslie Place, that she took scarlet fever; and so attached had she become to Miss Legh, that it aggravated her disorder to want her for an hour at a time from her bed-side. It frequently occurs that a child's attachment becomes rivetted on the individual who has awakened in it the first strong conscious emotion — an emotion which, unlike any of the others, becomes with it a subject of after thought. And so it was with Julia. She reflected often on the similarity of circumstances between herself and her English cousin; the reflection induced an increased sensibility, and, in consequence, a passionate friendship took possession of the child's heart. She had shown so much particularity in her attachment before her illness — much to the amusement of the Lentraethens — that Miss Legh had felt it rather unpleasant; while she had been secretly pained, at the same time, that she could not so unconstrainedly return the child's affection as her own kindly nature would have dictated. But now, in the hour of sickness — and at one period the disorder assumed a very critical appearance — hers was not the selfishness which could resist the child's constant wish to have her near. But she spoke little to General Maitland, when they met, of Julia. She was irresistibly led to conceal as much as truth would permit, where and how she spent her time; and the females of the family, with an amiable delicacy, penetrated, and in appearance, at least, seconded her motives. However, at the crisis of the disease, General Maitland sat constantly in a room adjoining the chamber in which his child lay, and passed in and out at frequent intervals; and these opportunities dear little Julia made use of to ask her father to read to her stories out of the Bible. She said she liked to hear them in her papa's voice. Jane, too, was frequently employed in the same manner. But it was singular with what intuitive apprehension the child avoided asking any of the Maitlands to read to her from the Sacred Volume. There was something in the manner of each of them, when so engaged, which served, instead of soothing, to irritate the little sufferer. Lady Grace and Lady Emily, when they made the attempt, tried in vain to suppress an occasional yawn; so that, by a tacit understanding, this department fell entirely into the hands of Jane, and of Mrs. Lewis, the kind and maternal bonne. Lady Grace procured some new story-books, with which she endeavoured to amuse Julia; who, in her turn, thanked her with a smile; but she always turned at last to her Bible stories, and to Jane, to whom, in a low voice, she made such remarks as showed that her little heart had begun to awake to the true meaning of the most interesting of all books. Miss Legh, too, began to feel a new and indescribable sympathy with the sweet patient, which made her all the more inclined to forget the selfish pride which whispered her, when the father came in, to throw up this sick-nurse occupation, let what might be the consequence.

When Julia began to get up to a sofa by the fireside, and when all appearance of danger seemed over, her father came less frequently to visit her, and Jane felt less constraint in lavishing on the interesting little girl that affection which had been really and strongly awakened in her heart, ready as that was to cling to anything so artless and affectionate. It happened one evening before Julia had left her sick-room, that General Maitland came in while all the ladies of the family were assembled there. They were gay and happy, and Lady Emily, with much liveliness, began to narrate the incidents of two or three balls and parties which she had attended during the period of Julia's illness, and to teaze Jane about the inquiries of sundry admirers, who, as she alleged, had behaved most ungallantly to herself by not being able to repress their mortification at the absence of her beautiful cousin. Julia, with the quick sensibility for which she was remarkable, came hastily up to Miss Legh, and clasping both her hands within hers, laid her head upon her shoulder. At that moment Lady Emily recollected an engagement, and left the room, and the other ladies almost immediately followed, leaving only Mrs. Lewis and General Maitland besides Jane with the little girl. Jane, too, would have followed, but for Julia's position, which detained her, and caused her some little embarrassment. "I fear, Julia," said General Maitland, smiling, as he followed up the conversation which had just taken place, "you have taxed your cousin's kindness too much during your illness. It cannot be other than irksome," continued he, the smile passing away, "to one who is so fitted to be the idol of the ball-room, to fetter her by attendance in a sick-room." This latter clause was spoken in a tone of bitterness almost amounting to irony — it might be from some association which rankled in the breast of the speaker. Jane's eyes instantly filled, and there was a felt injustice in the remark, which called the eloquent blood to her cheek. Balls! what had they ever been to her! A retort rose to her lips, but she smothered the inclination to give it utterance, as undignified and improper, merely saying, in a mild but cold accent, "I think you mistake me, General Maitland." "It may be so," said the General, as he read the speaking truthfulness of her countenance, his demeanour instantly changing into that of the most expressive softness, the more fascinating because so seldom assumed. "Some painful feeling — but it is past — and you must forgive me. Perhaps you have observed that I associate with worldly gaieties all that is most heartless and frivolous." "And I," said Jane, the cloud passing away, and a smile beaming through the changing colour of her cheek, "I have not found in them much that is otherwise." "Then why," said the General hastily, "why not renounce them at once and for ever?" "Because I dislike," said Jane, "to give offence to those who wish to give me pleasure. If I know myself, I do not think that I should ever seek the ball-room for my own gratification." "Ah, you will see things in a different light one day, my dear young friend," said the General; "and I! may God forgive me! why should not *I* have forbearance with such a one as you! Why should I wound you by unnecessary harshness? — *you*, above all, who have shown such self-denying kindness to my child! You will think me ungenerous, ungrateful — perhaps incapable of feeling! I deserve it all."

Jane would have replied; but these words were spoken in hurried and agitated accents, most unusual with the speaker, and that dark eye was fixed upon her whose full power she had felt but once before, though now it was without scrutiny, without doubt; but with a mournful tenderness, which seemed to say how devotedly his soul *could* love. All this bound her in a spell that she longed and yet feared to break. "Good night, Julia," said General Maitland, as he stooped to kiss the forehead of his little girl, and took her hand in his, which still held that of her friend. Ere the latter could withdraw hers, there was a momentary touch from that of the *father*, the name so unspeakably dear to her, which filled her with an undefinable dread. Light as it was, it was sufficient to show her that there was a tremor in the hand of General Maitland that no ordinary emotion could have occasioned. But he, on his part, instantly assumed, in appearance, his usual calm composure. He bowed kindly, but withal somewhat distantly, and left the room. Jane, on her part, yielding at first to the enchantment of the moment, touched with her lips the child's forehead; but she instantly shrunk from her own act, as if it had been one of unparalleled boldness, and the feeling came rushing over her heart that, standing on the verge of this sacred circle of the sweetest affections, which had drawn her irresistibly towards it, she was yet a *stranger* and *alone*. Earnestly had she struggled against this sensibility. She knew it was selfish, and might unfit her for all the realities of life. But this evening, at least, it overpowered her — subdued her. She retired to her pillow to wet it with bitter orphan tears; and the images of General Maitland and his child with that of her own beloved father mingled strangely and uneasily in her dreams.

CHAPTER XVI

*"Let men beware how they neglect and suffer
trouble to be prepared;
for no man can forbid the spark, nor tell whence
it may come."*

BACON

"Ah! you are here," said General Maitland, one forenoon, as he entered the small back drawing-room where Jane was sitting; "I come to tell you that your old friend the Highland catechist, of whom I have heard you so often speak, is in town. Would you like to see him?" "Of all things in the world," said Jane; "where is he to be found?" "I shall not tell you," said the General, laughing, "but if you are disengaged, and would like a walk, I shall take you where you may at least see him if not speak to him. We can, perhaps, procure an interview at another time." Jane consented; and after being equipped for a walk, put herself under the guidance of General Maitland, who conducted her in the direction of the Old Town. "Are we going in here?" asked she with surprise, as she found herself entering the Parliament House, where the law courts are held. General Maitland smiled, and threading aisles and passages, and ascending a staircase, they found themselves at once in the narrow oaken gallery of a handsome room, some forty feet high, looking down upon all the array of a court of criminal law.

In the back-ground near the farthest end of the hall was the judges' bench, and seated in three chairs behind it, sat three judges with their scarlet robes, white satin tippets, and formidable-looking wigs. Miss Legh knew them well enough; for they had before been pointed out to her elsewhere. In the middle was the Lord J — C — H —, and on either side, the Lords M — and C —. The most stately-looking personage of the three, was the Lord J — C —. He became his robes remarkably well; — at the same time, one could not help remarking, that it was the mere stateliness of bulk, and that in the countenance, though there was strong will, there was little trace of the great or intellectual. Lord C —, who sat on his left, had less to attract the vulgar eye; but there was evidently a power of expression in the physiognomy, which the other could never attain. At a table immediately below the bench, were a group of counsel, in their black gowns and stiff-curled grey wigs; on the left was the witness-box, resembling a pulpit or desk; and exactly opposite, on the other side, was the seat where the jury were impannelled. A crowd of men, either connected with the law or mere spectators, filled every part of the area and galleries.

All this was very formidable. But that which of all things attracted Jane's attention, was the catechist of Aird, with Kenneth Ore, and another young man whom she recognised, impannelled as prisoners at the bar; — policemen with glazed hats on, and armed with batons, flanking them on either side, as if to prevent their escape. Jane knew well that there had been an outcry in many of the newspapers of the day, about the terrible riot in the church of Glenmore; and General Maitland had given her information from time to time as to the state of things; but to see her once valued friend in such a situation, seated in that court as an offender against the laws of his country! this was altogether perplexing and shocking to her. Yet there he sat — his broad forehead, his fine grey hair, and mild sagacious countenance, glancing to the sunbeams that streamed in from the high arched windows above; — there he was — as unlike a man who, from heat of temper, or any cause whatsoever, should deserve such a place as might well be imagined. Sometimes he appeared to listen shrewdly to the proceedings, sometimes he fixed his eye on the light above, as if his thoughts were far away among his native hills, or farther away still — beyond the heaven above them. There, too, Kenneth Ore sat, with more uneasiness and seeming impatience. There was a flush upon his very handsome features, and a falcon-glance shot once and again from his clear blue eye, which seemed to say very plainly, If right were might, I should not be here.

The first witness called after Miss Legh's entrance into the gallery, was, to her no small surprise, a man exceedingly deaf, who was to depone as to something he had *heard* pass between the catechist and young Kenneth. The Solicitor-General and the counsel who interrogated him, had to roar extremely loud before they could make themselves heard. This singular ear-witness deponed, that he had been standing near the church door of Glenmore after the settlement was over, while the people were dispersing; that Samuel and Kenneth had been at a few paces distance from him; and that he had heard the latter threaten to break the bones of George Donaldson, the newly-settled minister, as soon as he should have an opportunity; while the catechist applauded his resolution, and told him, clapping him on the shoulder, that *he was a lad of spirit*! This man was cross-examined by the counsel for the prisoners, but he held consistently to his testimony. "Were you as deaf as that, my good friend! said Lord C — , looking up from his paper, while a smile of peculiar meaning played around his mouth — "Were you equally deaf on the day of the Glenmore settlement?" "I've been deaf this thirty years," cried the man, speaking as if Lord C — had been deaf too, and with the stolid look peculiar to his condition. A laugh rang from the galleries, sharp and triumphant, sufficiently showing the feeling that prevailed there; but the sound appeared to have a most irritating effect on the temper of the Lord J — C —. "If," said he sternly, "the galleries are not better able to regulate their expressions of feeling, I shall instantly order the officers to clear the house!"

Another witness now entered the box. It was Miss Legh's old northern friend, Mr. Davidson of Kilblair. After having been sworn, as a matter of course, to tell the truth, the whole truth, and nothing but the truth, as he should answer to God at the great day of judgment, the Solicitor-General proceeded to question him on behalf of the Crown: "You are Mr. Davidson of Kilblair?" "Yes." "You accompanied the presentee on the day of the Glenmore settlement?" "I did." "Did you remain during the whole of the proceedings?" "I did." "Were you a witness of any tumult in the church?" "Such an infernal uproar as never met my ears!" "Were the presbytery, or were you personally, assailed by any abusive language?" "There was nothing but abuse." "Do you consider that there was any *threatening* language held?" "Yes." "Will you mention what it was?" "I was told that there were many marksmen among the crowd, who could easily take my life." "Then you consider your life to have been in danger?" "I do; assuredly I do." "Do you consider the lives of the other friends of the presentee to have been in danger?"

"There were many missiles thrown, such as halfpence, stones, snowballs, pieces of wood, and plaster." "You say" — "Stop a little, not so fast, if you please," interrupted the Lord J — C —, addressing the solicitor; "I have to write that down." And he repeated slowly the name of each missile, as he wrote it, by way of asking the witness for confirmation. "You say," continued the Solicitor-General, when his Lordship had concluded his task, "You say there were *stones* thrown!" "Yes." " Did you *see* any stones thrown?" This question was put in a particularly bland voice, just to smooth down any ruffled feelings on the part of the witness, and, in fact, to get the answer out as pleasantly as possible. "Ahem!" said Davidson; ."I saw a stone which had been thrown." (He had been shown a small stone picked up by one of his reverend friends, who told him it had been thrown, and this — having the fullest confidence in his friend's statement — he considered as testimony sufficient.) "Did you observe any of the prisoners at the bar active during the day in promoting the riot?" Davidson turned full round, and made a set with his small, malignant eyes, towards the catechist, saying, at the same time, while he clenched his fist, "I believe that old man to have been a chief agent in keeping up the worst feelings among the people" "Do you know the other parties at the bar?" "I know them, both by sight and by character." "Did you observe them throw anything from the galleries, or otherwise make themselves conspicuous?" "I saw Kenneth Ore take a principal part in obstructing our entrance into the church; and though I did not see him in the gallery, I believe he was both an instigator and a principal actor in the day's proceedings."

The counsel for the prisoners then rose up. "You are an elder of the church. Mr. Davidson?" "Yes; an elder in old Mr. Donaldson's parish, the father of the presentee to Glenmore." "Pray, did you swear at all on the day of the riot, as it is called? Is it consistent with your recollection that you made use of any oaths on that occasion?" Davidson looked startled and exceedingly blank. He replied, however, "No, I don't remember swearing." "Do you not recollect saying anything about hell, and so on?" "Oh, I dare say I told some of the people that they were on the high road to the place you mention; but that was, of course, by way of serious admonition." "Or joke, perhaps?" "Perhaps, perhaps. I really don't recollect. A man can't recollect the meaning of every word he has uttered." "You may go, Mr. Davidson," announced the Lord J — C — . The succeeding witnesses all confirmed the fact of a riot having taken place, but failed in bringing forward any palpable evidence against the panels. One of the witnesses more bold than the others, ventured to state what he believed to be a great cause of the indecorous proceedings of the day, viz., the omission of the Bible on the part of the presbytery, and likewise the presence of the constabulary force, which he considered sufficient in the most peaceable district to create irritation and opposition. After having been examined, however, and cross-examined as to his *opinion*, he was rebuked by the Lord J — C — , who told him it was not *opinion* that was wanted, but fact.

Tired at length of this scene, Miss Legh signified her wish to General Maitland to retire from the house. The afternoon was still fine; the sun shone brightly, and after they found themselves in the open area of the square, the General inquired whether it would not be well to take the opportunity of seeing some parts of the Old Town, which were still new to his stranger cousin. She gave her consent; but during the first part of the walk was silent, and scarcely appeared to notice the different objects of interest which were pointed out. Observing her abstraction, the General inquired the reason of her extraordinary thoughtfulness. "I am thinking," replied she, sighing, "that if human beings *are* immortal, what an awfully important part some men are born to! — the multitude pressing behind, before! — our influence over their destinies!—the Judge above! I do not clearly convey my meaning."

"Yes, my dear Miss Legh," replied the General, "I too have felt such thoughts press appallingly upon me. What has suggested them to you at this moment? — yonder court?" "I think so. There was something *uneasy* about it. It did not seem to tally well with the voice of conscience." "True," said General Maitland; "conscience may be capable of mistaken manifestations; but still it is *conscience*, which ought ever to be treated as the thing it is. The poor people in the church of Glenmore *had* a conscience, an acute sense of right and wrong; that presentee whom they justly nauseated had none ; yet here *he* is the innocent person in the eye of the law — *they* are the defenders for a supposed crime committed against him. Yet who can doubt which of the two — yon fine old man, for example, or he — is the criminal in the court of *heaven*? It is a fearful thing when the magisterial authority, in whatever form, which has no valid title except as God's viceregent on earth, sets itself against his eternal laws. Warren Hastings, abroad, omnipotent and irresponsible, was at home arraigned before the bar of his country — a faint similitude of those high arraignments of kings and courts which shall yet have place, when their delegated authority shall have been surrendered."

"How *little* is man!" said Jane. "I seem to speak paradoxes; indeed, I sometimes feel man to be very great, and sometimes unspeakably little." "But both are *true*" said the General. "I believe man is feeble, helpless when he has nothing to depend on, save his individual resources; great only when he has obtained a mastery over some great agency The man who undertakes a journey of some five hundred miles on foot, feels but his own littleness. At the end of each day he has accomplished, by a vast amount of labour, a small amount of progress. How different from him who sets forth with all the appliance of steam, whose self-confidence is a kind of triumph over time and space, and who already talks of what he is to accomplish on the first hour of his arrival!" "Would," exclaimed Miss Legh, "that there were some great moral enginery for the accomplishment of man's happiness, his redemption from the abyss of nothingness and depravity in *this* world, as well as that which is to come!" "And is there not, my dear young friend?" said the General. "Has the Author of man's being left him so morally helpless, as to let him grope his way painfully and toilsomely along upon his own feeble resources towards the goal of his moral destiny, and that of his fellow-creatures — then hold him responsible for the smallness of his progress, or, it may be, for his retrogression? Ah! man can be responsible only for not availing himself of those great and certain means which God himself has provided." "You mean," said Jane, in a low voice, but with an expression of deep emotion, "the preaching of the gospel to every creature, according to the last command of the Saviour of men ?" "Yes I do," replied General Maitland: "that alone has absolute authority and all-prevailing influence — the high authority of Deity — the attractive influence of pure and loving humanity."

At that moment a poor woman, having a child in her arms, approached, and, as she passed, dropped a curtsy to implore charity. She was extremely filthy — her child squalid and miserable-looking, and neither seemed to have half the clothing necessary to protect them against the cold of the season. Miss Legh immediately took out her purse and gave her half-a-sovereign. The woman looked at the gold with surprise, and then supposing it had been given by mistake, walked hastily on until she had turned a corner, when she began to run, and quickly disappeared. "To judge from that woman's appearance," remarked General Maitland, "I fancy she will have a grand carouse with some wretches as filthy as herself before the day is done." "What!" replied Jane, "and not procure the necessary clothing for herself and her child when she has the means?" "Do you imagine," said General Maitland "that *that* poor creature has not long ago lost all taste for the *comforts* of life, to place all her gratification in its vicious indulgences? You must not judge of our town pauper population — from the knowledge of whom rank and fashion separate us, alas! too widely — by your country poor, who want nothing but what to be sure they too seldom enjoy — the efforts of a beneficent landlord to render them happy and comfortable. Millions of our town's people live on the farther side of a great gulf, which, as yet, has never been bridged across."

"I have read of such things," said Jane, with a sigh," though I have perhaps too rarely seen them; and I have felt an impulse, often, to devote my fortune, my time, and strength, to the redemption of the wretched; but the vagueness, the hopelessness of the attempt, has made me sink back into inaction." "I dare say," said General Maitland, "there are few generous minds which have not felt such an impulse at one period or other; and it only remains that these blessed impulses should be systematized, and that the apprehension of right means should lead them on, in order to make them carry their measure of success." "Ah, but the right means," said Jane, "surely *there* lies the problem. Now, would you consider the preaching of the gospel, which we know has done marvels for the savages of many countries, for the negroes of Jamaica, and the debased wreckers of Cornwall — would you consider it sufficient for those who have no *physical means of virtue*, if one may so speak? Savages, negroes, miners — all these could, however poorly, provide for themselves an independent livelihood."

"There are two sets of philanthropists, you are aware, I dare say," replied General Maitland, "who set themselves to work by opposite means. The first are the physical philanthropists, who employ means purely physical. The physically wretched, say they, cannot be virtuous. The standing man lives under the imperious bondage of the first law of nature. He hears his family cry for bread. The voice of virtue is drowned in that cry. Bread must be procured at all hazards, by whatever means. Those poor creatures lose hold of that virtue which, it seems to them, they have no longer any interest in maintaining. Vice alone offers them the means of forgetfulness and pleasure. Now, says the physical philanthropist, provide food, livelihood, and you take away the temptation to sin. But, on the other hand, reasons the spiritualist, you have to do with a population whose habits are already formed. Even though full bread-provision were possible for starving millions out of employment, you have to do with those whose depraved tastes have grown with their growth from childhood to maturity or old age. That which you give them to provide *bread*, do you not see, is every day spent in drunkenness and debauchery? Now I aim at the destruction of the depraved *will*, which, until you have destroyed, you have accomplished nothing. The love of God brings, as its necessary consequence, the love of virtue — holiness. Here is emphatically a new birth. All vices are thrown down at the foot of the Cross. I speak no chimeras. I can point to hundreds who, out of the very depths of misery, have cried to God. *Then* give your bounty; for not till then will it be well employed."

"Then," said Miss Legh, "you would, I fancy, belong to the second class?" "Of the two," replied the General, "I think it is to be preferred; because, in actual circumstances, it can point to the most certain results. Of the poor, individually, who have come under the influence of the spiritual philanthropists, many have been rescued from vice and misery; because the poor man has imparted to him that moral strength which enables him to resist temptation; and if he is enabled to pass successfully the hour of deepest trial, he is on that platform from which he can seize opportunities of bettering his condition, which will occasionally fall in the way of all. The beauty of the physical philanthropist, on the contrary, is in its nature temporary. When it is squandered, nothing remains. Again, such national provisions as poor-rates, inevitable though they be when the masses are sunk in a state of self-helplessness, are proved, by long experience, to increase the evil they are meant to remedy — they *attract* thousands to the condition of pauperism; whereas the moral remedy has *raised* thousands from the state of pauperism. By imparting the ability of self-help, it has made continual draughts upon that state; so that its tendency evidently is to reduce the bulk of the pauper territory."

"Yet," said Miss Legh, "I do not confess myself entirely satisfied. What you say I do not doubt; but is not the spiritual remedy only successful in so far as it cannot be universal?" "I do not quite understand you," said General Maitland. "Perhaps not," said Jane, smiling. "However, I think I understand myself; which is so far well. You talk of making *draughts* out of the pauper territory; of placing a *certain number* of poor on the platform of conduct, from which they shall be ready to avail themselves of opportunities as they occur. But does it not remain true, that there are starving *millions*, while there is only employment for a few thousands of these? So that if the spiritual remedy were successful with the millions, it would not create for them employment; and though happy opportunities might thus occur to the few, they could never occur to the whole. Thousands would have to beg, starve, or die, just as they do." "If," said General Maitland, "the spiritual remedy were universally successful, it is impossible to foretell what the consequences would be. Society would be placed on a different basis, and those well-springs of human charity — capable of infinitely more abundant resources than have ever been drawn forth — would not then be sealed by vice and misconduct, as they are. At the same time, I had said that I preferred the spiritual remedy *of the two*; but I must suppose the perfection of system to consist in considering man such as he is, a spiritual and physical being, and in bringing those supplies to each of those natures which, from the mere fact of their existence, they must need. So far for the principles of philanthropy; while, in like manner, I conclude that the *ultimatum* of *national* felicity, must consist in a pure temporal and a pure spiritual government, and these mutually assisting and working out one another's ends, instead of contravening and obstructing each other."

"Is not government too vague and too distant a thing," said Miss Legh, "to work out effectually the end of individual happiness?" "That is," said General Maitland. "because we choose, and every man chooses, to consider it in too indefinite a sense. Legislation ought to spread its ramifications through the minutest interstices of society, while the higher ought to be founded on the lower. I consider it as beginning, in the simplest form, under the paternal roof. The father and mother do in effect *legislate* for the moral and physical welfare of their families. With the first development of human existence under their control, they do in a mighty degree influence the destinies of their nation, seeing their legislation may be either of the best or of the very worst kind. And out of this most widely spread form of legislation springs its next aspect — that of property, which includes a jurisdiction over many families. This I do think one of its finest aspects. Would that our class would but strip the idea of its vulgar trappings, and come to feel it in its most natural and delightful sense! A home! with all its felicitous associations, increased ten-fold, by the consciousness of *property*, interwoven with the sense and memory of much of the beautiful in nature!. Our own happiness multiplied and reflected in hundreds of happy homes nestling under our protection! This is a legislation which is to be *felt* as much as reasoned on in all its bearings. I have no sympathy with that man who, in traversing his acres, sees in them all but the one solitary *I* — all that room on God's earth, which he destined to be filled with *many* beings, with their joys and affections, sunk and annihilated in that one, heartless *I!* I fear, I do fear, that the emphatic curse of Heaven must rest on men who so dare to reverse the end of their being."

As General Maitland's manner kindled into enthusiasm, his voice uttering sentiments once so familiar, sounded in his cousin's ear like a strain of dearest melody long unheard. She suppressed her emotion, however, and asked, "Well, supposing you to be fully impressed with the responsibilities of property, how would you proceed?" "I would begin," replied the General, "as I hope I have already done, by improving my soil to the utmost of which it is capable, for the sake of my tenants, and for my own sake through them. The welfare of landlord and tenants is, of course, indissolubly united, although this axiom I almost view with distaste, from its having been so often repeated in the form of a refined selfishness; as if the welfare of tenants was of importance *only* as it increased the rent-roll of the proprietor! If there is a balance in the scale of importance, I, for my part, freely concede it to them, as they are many, I but one; and if, individually, I am of greater consequence than they individually, it is only because I reflect and influence their united interests. Well, then, the *product* of physical well-being to the families under my protection, together with a moral impulse in the right direction, would be, with God's blessing, a fine and healthy *physical* condition."

"But," said Jane, "you would not consider yourself alone adequate to the discharge of the physical, moral, and spiritual duties which you hold man's necessities to create?" "By no means," said General Maitland; "assuredly I would not: and here comes in that all-powerful auxiliary which God himself — the great Author of our respective positions — has created; I mean the pastoral office, and the spiritual jurisdiction. But here I stand on quite another ground. In so far as this world goes, I am the superior of my tenantry, and in so far I contribute to their happiness or misery; but with regard to the unseen world I can claim no superiority. My soul, gifted as it is with endless existence, possesses no superiority over the poorest of my fellow-men. I cannot pretend to answer for the souls of others; — every man has to answer for himself at the bar of God. But I have extended to my people the blessings of an enlightened education. The book which God has addressed to us in common is in their hands. It is no *class*-book. It was originally addressed neither to an aristocracy nor to a hierarchy, but directly to the multitude, for whose benefit it was intended. By the equal light of that book, then, we should consult together on equal terms as to the choice of a spiritual guide. Our stake in the matter is the same; no man can have less — no man can have more. The product of enlightened spiritual guidance, which I am assured would, by God's blessing, be secured by these means, would be a healthy moral and *spiritual* condition. The elevation of the moral being may, indeed, be regarded as the true *visible* quotient (if we may so speak) of a correct arithmetic. The physical and spiritual culture do, with that harmony which pervades all the laws of God, powerfully assist each other, and, by a reflex influence, aid in carrying each other to a productive moral consummation."

"And what is your opinion," asked Miss Legh, "of the highest legislation which is generally made responsible alone for the national prosperity?" "I think," replied General Maitland, "that it is chiefly valuable as affording support and protection to the lower kinds of legislation, and enabling them to work truly and well. But unless we have the previous conditions fulfilled, of a faithful paternal and class legislation, the highest, which goes specifically by the name of *Government*, must always prove a most insufficient basis for the national happiness. How can men be interested in the welfare of millions, which become to the mind of the statesman a mere abstraction, who has utterly disregarded the welfare of the few hundreds of whom God has made him the natural protector? How can large and beneficent national views be expected from one who has through life pursued his egotistical ends of pleasure or ambition as his chief good? We must have virtue created by the paternal legislation in the class which elects; and then we shall no longer have the disgraceful spectacle of a house of representatives who have obtained their places almost exclusively by the appliance of venality and corruption. We must have the proprietor and the manufacturer — who are most nearly allied to each other in position — forced, either by a really acquired virtue or by a more highly rectified public opinion, to make the interests of those subservient to them co-extensive with their own, in their speculations of the good which they purpose to achieve, ere we shall have a class of legislators from which to choose. An ardent and profound consideration of the welfare of his fellow-beings, who stand in a subordinate relation to him in the three aspects we have alluded to — the physical, the moral, and the spiritual — is the only education which fits any man for the place of a national legislator." "But," said Jane, looking up with a delighted smile — for the subject, though to others it might appear dry and speculative, had been to her one of the deepest interest from her earliest years — "but, after all, is not *the creation of virtue*, where it does not yet exist, of all other things the most chimerical?"

  The glance of General Maitland, which rested but for an instant on the animated expression of her beautiful countenance, was hastily withdrawn and fixed itself again on the horizon. "The *creation of virtue of all other things the most chimerical*!" he slowly repeated. "Yes, it would be so, were it not for the interference of Divinity in man's behalf. The Word and Spirit of God can *create* virtue in the savage, of nearest alliance to the brute; in the negro, steeped in all the pollutions of slavery; and why not, then, in the most apparently hopeless classes in our community — in its self-seeking proprietors, in its vice-enslaved pauperism? "Do you see," continued the General, "yon obscure church, in that hollow on your left, with its spire rising at the foot of yon opposite hill, which is covered with houses?" Jane replied in the affirmative. They had now returned from a rather lengthened walk around the base of Salisbury Crags, and were at the moment coming in sight of the back of the Parliament House, whence they had set out.

"You may smile," said General Maitland, "but of all objects of interest in this old picturesque city, I cannot help regarding that church as the first. Our National *Kirk* is indeed founded, in her primitive constitution, on a noble theory — that of a universal adaptation to the wants of the nation. She has been prevented from doing justice to herself, from a full fruition of her theory, by foes without and foes within; and now that she is fully awake to her chief end, I feel thankful that, if she receive a death-blow, it is with her face to her enemies, and not in cowardly retreat. This little church of St. John's is, perhaps, the last attempt she can make in connection with the State to carry her theory fully and adequately out. There it stands in the very centre of a mass of pauperism and vice. It has been built to contain one thousand persons. The area of the building is free to the surrounding poor, but each has his sitting appropriated to himself, which is as much his own as if he paid for it in gold. The galleries, on the contrary, are let at high rents, in order to clear off some debt contracted in the building, and because, likewise, in the embodiment of a great principle, the rich as well as the poor have their part to perform. The pastor, who is, and ought to be, the moving soul of the whole, is a man of great talent, of stirring eloquence, and of unwearied energy and benevolence. To preach Christ crucified to the crowded audiences that fill the church every Sabbath is his delight — the very end of his being; and he conjoins with it unceasing week-day efforts, to make an impression on the poor of his district. Still the energies of one man are unequal to daily and weekly ministrations to one thousand persons; the better portion of the congregation are therefore enlisted on the side of their minister; twenty elders are chosen by the voice of the congregation, and are amongst the best men of which it can boast. These have the superintendence of fifty persons each, which may amount at most to twenty families. They are assisted likewise by a certain number of deacons, who have the more exclusive administration of temporal affairs. In this manner the circumstances of every individual are accurately ascertained; their habits fully known, and what use they are likely to make of such assistance as they seem to need. A society is formed among the ladies in the class of gallery sitters, in order to supply the most needy with decent apparel, in which to appear on Sundays in their sittings below. This they can neither part with nor pawn without the circumstance being immediately apparent. Were the church quite unfettered in the matter of door collections (which it is not, as these collections are seized on as a right by the city magistrates), they would be greatly more liberal than they are, as they would be understood to be applied to the relief of the poor in the district, and would thus go a great way in relieving pressing want. As it is, every exertion is made by the deacons to procure employment and relief for the respectable poor who are out of work."

"Now," he continued, "what I wish to point out to you is the machinery which is brought to bear on a *certain definite portion* of the vast masses of pauperism which overlay the energies of our country. A wretched family, the children of which are sunk in starvation and misery, with scenes of debauchery perpetually passing before their eyes — which is the kind of paternal legislation under which *they* live; this family is visited by a messenger of good, either in the person of the minister or one of his assistants. 'Do you go to church?' is one of his first inquiries. 'No' replies the father, 'I am too poor, I cannot pay for a seat.' 'Well, you need not pay for it,' continues the visitor; 'come to our church, which is just in your neighbourhood, and you will have your own sitting appropriated to yourself as much as the man who comes in his own carriage' But still, urges the man, 'I am too poor; I have no decent clothes in which to appear — I cannot go.' 'Come to my house' pursues the visitor, 'and you will be furnished with a suit of clothes good enough to wear in the house of God; but remember if you part with them, you will show yourself unworthy of future assistance.' The man and his probably miserable wife, who may have existed for weeks in a state of half intoxication, come for once to sit under the benign preaching of the gospel. Some of the expressions of the preacher arrest their attention. Their feelings are full of a novel excitement. They are for once within the pale of humanized life, and are, besides, under a renovating, vivifying influence. At night unwonted discourse is heard in their wretched dwelling-place. They repeat portions of the sermon in the hearing of their children. Again, the next day, before the good seed has yet been picked away from that beaten track, that stony highway of depravity, the messenger of life returns. He now begins to question the father as to his habits, his means of livelihood. He has possibly been a tradesman, but having been long out of employment, has subsisted on the precarious begging of his starving infants. The visitor endeavours to open the sluices of natural affection. He speaks of the dreadful crime of bringing up immortal beings for perdition. He opens up a glimpse of returning respectability. What an achievement, if this man can by any means be brought to *legislate well* for his family, and so reclaim them from the ever-sinking, ever-accumulating mass!"

"And has there been much practical success here," asked Miss Legh? "Yes, very much," replied the General. "I shall give you an example. A poor woman who had been brought to acquire church-going habits, and had given evidence of a change of character, attracted Mr. G — 's observation at an evening meeting, at which were assembled many poor persons like herself. The minister had chosen for comment the 51st Psalm, in which the royal bard gives expression to his deep feeling of penitence, his sense of the wrong he had committed against God, as against his beloved friend and benefactor. The poor woman began to weep, and during the whole of the address, tears and sobs burst from her heart. At the conclusion, when she had waited to be alone with her pastor, she spoke thus: 'Sir, I have been guilty of a great sin — I no longer deserve the favour of God. I have felt every word you spoke as if it were addressed to myself.' 'Compose yourself, my friend' said the minister; 'whatever you have done, there is compassion with God through the atoning blood of Christ. If he has given you a *sense* of your sin, he may preserve you from repeating it. What have you done?' 'You know, sir,' she said, 'that I used to be often the worse of liquor, and the neighbours and myself used to meet in each other's houses to drink. But after I began to go to St. John's, God opened my eyes to see the ruin I was bringing on myself and my children for time and eternity. When the neighbours saw the turn I took, and that I no longer joined them in their carousings, they not only jeered and mocked, but laid plans to draw me again into my old ways; and on New Year's Day, by asking me to drink their healths, and telling me not to be unneighbourly, they drew me into the snare, till, with shame I confess it, I became much the worse of liquor. But when my senses came back, I thought my reason would have left me; I thought, indeed, I was like the 'sow that was washed returning to her wallowing in the mire,' when even a glimpse of the grace of God and a sight of the blood of Christ could not keep me clean. Do you think, sir, there is any mercy for such a wretch as I?' The faithful minister, without lessening in her eyes the enormity of her sin, as God had shown it to her, drew consolation from the psalm which had so much touched her conscience; he told her where to go for strength in the moment of need; and above all, gave her the judicious advice never to confront temptation when she could fly from it; and I believe that woman has been consistently correct in her conduct ever since."

"A most interesting history " said Miss Legh, "and curious too, as showing *the tone of society* among the more wretched classes. We are apt to confine that term to our own circles, and it surely exerts the strongest influence over our minds; but what a low and abject *tone* must exist in the poverty-stricken grade which is farthest beneath us, and how it must exert its power to stifle every virtuous emotion! Would it not be a blessing if the tone of that society could be changed so as to exert its power for good, and not for evil?" "Assuredly," replied the General, "but unless Christian exertion so change it, I know not what can. Poor-rates will not do it, as England can tell; plenty of food will not do it, without *motive for exertion*. Witness, for example, the Lazzaroni of Italy."

"Then," said Miss Legh, "if your country were supplied with churches upon the plan of St. John's, to the extent of one to every thousand, would it not be a grand idea brought into the every-day practice of all your people? Every Scotchman would be supplied with the machinery adapted for a great end of living — the fulfilment of the will of God for himself, and the redemption of his fellow-creatures." "Why confine our wishes to Scotland?" said General Maitland, smiling. "Would that every human being had the same end of living, and then we should indeed see a millennial time! But this is exactly the aim, with respect of their country, which our reforming clergy have now in view, and restricted to less than which they cannot conceive themselves fulfilling their duties to God and man. It was, indeed, the grand aim proposed by our Church from her very formation, but which the intervention of patronage, with the set of sleeping and self-seeking men it introduced, served to foil; and it is this end which the civil power sets itself determinedly against. Whatever hucksterings there may have been with it regarding emoluments and the interests of worldly patrons and presentees, *this* is the real cause of its hostility. It will not have the Creator of the spiritual nature of man to reign as the spiritual head of men — *it* will govern this nature in its own clumsy and inadequate manner; and the result is anarchy and wrong, not only in the spiritual, but in the moral and physical departments they have to deal with."

"And do you not conceive," asked Miss Legh, "that your Church would work out her ends equally well without *State alliance* at all?" "Not *equally well"* replied the General, "but certainly better than under the bondage of an alliance by which she should surrender her independence — which means, in other words, her *spirituality*, her acknowledgment of God the Spirit as superior to men — to all men, whether individually or in their collective legislative capacity. In whatever capacity, man cannot be more than man; God must be HIMSELF. And if man be, as we have said, a spiritual, a moral, and a physical being, whatever affects *one* of these natures, *indissolubly* united, must, without question, tell upon the other two. It is palpable that the withdrawal of State support from the clergy would compel the people to do that which the State refuses; and the resources of the *giving* classes, which, I am ashamed to say, are not the most wealthy, would, notwithstanding their utmost liberality, prove utterly inadequate to the support of the clergy, and of the pauperism of the country likewise. No sooner, therefore, will poverty become dangerous to us — for it is in this aspect alone that it at all affects our peace — than it will come upon us in the form of poor-rates, which, in their turn, will have the admirable effect of aggravating, by an ever-increasing ratio, the physical, moral, and spiritual evils of the country." "Then," said Jane, "in that case the multiplication of *St. John's* over the country, nay, St. John itself, such as it is, with all its parochial advantages, would come to an end."

"Christianity," said General Maitland, "is an ever-living active principle; it cannot lie dormant — it will do what it can; it will struggle on, it may be in one sense triumphantly, and will undoubtedly save its chosen few; but it will have been banished from the highest vantage-ground it can possess — which, in an *uncorrupted state*, it ever possessed — for adapting itself to the whole wants of all classes of a community." "And do you think," continued Jane, "that statesmen will ever really awake to the highest interests of mankind, and learn to keep these steadily in view as the only true end of their official existence?" "That is with me," said the General, "rather a matter of faith, than a conclusion deduced from reason. Scripture does give us decided promises of such a time, and I would venture to hope that the eye of the Christian philosopher may trace the achievement of several important steps towards the Christian millennium. The representative principle, of high value when the population shall have become more truly Christian; the balance of power among nations; even *the value of peace* — all now recognised principles — have made their way through a frightful amount of antagonism from personal and class selfishness. Then why may not the fulfilment of personal and class duties come to be recognised as the true foundation of pure national legislation? and why may not the grand moral and spiritual enginery which God himself has adapted for the regeneration of the human race, come to be recognised by such a Legislature as its indispensable ally?"

CHAPTER XVI

*"True genius is the ray that flings
A novel light o'er common things;
And those that dread most followers boast
Alive — with others differed most."*
COLTON

May Morrison had been despatched on several missions by her mistress for the discovery of the residence of Samuel the catechist and of Kenneth Ore, but the search seemed likely to have an unsuccessful termination. May, who was now growing into an extremely pretty if not a beautiful woman, was returning along Princes Street towards the west from one of those fruitless pilgrimages, when the active and manly form of Kenneth, bonneted and plaided, hastily brushed past her. The girl's pace had been tardy, and the expression of her countenance beclouded. She was thinking that Samuel and Kenneth might at least have tried to find her out, for old acquaintance' sake; she did not take into account the proper bashfulness which would shrink from intruding unsought into an earl's residence; for having herself somewhat forgotten the excessive awe with which she once looked upon rank and title, she forgot, in consequence, to make allowance for the feeling in others: she fancied her friends, therefore, merely forgetful and unkind. "Kenneth, Kenneth!" she cried aloud, losing sight of the crowded street on which she walked, as he, not having recognised her altered figure and nearer approach to the step and grace of the lady, was stalking on with his mountain stride, which would soon have carried him beyond her call. He recognised at once, however, the sound of her voice, and quickly turning, gave her such a hearty greeting as brought a smile into the faces of the passers-by.

"And so, Kenneth," May began, as they walked onwards together, "you were going to leave the town without even coming to see me!" Kenneth's brow darkened at this apostrophe, as if he were at a loss how to reply. At length he made answer, "Well, May, I'm sure it was not for want of thinking about you." Poor Kenneth! he spoke truly. He had thought of her more than once when, seated at the bar of the criminal court, some evidence had seemed to come out strong against him, and his heart palpitated at the recollection of those suggestions which some kind comforter had made, that he might possibly be transported for seven years, or perhaps for life! He had thought of May, too, when, with transport, feeling himself once more a free man, he walked through the magnificent city of the stranger, and gazing at the streets and houses, wondered in which of these she might be dwelling. "Hech!" resumed Kenneth after a pause, and sighing as if his heart had been recently relieved from a heavy load, "it's an awful place yon court, May! It minded me of the day of judgment, and put thoughts into my head that should maybe be there oftener. But there's one great differ; and that is, that the judges yonder canna get a blink o' the heart, but have to get witnesses questioned and tormented — some o'them poor stoitering chiels enough; whereas, at the last, the Judge will be the ae witness o' the heart himsel." "That's true, Kenneth," said May; "but ye're free now: they're not to do anything more to you!" "Yes, thanks to ONE above, and to yon twelve men!" said Kenneth fervently; "not forgetting," added he, "the *counsel*, as they're called, who did as much for me without fee or reward, as if they had been my own brothers."

With regard to the latter, poor Kenneth's heart had exhausted itself in thanks and benedictions. He and his companions, having been previously out on bail, had to travel to Edinburgh at their own expense, and had no money to fee counsel. They would thus have been completely at the mercy of the court, had it not been for a few spirited lawyers, who, breaking through the trammels of professional prejudice, were able to appreciate the cause of truth, and brought their talents to bear in behalf of the oppressed. "I was ashamed," continued Kenneth, "that I could not thank them better; but never, never will they go out of my heart. If I could serve them any way, by night or by day, I would die the happier. You dinna know what it is to be a prisoner, May. From the day I was taken up, though I got out on bail, till yon men said the word '*Not guilty*,' a load never rose from my breast; and that word, when it came, made my heart jump to my mouth; — I believe it's not in its right place yet."

"But how," asked May, "were you ever taken up at all?

and what, in all the world, had they to say against Samuel? He was a man that always was for peace." "Between you and me," said Kenneth, "but it doesna do to speak much about it, Davidson's cash was at the bottom of it. Himsel' and Geordie Donaldson — what a cloit I gied him yon day when he was kissing you, May!" and Kenneth laughed gleefully at the recollection — "that Davidson and him have never been separate since the day of the settlement, and I well believe it's not them that had the greatest concern in the riot, but such as *they* had the greatest spite to, that were taken up. For mysel', I helped no way but with my good wishes; for, to tell the truth, I dinna care much about flinging o' half-pennies; though, if it had come to the real fighting work, I could have stood to that well enough. And as for Samuel, the day's work vexed him sore; for he was for nothing but just the Glenmore people to rise and go out, and leave Geordie and his crew wi' the empty walls. 'Deed, he stopt in for nothing but to keep peace, so far as he could; and not as much as a lozenge or a cold potatoe was thrown from the part where he sat; but it's just that they dinna like good men, in the pulpit or out of it. But I heard none of *your* news, May," continued Kenneth. "Would ye like to go back to Glenmore?"

"*Would* I, Kenneth!" replied the girl, looking up in his face reproachfully. "You were going away without once seeing me, and now you think I could forget the place I was bred in!" Kenneth strode on more quickly, so that May too had to quicken her pace, but he did not reply. At length, stopping abruptly, he said, "Have you got the blue ribbon I gave you off my bonnet, May?" May replied in the affirmative, the crimson deepening on her cheek, already sufficiently dyed with the excitement of this rencounter. She did not tell, however, that she had taken the ribbon from the bottom of her trunk, where it had been first deposited, and that she wore it at that moment round her neck. "Do you see this?" continued Kenneth, drawing out May's neckerchief from beneath the plaid and vest which covered his manly breast. May glanced at it for a moment, and then turned her head the other way. Kenneth again strode on more quickly; and when he spoke, as if by a wrench given to his feelings, he changed the subject. "It's all the same, May," said he; "when you go back to Glenmore with your lady, you'll not see a bothy that you ken the face of. They grind us — they put their feet upon us," said he, grinding his nailed shoe on the pavement which grated beneath his heel; "they think there's no hearts that can feel but their own." "Come in, Kenneth," said May stopping, and in a half-choking voice, "come in — here's our house." "No, no," replied Kenneth hastily; "what should I do in *there*? Good-bye, May — one shake of your hand. Dinna forget me. Yes, yes," he added, looking back when he had gone on a pace or two, "do forget me, think of me no more — *It'll be owre seas yet.*" "The lassie's well where she is," thought he as he retraced his steps by himself; "what for would *I* make her young heart sore? The poor should never be born with feelings; they were made for the rich. *They* may woo, and wed," and he pressed convulsively with his arm the little token which he bore upon his breast; "but for us," continued he, "it's nothing but burn our haddins over our heads, and send us ayont the seas. It's a pity," he added, almost speaking aloud in a tone of deep bitterness — "it's a pity they couldna find a place out of the world a' thegither to put us bye out o' the road, without the guilt o' clean murder on their souls. Well, this shall go with me, go where I like," continued he, taking out the handkerchief and surveying it. "*She* wore it on her bonny neck, who used to climb my knee when she was a bairn, and put her fingers through my curls, and lay her head, like a wee lammie, on my breast; and it'll go wi' me to the world's end."

May stood alone on the elegant portico. Alone! Kenneth had really been there, and was gone! She looked upwards and all around her, and there was something in the very splendour of the finely built houses, and in their regularity — their rows of windows and cornices drawn smooth, as if by pencil lines — that pained her eye-sight. Old John Morrison's one room in the mountain hovel — the hearth fire, with its smoky buttresses — her grandfather seated in his arm-chair — his staff and his silver hair — Kenneth on a low stool, and she playing around him; all this seemed to supplant the circular rows of hewn stone actually before her. What would she not give to live one of those hours of long, long ago over again! The very roughnesses in the earthen floor, the shelf, with its old black books, the plates against the wall, seemed to live at that moment with a double endearment in her memory! And Kenneth was in this city of the stranger, and had left her! Poor May! She felt, for the first time keenly and really, that she was no longer a child. She felt it by the anguish biting at her heart, as Kenneth's last words echoed there — "*It'll be owre seas yet.*"

Many loungers had on that morning filled the Earl's drawing-room. General Maitland had gone out early, and had not yet returned. Lord Lentraethen sat reading the newspapers, which always occupied a considerable part of his day, in the back drawing-room, not troubling himself very much with any one that came or went. His lady and her two daughters had done their best to be entertaining; but at length their spirits began to flag. Jane's head ached with hearing the same things repeated over and over again; and Lady Emily, who saw her look pale, whispered, "What a host of uninteresting people to-day! It really must be, *Not at home* on the first cessation!"

Just then the door opened, and General Maitland appeared, ushering in an old man whom he now led forward — an unwonted kind of guest in an Earl's drawing-room: — it was the catechist of Glenmore. Little change had taken place in his appearance since Miss Legh first saw him by the death-bed of John Morrison. He wore the same kind of coat of light blue cloth, with leaden buttons, and of peculiar make; his broad-striped breeches were buttoned at the knee, and he held his staff and blue bonnet in his unoccupied hand. "Samuel, my good old friend!" said Miss Legh, hastily rising and going towards the door to meet him and take his hand in her own. The lady visitors turned half-round on their couches, with feathers waving; Lord Moir, who was there, stared and used his eye-glass; other loungers of the male sex were thrown into attitudes of astonishment; and even the Earl, perceiving the sensation that was created, left his newspaper, came forward, and stood for a moment with his back to the fire, then muttering, "Some whim of Frederick's," went back to his easy-chair and the columns of the *Times*. No sooner did Samuel, with intuitive perception, become aware of some unusual feeling prevailing, than he stopped and protested to General Maitland against going forward; but Jane, in her turn, protested against his going back. "No, no," said she, leading him on; "I am too glad to see you to let you go away in that manner. Come into the recess of this window, and there we can talk without interruption." "Ha!" exclaimed Lord Moir, in a half suppressed voice, "quite a picture! a rustic old man heralded by two distinguished-looking individuals! For my part, I am sorry I do not sketch," he added with a sneer and an appealing look to the nearest lady. Miss Legh meanwhile sat down, and would have had Samuel to do so likewise, but this he persisted in refusing. He stood leaning on his staff, bent forward in an attitude of respectful deference, waiting the lady's pleasure, yet with more native grace than many a well-trained cavalier. General Maitland threw himself on a tête-a-tête chair at a few paces' distance, which he had no sooner done, than Lord Moir approached, paid his morning compliments, and then took the other side of the chair, where he could easily remark what passed.

"Well, Samuel," began Miss Legh with a smile, "you have been a prisoner since I saw you last — I am sure undeservedly?" "I hope so" replied Samuel, with a tranquil expression of countenance; "I trust I endeavour as much as lies in me to live peaceably with all men, according to the Word. But you know, my lady, that the same Word says, 'Have no fellowship with the unfruitful works of darkness, but rather reprove them.' For that cause the Lord promised some measure of persecution to all his followers." "But they say, Samuel," pursued Miss Legh, "that you are a rebel — that you have been acting in opposition to the law of the land." "That is an old cry," replied Samuel, with a shake of his head — his countenance at the same time becoming more illuminated with its own peculiar expression —a radiant benevolence, with a cast of shrewd humour — "it is a cry as old as the days of our blessed Master; and as far as we have any record, it followed his disciples. I doubt it is a cry that will not be stopped until *He*" — he lowered his voice into tones of deep reverence — "take unto *himself* his great power and reign." "But Samuel," continued Miss Legh, "do you justify the riot which I suppose did take place, and the throwing of missiles, not, I dare say, intended to hurt, but which showed a spirit that I would not have expected from patient and well-instructed Highlanders?" "So far from justifying it," said Samuel, with the same imperturbable temper, "I trust I can say with a clear conscience, that I did all in my power to prevent it; but as for poor creatures like us — and in this the judge and the prisoner are all alike — we are glad to pluck the filthy rags from the tattered garments of others, to make a cloak for our own sin. The cry of souls," he continued, again altering his tone to one of deep seriousness, but without acrimony — "the cry of souls for the bread of life is arising from the face of the land. Will the clamour of a few famishing children in the church of Glenmore keep that cry from entering into the ear of the Lord of hosts?"

"True," said Miss Legh; "but you know that the patrons and the Government have the undoubted disposal of the temporalities." "If," said Samuel, with the same undisturbed seriousness, "if they take it upon them to dispose of these things according to their own worldly views, and not according to the spiritual necessities of the land, they have the heavier account to render. But, as I was endeavouring to impress upon the minds of our people, let God deal with *them* — let them alone in his hands; He has better weapons than pieces of wood and plaster. Can he not turn even that great leviathan that laugheth at the shaking of a spear?" Jane was struck with that sense of the grave sublime, which an adequate faith in Omnipotence never fails to inspire; and which she knew deeply pervaded the minds of the Christian mountaineers. "Yes," she replied, after a pause, "it is well when *we* fill the parts which the great Disposer of all has assigned to us; fully content that He will do *his* part, and assured that he *will* do it. But how have you been treated, my friend, since you came here?"

"Indifferently" replied Samuel, "at the first; but that is of small consequence. Yet God has followed me with undeserved mercy and loving-kindness. I have cause to thank him for the great goodness of the gentlemen that undertook our cause. Surely the hearts of all are in His hand. On the second night of my being here, our case not having been concluded on the first day, the counsel that pleaded for me came to me as I was going to leave the court under charge of the police, and said, "I have gone forty pounds bail for you. I trust you will appear to-morrow. You may now go where you please." I was not able to say much, except pledging myself to appear; but it *did* touch me nearly that the gentleman should have gone bail without my knowledge, and never ask my promise till after it was done. May *the blessing* descend richly into his bosom!" "And have you now any wants?" inquired Miss Legh.

"No, my lady," returned Samuel hastily, "no wants, no wants. My wife and I laid by for these thirty years back a pound in the twelvemonth, and as I have a salary of £25 regularly, I have been enabled, by the divine blessing, to provide for all wants, and for the expense in the meantime without trouble." " But the others, too," said Jane, "have they had all their own expenses to pay?" Samuel did not mention how much he had assisted them, but he expressed a belief that they would all get well home, thankful to have been freed by a jury of their countrymen from the imputation of any offence against the laws.

Miss Legh went to her desk, and took out unperceived a purse of gold, which, having beckoned Samuel to follow her out of the room, she pressed upon his acceptance. "No, my dear young lady, no," said he; " my pilgrimage is nearly over; my heavenly Provider has amply supplied my wants hitherto. What use could *I* find for gold? but," he added modestly, as if asking a personal favour, "if you could find some honourable gentleman to send the money in charge to for the deserving poor of our parish, there are many, many who would bless God for but a little of it." Miss Legh willingly promised to comply, and went to the adjoining room to ring for May, to whom she conveyed the charge of seeing the worthy old man provided with some refreshment, and of conducting him to his place of residence. As she put her hand in his to bid him farewell, he paused, as if he had something to say, without which he could not part with cheerfulness. "Do not be offended, my dear young lady," said he; "you have all the best gifts of Providence as to this life. Oh! seek the pearl of *great* price, which, when one has found, he is willing to sell for it *all* that he has." Jane did not reply; but she looked at the earnest speaker with a tear trembling in her eye; she bowed her head — and, did it defile those beautiful lips that she touched with them, lightly and reverentially, the old man's peasant hand: He, on his part, drew it hastily away, as if he felt that such expressions of respect were not for him; but he placed it instead on her young and noble head, and with the deeply-breathed expression of "blessing" in his native language, he turned with May and went his way.

"In what an atmosphere of heavenly truth that man lives!" remarked Jane to General Maitland on her return to the drawing-room, without minding Lord Moir, who looked at her with rather wondering eyes. "It diffuses a light of intelligence — a sunshine of high-toned feeling around him wherever he goes." "Pray, may I ask," said Lord Moir, with a more than ordinary lisp — "may I ask Miss Hamilton Legh if you keep any pet dogs?" "May I know," returned Miss Legh, "why I have the honour to be asked the question?" "Ah !" said Lord Moir, "because you seem to have an odd *penchant* for pets in general — old rustics, for example." "Why, then," replied Jane, "I like dogs well enough, if they are good respectable animals of their kind; but," she added in a sarcastic tone, "*I abhor puppies.*" "Ah!" said the young lord, slightly colouring, while he looked rather like a puppy that had been whipped; and a laugh looked out from General Maitland's eyes. *There were reasons* why Lord Moir should dislike this particularly. He coloured still more, and rising with a look of some displeasure, joined the other ladies, whom he horrified by informing in a whisper that Miss Legh's *protégé* was actually one of the rebels who had been cited for taking part in the northern riots! In general, Lord Moir constituted himself Miss Legh's sworn champion. He asserted that she "was not only a star, but a sun, in the horizon of fashion; and that if she *had* odd notions, she was quite beautiful enough to sport what notions she pleased; indeed, mere beauty was insipid without something to give it poignancy," &c., &c. Whether her fortune had anything to do with his extreme toleration, Lord Moir did not say.

" I am the bearer of an invitation which I think you will not dislike," said General Maitland to Miss Legh in a low tone. It is to Lady Douglas's this evening. She is to have a quiet evening party to meet Dr. Chalmers, whom she thinks you would like to know. I met her on her way here, and as she was hurried, I told her that I thought you would take the invitation from my mouth. She hopes you will excuse its shortness, which arises from the uncertainty of the Doctor's visit, of which she was only made perfectly sure this morning, owing to his numerous engagements. You will look in with me for a couple of hours?"

Miss Legh expressed her unqualified delight at the opportunity afforded her of seeing one whose name she truly venerated, and from whose circle of acquaintance she was almost excluded by her own very different set.

She found at Lady Douglas's neither rout nor private ball, but a small intelligent circle, met to spend the evening in rational conversation. She was introduced to Dr. Chalmers, who received her with distinguished kindness; while she, on her part, felt an unwonted, and almost awkward, bashfulness take possession of her. Strange power of mental greatness! whose presence compels a homage which swallows up all thoughts and personalities in itself! Jane felt it, as perhaps only a very superior mind can feel. Young, wealthy, independent, accustomed to deference, and caring nothing to express her sentiments in all sorts of society, she now sunk at once into the shy and timid girl. At first, especially, she scarcely found courage to reply with any collectedness to the Doctor's remarks. Yet was there a refulgent goodness in his every look, whose sunshine it was delightful to feel falling on herself. He, on his part, seated himself, apparently well pleased, by her side, and rising occasionally to carry on a little desultory conversation with this individual or that, as courtesy seemed to require, returned often to the same place, attracted evidently by those pleasant influences of countenance and manner to which he was peculiarly open. How did she, on her part, delight to contemplate that honoured face and venerable figure! They filled her eye and mind during the whole evening. His physiognomy large, and features rather strongly marked, with any other expression might possibly have been harsh. They were harmonized and softened by the mind which animated them. Yet, although those features wore the habitual impress of goodness, the eye did not habitually express intellect. A kind of dreamy mistiness hung over it, which might either mean the absence of thought, or else that the mind had withdrawn within itself, to revolve and contemplate those habitual ideas which so powerfully impressed the countenance. What those were, if it had been possible to misunderstand them, would have been revealed by the sudden flash which lighted up the whole expression, when any according sentiment from another brought those inner thoughts to the surface; — they belonged to the most comprehensive philanthropy, the highest well-being of man! Miss Legh had been taught this idea as a problem — a duty devolving upon her by inheritance. She had, indeed, felt that pleasure which a benevolent mind must ever feel in acts of benevolence performed; but her duty towards mankind in its *futurity* was an anxiety — a weight which often lay heavily upon her. But in sitting beside Thomas Chalmers, who owed half his greatness to the magnitude of his philanthropy, it was impossible not to feel that with him the sense of duty itself was absorbed in the higher principle of *love*. It had become the governing law of his nature, not to obey which, was not to live. Never was any man's being more absorbed in one grand idea — in rising, in lying down, in walking, in conversing, in public and in private, this idea of elevating the spiritual condition of his fellow-men never forsook him. The uneasiness of responsibility was, with him, swallowed up in unwearied, undeviating efforts to put this in-dwelling love into the shape of positive exertion, and in unwavering confidence in those means which the Author of man's being had put within man's reach — the renewing and elevating influences of God's Word upon the depraved heart. As for the *personality* of his responsibility, it rested on this, "Believe on the Lord Jesus Christ, and thou shalt be saved." Conscious of the *reality* of this belief he left all besides quiescent in God's hand. This great man's mind, in its renewal by grace, bore upon it the majestic impress of the God of nature; it resembled the impulses of the heavenly bodies in this, that, pursuing its sublime course with amazing rectitude, it borrowed its power of progression only from the Creator's hand.

Our friend had heard much of Dr. Chalmers, had read many of his works, and had known how to appreciate him as a good and great man; but not until she felt the influence of his *presence* did she conceive *how* good and how great he was. Yet there was about him a certain simplicity which, as much as any other of his characteristics, distinguished him from other men, and gradually the awe which she at first experienced, was changed into a deep, venerating, never-to-be-forgotten love. This simplicity pervaded every movement, and even communicated, itself, as one might easily imagine, to the very dress which he wore. His clothes sat upon him without slovenliness, yet so as plainly to indicate that they were no part of *himself*, that they had never in the course of his life cost him an anxiety or care. The folds of his neckcloth, and the very tie upon it, without an indication of eccentricity, told of a toilet devoid of concentration, though performed, probably, with a sincere endeavour to give it all that propriety required. But there was a charm in this simplicity quite beyond the reach of imitation. Miss Legh was struck, too, with the remarkable beauty, as well as size of his head, with its thinly-curled locks of a silken grey. She compared it with the others present, and found it unapproachable, not only in intellectual development, but in the grace of the whole contour.

As the evening advanced, and the Doctor continued frequently to address her, she found courage to ask his opinions on some of the leading topics of the day. She ventured, among other things, to remark, "How very extraordinary, that those means which God himself had appointed for the regeneration of mankind should receive so little attention from men."

"I have indulged," said the Doctor, in his strong accent, marked by peculiar emphasis, and a momentary pause on every important word — "I have indulged in the fallacy, that I might show the vast superiority of these means by a numerical calculation — a kind of arithmetical demonstration." "And have you not succeeded by your labours in doing so, to a certain extent?" asked our young friend, timidly. "To a most inadequate extent," replied the Doctor, catching the words as if they had been his own, "and I have come at last to the conclusion that nothing short of a renewal of the mind by divine grace can create a right appreciation of the blessings of divine truth." "Still, one would imagine," argued Jane, "that what has actually been accomplished, and remains no longer a matter of theory, requires but the portion of attention which we bestow on other subjects, to ascertain it as a *fact*, which is distinct from an understanding of the means through which the end has been attained." "I indulged in the chimera," said the Doctor, "that I might even bring it down to the level of the eyesight — bring it down from its occupation of any high intellectual position altogether; and with this view I took, — — ,when he was in Glasgow, to visit some of our newly-excavated congregations, where the people had all, without exception, been lately brought within the pale of the decencies of life; and I imagined that, by this kind of demonstration, I might gain access to his mind as a statesman." "And did you not make any temporary impression?" asked Miss Legh. "No, I think not," returned the Doctor, with the most decisive simplicity, "*I think not.* He is a cold man — cold and selfish; a state mechanician, but no statesman; an adept in the intricacies of leadership, well acquainted with all the springs and leading-strings of party. But he seems to me like the master of a vessel, who is a perfect master of its management, with a thorough knowledge of his crew and the whole of his sailing machinery, but without the least idea of the wide ocean over which he is sailing. So — ,with his party well drilled and thoroughly acquainted with Parliamentary manoeuvring, which has been the study of his life, has *no notion* of the human nature upon which he has to operate."

Jane would have inquired, in return, whether the elevation of that human nature was in reality his object, but she was interrupted by the novel appearance of a footman bearing an arm-full of Bibles, the largest of which he placed on a table near the centre of the room, while Dr. Chalmers immediately rose and seated himself beside it, and the company formed themselves into a circle around. Never, Jane thought, had she heard sweeter melody than that in which this circle — united for the time into one family — began this act of worship to the Supreme, with this apostle of beneficence leading their devotions. The portion of Scripture chosen for the subject of a short exposition, was the 8th chapter of the Romans, which gave the Doctor an opportunity of dwelling on his favourite theme of justification by faith alone. This he viewed in the aspect most familiar to him, as being in the mind of the believer the germ of future righteousness; and he repelled indignantly, the charge brought against this maligned and misunderstood principle, that it was the enemy of personal virtue or holiness. He dwelt with enthusiasm on the value of that experimental knowledge of the truth of revelation, of which *faith* was the primary cause; asserting that, upon grounds of high philosophy, it was no fanciful or chimerical evidence of the divine origin of the Scriptures, of which the uneducated peasant was possessed, who, ignorant of all their *external* evidences, was occupied only in the study of his own heart, and who, finding its experiences always coincident with *Scripture* declaration, argued that the Author of his being was the author of the Christian revelation likewise. To this exposition Jane lent an interested and delighted attention. But what humility yet elevation of mind she experienced when, kneeling to worship God in such near communion with this his servant, who, she felt, stood immeasurably nearer the presence of the SUPREME than she did! She thought of those glorious spirits, who partake in so much higher a degree of his communicable attributes, and yet between whom and *the Source of Life* the distance remains INFINITE; and the infinity of mind itself seemed to expand into greater vastness, even as the infinity of space becomes more immeasurable by the comprehension of an immense series of its parts. And thus an intense admiration of the creature deepened into a profounder adoration of the Creator.

When the company had arisen from this unusual, but surely not irrational nor ungraceful conclusion of the evening, the Lentraethen carriage was announced, and having once more had a kindly greeting, and encouraging farewell from the Doctor — not unusual things, with him in the overflow of his social benevolence — Miss Legh took her departure.

During the ride homewards, remarks were naturally made on the individual who had formed the great attraction of the evening. "He is indeed an extraordinary man," said General Maitland, "and that, too, in many ways in which he is not always duly appreciated. No man, for example, can be more free from the mere secularities of party or profession. Many clergymen, men of high aims, too, are apt to lose sight of these aims, especially in their intercourse with each other, and to descend into the slang business-style generated, it may be, by the necessities of the means which they have to adopt. But those ends, those high aims — the glory of God and the good of man — never assume for a moment, in the mind of Thomas Chalmers, any secondary place. They never cease to be to him *direct* objects of thought. And this constitutes him in no small degree the great leader he is. With regard to the grosser secularities of station and luxury, I believe he is simple as a child. He has a standard above which he does not permit himself to rise. I have heard it related as fact, that a present of finely-flavoured wine — Burgundy, or something of that sort — was sent him from some friend in England, and that an English nobleman, who had brought a letter of introduction, happening soon after to dine at his house, his family wished, as a matter of course, to produce some of the wine which had been thus provided. But the Doctor positively refused his permission, while he gave them ample liberty to disperse it among their acquaintances in any other way; lest the introduction of this new element of luxury might form a dangerous precedent; and likewise because, as he said, anything beyond the plainest wines ought never to be seen on the table of a Scottish pastor."

"I cannot tell you," said Jane, "how delighted I am that I have conversed with him. The enthusiasm I feel will last with my life. He is surely a very wonderful character. Has he *any* fault?" "If you believe his enemies," said General Maitland, laughing, "no one has more." "Oh but," said: Jane, "they are ignorant; they have not felt the charm of his presence; or else, not being able to appreciate his greatness, they wish to bring him down to their own level. But I mean any *real* fault — any thing which might approximate him to the rest of his fallen species?" "I understand," replied the General, "that he permits nothing which is akin to private scandal, nothing that could reflect on the character of any one, to be retailed at his table; and thus carrying out the principle of charity to the very letter, in so far as he does, he is sometimes kept in ignorance of facts upon which to found his judgment with regard to private character. This may occasionally lead to misapprehension of character and mistakes in public business."

"Yet he is tolerably severe at times on public men," remarked Jane. "Oh yes," said the General, "these are men who have identified themselves with certain classes, and who represent, in so far, the interests of mankind. Not to appreciate *them*, would argue him unequal to grasp with the interests themselves. But I believe that, more than any living man, he has acquired the habit of considering individuals only as they advance or retard a certain desired consummation. The long habit of considering human beings under a single relation, does very much, I conceive, contribute to make them lose their individuality. Napoleon learnt to consider human life as an abstraction entirely subserviated to his purposes of ambition; and Dr. Chalmers views human character through the exclusive medium of his own mind, in its bearing upon the moral destinies of man. But what there is most singular in the matter is this: Napoleon subjected all happiness or misery to his own personality, which was the grand, if not the only, object of his ultimate contemplation; — Chalmers is with himself almost as much an abstraction subserviated to *another* great end as any other being." " Of all greatness," remarked Jane, "that must be the greatest; for it is the most godlike. But of what value are *we*," she added, after a pause and with a sigh, "if we do not in some degree advance the same ends? and how much we, of our class, *might* subserve them, if we would!" "Ah! if we would!" replied the General. "What a spectacle would Britain now present, if its proprietors and clergy had been universally indoctrinated, but a single quarter of a century ago, with the large views and fervent charity of Thomas Chalmers! For that and much and ardently has he laboured; but we will not hear — enveloped as we are in the mists and prejudices of caste — until the accumulated vice and misery of our people speak in a voice of thunder to the selfish principle within us. If we fall, the world may-hap shall not sorrow for us!"

CHAPTER XVIII

But all unrivalled must the Godhead reign;
Then stand resolved, through peril, storm, or cloud,
To doff thine armour only for thy shroud;
To such alone, fulfill'd their mortal strife,
Defeat is victory — and death is life.
COLTON

The memorable Assembly of the year 1841 drew near. Miss Legh would have been ignorant of the circumstance, but for General Maitland. So soon, however, as she did know it, she expressed a wish to delay her intended departure for a few weeks, that she might have a better opportunity of seeing the leaders in the reigning controversy, and likewise acquire a clearer idea than she yet had of the order and discipline of the Presbyterian Church. She therefore made arrangements to make one of a party with Lady Douglas, who easily procured tickets for the Commissioner's box.

It was on the 27th day of May that our friend, on entering the house of Assembly, held in St. Andrew's Church, had her attention powerfully arrested by the speaker addressing the house at the time, whom she recognised, from having heard him preach on a former occasion, as Mr. (afterwards Dr.) Candlish. And it might well be so arrested; — she had arrived to hear one of the most extraordinary displays of oratory which that remarkable man had ever made. It was his address upon a proposed measure of the Duke of Argyle's, spoken rather to the opposition, as it would be termed in Parliament, than to the members of his own party. The speaker stood on the platform in front of the throne, with his face turned, and his arm stretched towards the side benches on the right of the Commissioner. His figure, diminutive and slight, was retrieved by a head of extraordinary development in the intellectual region, and by an expression of earnest and sustained energy which communicated itself to his whole frame. His voice, not fine in the common acceptation of the term, yet possessed the capacity of awakening and fixing the attention in an uncommon degree.

The whole house — the crowded galleries above, the members

below, of whatever sentiments — now hung on the lips of the orator, while he delivered his urgent appeal, as if he felt that the fate of his Church, the future weal or woe of his country, depended on its success. Its substance was concisely this: — "We, the reforming party, harassed at every step by the courts of law, and found liable at every step in pains and penalties, cannot, under this state of things, continue to exist within the Church. But from the reformation of certain deadly abuses — the imposition of hands, for example, in the solemn rite of ordination, on the creature of the patron, against the mind and consciences of the people — we cannot desist. We must likewise continue to assert our independence of the State in things *spiritual*, as secured to us by ancient statute. Upon the maintenance of this principle we deem the future purity and usefulness of our Church to depend. Our consciences, our word, our *all*, is at stake. Here is a proposed measure which will recognise the Treaty of Union, will re-enact the ancient statutes in our favour, and will free our position from all mistakes and misunderstandings. Is there any thing in it, which, if it were carried, would violate your consciences? If the *law of the land* be that which you inscribe on your banner, unite your forces with ours in procuring this measure — so reasonable in itself, so much in accordance with the ancient constitution of our Church — to be the *law of the land* in your own acceptation of the term; and you will heal all divisions, unite all hearts, and prevent the schism so much to be deplored in its consequences, which must otherwise rend our Church and nation."

Such in substance, though not in words, was this very powerful appeal. And for a moment it had its effect; not a breath could be heard as the sustained and tensely-strung voice of the speaker rung on the ears of the audience. And at its conclusion, the members of his own party and the galleries were silent, moved by a sentiment too deep for applause. The power of eloquence prevailed for a time with even the opposition over the prejudices of party. Loud cheers burst from them — as if every man had broken his leading-strings, and was giving expression to the feelings of his own bosom — cheers which thrilled the rest of the spectators with a pride in the oratory with which they had just identified themselves — with a hope of its success not to be described. Pride most just, but, alas! hope most fallacious! At the evening vote the old majority remained with the reformers, but the transient blaze of feeling soon subsided in the breasts of those accustomed to weigh the interests of party against everything besides. Every man of the large minority remained to harass, to misstate, to misrepresent, and finally to establish, the *Moderate* ascendency on the ruins of the best interests of their Church.

On the succeeding day Lady Douglas' party was earlier in the house. A great crush was anticipated, and the numbers who assembled at an early hour exceeded expectation. The spectacle presented was imposing. The whole lower area was filled, as usual, with clerical members, whose grave attire was relieved to the eye by the number of well-dressed gentlemen representing the eldership of the Church; and there was a strong muster of the forces on either side, as if a decided movement, a hard contest, were expected. The two parties directly faced each other to the right and left, and the cross benches in front were occupied, as our friend understood, by those members who wished to maintain a neutral position, and vote with either side as conscience or interest seemed to demand. The galleries above were divided into two compartments — one being reserved for the students of the Church, and the other thrown open to the public. These were early so crowded, that it would seem impossible to insert an additional individual into the mass. Controversies, in consequence, were heard to arise from time to time in the background, between the door-keepers and parties urgent for admittance. The throne, canopied with crimson, and quartered with the royal arms, occupied the place where the pulpit of the large church, now converted into a house of Assembly, usually stood. The chair of the *moderator* or president, chosen by suffrage, was immediately below; and a table covered with papers, at which the clerks and some of the senior members sat, filled the greater part of the small open space in front. The boxes on either side of the throne, covered like itself with crimson, were filled with well-dressed ladies, mostly friends or acquaintances of the Lord Commissioner.

"The Dissenters object to the appearance of the Commissioner in this place," remarked an elderly and gentlemanly-looking man, who had been a foreign consul during the greater part of his life, to General Maitland. "They call it, I believe, the badge of the slavery of the Kirk. I cannot see it in that light. It seems to me fair enough, that when two nations enter into terms of alliance, each should have its representative or ambassador, to see that the terms are not infringed. Such is usually considered a pledge of mutual independence, and I think that such is likewise the case with Church and State." "You an Episcopalian," said General Maitland in reply, "and yet an advocate of spiritual independence! How comes that about ?" "It is my opinion," said the old gentleman decidedly, "that our Church has too much succumbed that principle. Still I cannot but think she possesses it, though she does not now choose to assert it. I argue in this way; if every man's conscience ought to be independent in religious matters, should not a Church, which is but an aggregate of men's religious consciences, be an independent body?" "Aha!" said the General, "a dangerous way of reasoning for you; for, if a *man* prostrate his conscience before the will of another, he can be no true man, and if a *Church*, yield up her conscience to the arbitration of a foreign power, that fact proves her to be a Church untrue to herself. For though a sincere conscience may err, a conscience willing at all times to be put down by a foreign power, must cease to *be* a conscience."

"Well, well, I should certainly not be willing to carry the argument so far," said Sir John. "I love the Church of England, and I must do so as long as I love the old pew where I used to kneel every Sunday by my mother's side. I feel some interest in this Kirk of yours, but it is a stranger to me; and, besides, I cannot get myself reconciled to the constitution of this court. I would have our English convocations revived; but I would have them to consist wholly of the clergy. I understand, too, that there are sometimes here indecent exhibitions of popular feeling." "So our enemies say," replied the General, "but I can scarcely see on what grounds. The fact is, that our early Reformers, newly emerged from Rome with its corruptions and its sort of *close-burgh* system, determined to throw open their Church in every department, to the wholesome action of public opinion, or rather, we should say, to the common sense and conscience of the country. They reckoned on their successors being but men, and liable to the same self-interested influences which had gradually corrupted primitive Christianity, and they thought that a religiously educated country, where every individual had the Bible in his hand, was one of the best safe-guards for the purity of its Church. And why not? The most iniquitous courts have been often the most solemn. What court has ever surpassed the Inquisition in gravity? While in any thing which bears the character of an open court, a popular assembly, the natural feelings must find vent."

"Ah, probably," replied Sir John, who, clear-headed and shrewd in matters of politics, disliked following out any argument connected with religion, from a kind of suspicion that it might lead him into a jumble of inconsistency. "But these laymen in the body of the Church," he continued, "why should they be here?" "They are elders regularly ordained according to Scripture precedent, by laying on of hands," replied General Maitland; "and from being destitute of clerical interests, they form in our Church courts a barrier against clerical encroachments, which renders it nearly impossible for Presbyterianism to degenerate into spiritual despotism." "Ah, probably," replied Sir John again, "*Chaque pays chaque coutume*; every Church is pure," he added, laughing, "in its own country — the child of the soil. I have lived too much from home not to know that."

The General shook his head. "But, my dear Sir John," he said, "there must be a *standard* for Christian Churches. Every man who believes God's word, should, as a responsible being, bring his Church to that test." "Ah, true, true," said Sir John; "but see, there are the famous *seven*; they are taking their places at the bar. Well, after all, it is a hard matter to depose seven men for obeying the law of the country they live in." "I rather think," said General Maitland, "that in this instance the law has obeyed them. I have followed the controversy closely, and I am convinced that these men are but the tools of their party. The body of worldly men introduced by the act of Bolingbroke, and for a long time in the ascendant, have sought by all means to get rid of the spirit of piety, and of the reformers of abuses. They have now found two or three old law-lords brought up in the prejudices of their party (for all men in Scotland have their Church as decidedly as their State politics, and usually the more engrossing of the two), and these lords, relics of a period not the best in Scotland's religious history, have turned for them the majority in the Court of Session; while they, the Moderate party, in turn, are willing to sell the independence of their Church to that court which the Scottish Parliament and the Treaty of Union recognised but as of co-ordinate rank with their own; the Court of

Session, in return, giving their measures the ascendant. These seven men are but, as my Lord Castlereagh said, 'the features on which the question hinges.' They have not preached nor administered the sacraments while under sentence of suspension, without first ascertaining that the law-court would lend them the weight of its authority; and every interdict against the decrees of this Assembly has been obtained *expressly at their instance*."

"Why," said Sir John, "I suppose they considered themselves unjustly suspended." "Of that," said the General, "their ordination vows made their ecclesiastical courts, not themselves, the judges. But in itself, what could have been more reasonable than that sentence? A man of the name of Edwards, had performed the duties for the old incumbent of the parish of Marnoch for three years and a-half. The people found his ministrations so unmeaning and unprofitable, that they could scarce keep up the form of attendance at church. At the decease of the old man, this very Edwards was presented to the living. The people remonstrated — their remonstrances were unheeded. The supreme Church court, like a parent that protects her children, interfered in their behalf. They forbade that presbytery, whose majority is now at the bar, to proceed with the first step towards ordination. This majority proceeded in defiance of their orders. It was necessary then to suspend them for a time from the functions of clergymen, in order both to protect the people and to maintain the authority of the court. In spite of all which, having first ascertained that the Court of Session would maintain them in their temporalities, they have continued to perform the functions of clergymen, and have actually ordained the man Edwards to the cure of the parish of Marnoch. continuing all the while to procure interdicts against this court in every step of its subsequent procedure. What court is there, of whatever kind, which would not, in similar circumstances, proceed. to the last sentence within its power? Secure in their livings, supported by the greater part of the patronate and law interest of the country, and with a powerful party in the Church to sanction, or rather instigate, the barter of the Church's independence, these men are not objects of pity, for they are assailed only in principles which they do not feel."

This conversation took place before the arrival of the

Commissioner, who now entered, followed by his suite — a tall, handsome nobleman, dressed in scarlet uniform, with hat and feathers. The Assembly rose, as on the appearance of majesty, and after the mutual courtesy of recognition between him and the moderator, as between the representatives of two estates, the meeting was constituted by prayer.

As the business was about to commence, Miss Legh looked with increasing interest at those who were to be the leaders in the day's debate. As the acknowledged head of the Moderate party, an old heavy-looking man, was pointed out to her, seated at the table where the minutes, &c., were taken down, whom she understood to be Dr. George Cook, one of the professors in the University of St. Andrews. There was something in his face and person, which assigned them a place in the extreme reverse of the ideal, and our friend felt no strong interest in contemplating them. But in the aspect of the one other individual on the same side, who was looked upon as a man of talent, there was considerably more to arrest the attention. A figure, large and strong, though not above the middle height —a head of great size, and yet in no ways remarkable apparently in the region of intellect — coarse firm features, with hair of an iron-grey drooping over his forehead, and a stoop from his shoulders, altogether gave the idea of great firmness and energy of character, though not in an equal degree of openness and candour. He was a man, one would have thought, who, had he been born in France in the earlier times of the revolution, might have somehow cut a figure in the troubles of the time; or a few years later, might have distinguished himself as one of Napoleon's generals, both daring and wary in action.

On the other side, on the front bench, with other members, not distinguished by any particular prominence of place, sat Dr. CHALMERS, leaning on his silver-headed staff. He was silent and abstracted. In him likewise there was something to be read — nothing *less* certainly than his usual beneficence, but as certainly something more. Our friend looked for the other leaders on the same side. They occupied a retired place behind the corner of the Commissioner's box, and were scarcely discernible. She then glanced at the bar. Six men sat there in the attire of clergymen, instead of seven. "What has become of the seventh?" she inquired in a low voice of a pleasant-looking lady who sat beside her. "He is an old infirm man, not able to appear," was the reply. "But see, there is young C — , the son, leaning forward with his head down. I have heard that he is one of the best of the seven; which means, I believe, that he has little mind of his own, but has been kept in his position by force of influence and against his will." "Two of these men," said Miss Legh, "look more like gentlemen than the others. Who are they?" "A — of R — , and W — of H — , "replied the lady. They are of those among the Moderates, who, by dint of loving much to mix with their superiors, have polished somewhat by contact; and on the strength of such the party take great credit to themselves for being an exceedingly *gentlemanly* set; but really, so far as my experience goes, I think the greater number are more like those other men whom you can easily see are vulgar enough." "Then you think," said Miss Legh, "that the Moderates, as you call them, are, with few exceptions, divided into those who have a kind of worldly *beau ideal*, and those who have no *beau ideal* of any kind, but are content to live as instinct directs." The lady, a smart lively-looking brunette, looked at Jane with an expression of the ludicrous, mingled with surprise, and nodded. "Yes," she replied, "chiefly with a few weaklings, a few babes and sucklings, like young C —. But hush; here is — going to begin his address."

Miss Legh looked up and saw a figure standing at the bar as counsel for the accused, of remarkable dimensions, but possessing no other striking advantages. The *animus* of this gentleman's address soon made itself apparent. He came with a scold by deputation from the Court of Session. That court — the idol of every lawyer's heart with whom an enlightened regard for his Church and country did not assume a still greater pre-eminence — he invariably designated the *supreme* court of the country, although he made no appeal to any act of the Legislature which had so constituted it. Neither did he make any allusion to those clauses in the Treaty of Union which declared the General Assembly to be the court of *last resort* in all causes ecclesiastical. He was content with merely denouncing the body of men he was addressing as "rebels against the law." The idea of *spiritual independence*, it was evident, had never found, *and could never find*, a place in his mind. The words, "*spiritual*, forsooth!" emanated from his lips with supreme contempt. To a mind like that of our young friend, which always sought for first principles, his arguments appeared inconsistent and baseless. He accused the Reformers of wearing the State livery, and drawing the State pay, and yet raising their rebellious heads against the law which protected and defended them. The plea that Christ was the Head of the Church was a plea, he urged, totally irrelevant. True, the Confession of the Church of Scotland's faith, recognised as part of the *law of the land*, stated that there was *no other Head of the Church than the Lord Jesus Christ*; but that, he said, was a theme too sacred for argument. It was above all human institutions; it applied to the Church universal!

A singular enough phenomenon, thought our friend, that a lawyer, whose mind, for all she knew, was confined within the clasps of some few law-books, should thus stand with face inflamed and vehement gesture, his clenched fist sounding frequently on the desk before him, rating with the violence of a pedagogue that other man whose name was venerated, and was yet more and more to be venerated throughout the world! and those, too, who understood his aims! who saw clearly the same good, and stood ready unflinchingly to make the same sacrifices! After this preliminary to the proceedings of the day was over, the lawyer retired, with an assurance that whatever were said or done he should take no further part in the proceedings (as if that had been a matter of importance), and was followed by Mr. A —, the foreman of the accused.

All this the court took good humouredly, as a form necessary to be gone through. Dr. Chalmers had sat in the attitude of a patient listener; — he now rose, and advanced slowly forward, a more than usual gravity resting on his features. Cries for silence rang from all parts of the house, and there was a general change of position, as if the audience were disposing itself for an intense and respectful attention. It was only the first few sentences of Chalmers which made the lawyer sink into his proper place. What a mastery has the mind accustomed to resolve all modes of thought into each other, over other minds encircled within one narrow sphere! Like almost every other great thinker, Chalmers could not resist treating the external phenomena of the mind's action, whether developed in action or opinion, as the mind itself. From a complication or confusion between the obligatory or that which *must be*, and the lawful or that which *may be*, much injury, he alleged, had arisen to the cause "in having placed it beyond the reach of ordinary minds, which have room but for a single engrossing idea on any given theme. Other parts of the question, parts relating to the controverted *veto*, might belong to the lawful; *the Church's discipline* is not merely the lawful, but *the obligatory*. The question between the Church and the Strathbogie ministers, is not whether the *veto* be a good or a bad law, but whether disobedience to the Church's discipline be a good or a bad action. Unless we confound the *essence* of a thing with the occasion of a thing, we shall read in the disobedience of the Strathbogie ministers, a blow struck at the entire jurisdiction of the Church, — a distinct matter, truly, from the merits of any of her particular ordinances."

An assertion followed these sentences which the world will certainly, in the long-run, come to understand, or come to the necessity of understanding, viz., the totally distinct nature of the civil and ecclesiastical jurisdictions. In Scotland they had hitherto been kept apart in their provinces, "When, about one hundred years ago," continued the Doctor, "the Court of Session were moved for an injunction on the Presbytery of Cupar, to *receive* and *admit*, as the minister of Auchtermuchty, one whom they had just found to be the rightful presentee, they refused to entertain the motion, because relating to a matter which belonged to the internal government of the Church, with which they, the Lords, thought they had nothing to do. It was thus," continued the Doctor, "that they kept clear of the mischief arising from a conflict between the different powers and authorities in the commonwealth. We do not overlook the consideration that while there lies a power in each court to decide between man and man, there must be a power somewhere to decide, or rather to regulate and ordain, between court and court, when a conflict shall have broken out between them. That power lies in the Legislature to which we have been addressing ourselves. We are not willing to be overborne in our principles, or extinguished in our being as a national establishment by the *Court of Session*. We have gone more constitutionally to work. We have been knocking at the door of Parliament, and seeking for adjustment there. We are still hopeful that they will decide this question, otherwise than by an experiment whether on our firmness or our fears. In the meantime, there must be resolute principle on our part, and resolute endurance; and then we shall know what to do when once the Legislature has spoken — whether, on the one hand, they shall keep it possible for conscientious men to work their endowed institute; or if, on the other, they shall charm the heart of Radicals and Voluntaries, by letting the world know that any establishment of theirs implies an utter prostration of the ecclesiastical to the secular power."

The delivery of these sentences — still more the conclusion of the address, which bore more especially on the delinquency of the seven men at the bar, the time-serving nature of whose conduct could be best appreciated by a great heart — was characterized by an indomitable firmness, which only an adequate occasion could fully call forth from this man essentially a philanthropist — an occasion when the welfare of humanity was identified with the interests of his Church and country. Surely nothing is so appalling as goodness when alchymized by men's guilt into a stern severity! Heaven, ere its own awful turning point come, have mercy on those consciences where a good man's voice finds a dread echo! Our friend, with sinking heart, glanced at the men at the bar. Young C — , pale and trembling, grasped the seat before him; beside him another man, of another stamp, was coolly sucking an orange! Some men's consciences it will need the voice of Heaven to awaken.

The Assembly soon after adjourned. Lady Douglas' party went home with her with the intention of returning in the evening. But so intense was the interest excited, that in the galleries, where the public had free admission, numbers of persons kept their seats, which they would otherwise have lost, for eighteen or twenty hours!

The first important speech of the evening was that of Dr. Cook, the leader of the Moderates. It was considered by those who had heard the same ground frequently gone over, dry and stale; but our friend, to whom the whole was new, thought, it would have *read* sensibly, if freed from the monotonous and unimpassioned tones of the speaker. He, in effect took up the converse position to that of Dr. Chalmers, viz, that because the *veto was* a bad law, the disobedience of the Strathbogie ministers to their ecclesiastical superiors was not in this instance a bad act. Being chiefly historical and full of detail, this lengthened speech was destitute of points of prominence.

In reply, a speaker stept forward, whom Miss Legh had not before seen. His step sounded like a challenge, as he overleapt the front bench, and appeared on the platform. His frame was powerful and muscular; his air bespoke a man confident of the justice of his principles, and inflexible in maintaining them. His tone and manner were strongly demonstrative and suited to carry conviction; while in argument he did not fail to seize on the most impregnable point. Miss Legh was for the moment reminded of Luther before the diet at Worms. The main point of his speech now went to traverse the defence in favour of the accused. He undertook to prove three points: — "That they had broken the laws and ordinances of their Church; that they had broken their ordination vows; and that they had been guilty of sin against the Lord Jesus Christ." The two first points he demonstrated with a thorough knowledge of the constitution of the Scottish Church; the last was received, as soon as it was announced, by the minority with an outburst of hisses and contempt. That party identifying themselves with the accused, had during the day met the evident wish of the rest of the house to treat the subject in a becoming manner with petty annoyances, with hisses, interruptions, and shouts of laughter. With them it was no very serious business. The language of their conduct was, "We shall keep our temporalities, whatever you may do. *We* undoubtedly shall not risk this, to us the most momentous concern in life." The speaker, however — Mr. Cunningham — calmly reiterated his statement. He expressed his feeling that without a deep conviction that these men at the *bar* had been guilty of sin against the *Lord Jesus Christ*, in appealing to a civil tribunal from a Church where the Bible was the statute-book, and Christ the sole Head — he could not conscientiously vote for their deposition.

In reply, as the proper opponent of Cunningham, came forward Robertson of Ellon; decidedly the ablest man of his party, and listened to with a corresponding attention. His voice, strong, ringing, and harsh, was not unpleasing; nor were his gestures repulsive, though uncouth, because they had in them somewhat of the truthfulness of power. It was his wish, evidently, to stand aloof from his coadjutors, in good sense and sentiment, as well as in oratory. He saw well where the proprieties lay, and strove hard to avoid whatever should seem to offend against good taste. Apologizing for the reception which the most solemn charge of his opponent had met with from his party, he rested his defence for the accused on the supposition that they might have continued their ecclesiastical functions, in respect of a *secret* appeal to the great Head of the Church, against a sentence of suspension which they felt to be unjust; and that, in virtue of this appeal, and not any assumption of the keys by a civil court, they had persevered while suspended in preaching and dispensing divine ordinances. To reply to this plea so plausibly urged, there rose up the ablest Scotch lawyer of his time —- one of the most devoted friends of the Church Reformers. It was Alexander Dunlop, the author of a law-work which had already become of standard authority in the superior civil court of his country — a very rare thing in law during the life-time of an author. At once he negatived Mr. Robertson's argument by simply reading a clause of the defence brought forward by the accused, in which they stated that there was no charge brought against them of any act done by them in violation of the orders of the General Assembly, while such order was binding on them by the law of the land, or *before* the supreme civil authority had interposed against the execution of such order or sentence. "Their defence, therefore," said Mr. Dunlop, "amounted to this: 'We have violated our sentence of suspension, because we had the authority of the civil courts so to do' " And now came on the supreme annoyance of a representative assembly, viz., that numerous inferior members, afraid of remaining unheard till the discussion came to a close, rose up "to exonerate their consciences," and exhaust the patience of the house. The clock struck two of the morning. Many of the audience above had remained immovable from the early part of the previous day, and their impatience became uncontrollable.

The six brethren came in, and placed themselves at the bar, which gave promise of a close to the proceedings. None of them had been present since the commencement of Mr. Cunningham's speech. A — of R — , at the request of the advocate who accompanied them, began to read a written document prepared in their defence. Scarcely had he begun, when an officer approached the table for the keys of the house, announcing that Dr. Chalmers and a party of gentlemen waited for admission outside the door. A slight interruption was thus occasioned, and Mr. A — was requested again to begin his defence. His manner of reading was bold and uncompromising. He might have been mistaken for another gentleman of the law. His defence seemed mainly to rest on the statement that they, the accused, had not been the original moving agents in the part they had acted. They did not deny that the civil courts could only receive, and could never originate, causes. Who, then, had stirred up that court to assume its attitude of collision with the orders of Assembly? Mr. Edwards, it would seem, the presentee to Marnoch, had procured those stringent injunctions under which they had acted! Our friend could not help considering this a strange line of defence. If appeal to a foreign court really constituted in this Church a high ecclesiastical offence, it must have been in itself an essential delinquency, for which the parties at the bar, not suspended at the time from their ministerial functions, ought to have refused to grant this presentee ordination. But to these injunctions, although thus unlawfully procured, they stated that their consciences compelled them to yield implicit obedience!

This address being finished, the motion for deposition was put into the hands of one of the oldest and most influential of the clergy present. But at this moment, Dr. Chalmers and his party, who had kept back in the passage, in order not to interrupt the proceedings, came forward. The announcement of the officer had not been generally heard, so that his sudden appearance had all the effect of surprise. A burst of applause resounded through the house, especially from the gallery of the students, whose enthusiasm for their professor knew no bounds. It was met with a storm of hisses hurled at the venerable head of Chalmers from the partisans of the accused. Both at length subsided, as all applause or censure of men finally must, and then the important motion on which hung the future fate of the Church of Scotland, was put into the hands of one whose heart was intent chiefly on one sentence of approbation — "Well done, thou good and faithful servant." Two or three there were in the party of the reformers, who at this momentous crisis felt appalled at the step about to be taken, which they saw might involve to them the loss of all worldly things. These, under the plea of conscience, sought to gain the ear of the house, but impatience was by this time wound up to intolerance, and cries of. "Vote, vote" and "Question, question," became imperative. A new division on the deposition was agreed upon by both parties as unnecessary, seeing that a majority had already voted for the relevancy of the libel. A prayer was offered up; and then the moderator, Dr. Gordon — a man of mild and venerable appearance, of fine feature and lofty forehead, and a true representative of the noble and simple-minded pastors of the Scottish Church — pronounced with solemn voice that sentence which left seven men to such strength in the exercise of their ministry as the civil power might afford them, and threw the Church, whose best nourishment had ever been blood and prayers and tears, once more for her support on the arm of the Omnipotent!

"It has been a hard struggle to-day — a determined conflict" remarked Miss Legh to General Maitland, as they returned at three of the morning in Lady Douglas' carriage to Ainslie Place. "Do you not think it is natural to look for *rest* in a true Church? should it not be an emblem of heaven?" "What kind of *rest*?" asked General Maitland. "Peace, — unity, — love." "Yes," replied the General, "rest is all the Christian's desire, and all the Churches' hope. But it must be rest achieved. A pure heart cannot *rest* in iniquity — a pure Church cannot *rest* in impurity; and while there are so many hostile forces brought to bear outwardly and inwardly on Christians and Churches, how shall there be rest complete and absolute? It will come ;— on earth comparatively — in heaven consummately. In the meantime, while there *are in matters of fact* impurities to be got rid of in this Church, or in that, so long as that impurity is the object of warfare, the *struggle* not the *sleep*, is the symbol of *truth*. 'I am not come to send *peace*' said our Saviour, in that same sense, 'but a sword.' "

Jane remained silent. A new idea had flashed upon her — the beauty of that rest where purity shall be the deep, everlasting joy. It was one of those lights which God vouchsafes when he is training a favoured child. She thought that even now she tasted, understood the heavenly rest. It made her prostrate herself as a creature before the infinite Creator. She parted from General Maitland absorbed in the idea. She heard his footstep in the room over hers — that in which Julia slept. He had the habit of going, at whatever hour he might come in, to kiss the child, and bid her a silent good-night. These sounds, those footsteps, used to trouble our friend, partly with dear and sad remembrances — partly with an emotion she could not define. To-night they were unheeded; and with her mind full of another than an earthly *rest*, she laid herself down to an untroubled sleep. It was almost the afternoon of the succeeding day ere she appeared down stairs, such had been the exhaustion of the atmosphere in the crowded Assembly; but this was a circumstance to excite but little remark in the family of the Earl of Lentraethen.

CHAPTER XIX

*"Return hameward my heart again,
And byde quhair thou was wont to be,"*
                                    ALEX SCOTT

One of Miss Legh's last visits, before leaving Scotland, was to the cottage of poor Miss Matheson. She had repeatedly been there since the time she had first accompanied Lady Grace, sometimes with one of her cousins, sometimes alone; and at every succeeding visit she felt her first anxiety deepen, and saw more glaringly the heartlessness of leaving a dying creature, with only the frivolities of the world for death and eternity. Of this heartlessness she did not accuse her cousins; they did their all to soothe the bodily sufferings of the invalid, and the good they did not perceive, they could not impart. But how should she excuse *herself*? And yet how address herself to the great task of presenting immortal things to an immortal being! She could talk of the *rationale* of religion; she loved to view it in the light of poetry and philosophy; but in this case it was not an outside inspection of religion that was wanted — it was religion itself. How awful this — *I*! a dying creature! — all things *outside* my soul passing away. And that single point in all the coming infinite to which my soul may cling — God the Saviour — he who alone has passed the awful abyss which separates the infinite from the finite — the Creator from the created — good from evil — God from the sinner! Who beside can bear across the shrinking immortal? The greater these thoughts became to Jane's mind, the more diffident she became of her task; for this poor Miss Matheson, with her plays, and her cards, and her dress — a new piece of dress continued to delight her hugely for a few moments — seemed to want some sense wherewith to comprehend the spiritual. At length it occurred to her, that *God's Word* might speak for itself; that this Word, as it flowed from Christ's lips or the pen of inspiration, *ought* to possess in itself the power of awakening the sleeping or the dead sense. It was as a matter of simple faith, then, in the power of that Divine Word that, one morning, she put a small Bible into her reticule, lest one might not easily be found at the cottage; and that when she found Miss

Matheson somewhat composed, she timidly asked permission to read out of it a little. Miss Matheson almost shrieked with surprise, telling her visitor it was a cruel thing thus to remind her that she was dying. Jane, however, persuaded her that she herself studied the Scriptures, although she was in perfect health, and so gained permission to read a single chapter. She chose that in which, towards the close, it is said: "Come unto me, all ye that labour and are heavy laden, and I will give you *rest.*" The word was full of meaning to her own ear. "*Rest!*" repeated the invalid in a querulous tone, "I find no rest night nor day — who can give *me* rest?" Jane fixed on her an anxious and moistened eye. She laid her hand, gently on the arm which lay outstretched on the couch, and repeated in a tone of tenderness the hallowed name — "Jesus." In that one word she felt that she had become, for the first time, a missionary of the blessed Cross.

When she next saw Miss Matheson, she had the pleasure of hearing her ask to be read to; and on this account she repeated her visits the oftener, till by degrees a sense of the spiritual did seem to arise in the poor dying one's mind; but it was not in the form of *rest*. She complained that the Bible made her dissatisfied with herself, and said it would have been better for her to be let alone. "God," thought Jane, recalling the lesson she had learnt, "may give *purity* first, or at least a sense of it, and then he will give *peace*." However, she did not leave Miss Matheson, when she saw her for the last time, in possession of that rest she had so longed to procure for her; but she left her with an *apprehension* of it; which was doubtless a marvellous renovation in such a mind as hers. "Do you think," said Miss Matheson, with an anxiety which seemed to make her forget her sufferings, "that the Saviour will give *me* rest?" "He himself has awakened a desire for it," replied Jane, "and it is HE who has promised it to those who come to him. Only, dear Miss Matheson, *go* to HIM, and he *will* give it."

And now there was nothing left for our friend but to prepare in earnest for turning her steps towards her own desolate home. She had not yet written to her house-keeper or steward to fix the day upon which they should be ready to receive her; and for that purpose she chose a forenoon when the Maitlands were paying a visit to a gentleman's seat in the neighbourhood whither she declined going.

She sat down to her task in a boudoir off the back drawing-room — a little retired place, which held only a few books and a single table, but agreeably shaded with rose-coloured drapery, and couched and cushioned around. She began with fortitude, but had not proceeded very far, till her cheek became pale, and her forehead ached. For a few moments she forgot the spirit of meek submission which is one of the noblest lessons of the *creature*, and which, indeed, she had made some progress in learning. "Why," said she to herself, "am I bound, by a stern duty, to these lonely halls which the voice of love may never cheer?" She felt too surely that the mere votary of pleasure could never find a place in her heart; and a cheerless vista of a life unblessed and solitary, and a death-bed which only menials should surround, rose to appal her. " Oh!" she said, "but for one sister or one brother's voice to welcome me, and I might be happy." But a nearer than any earthly friend was with her, to strengthen her heart — and the tide of bitterness receded. A life spent for *herself* alone, whose only aim and object should be to exalt herself, seemed still more appalling; and there, among the sweet woods and glades of Chesterlee, where the hours of her childhood had been passed, was the sphere which her Creator — her Father in heaven, as she ventured to think — had assigned her! The friendly voices of her own home-born peasantry seemed to greet her. Once more she was about courageously to resume her task, when, looking up, she beheld General Maitland! She could not suppress an exclamation of surprise; for he, of all others, was the one whom in that hour she had least wished to see, and she had thought him gone from home with the others. He had stood unobserved at the open door for two or three minutes, and it had troubled him to hear the heavy sighs which swelled the bosom of his young friend, and to see her beautiful head droop like a broken flower. He sat down uninvited on the couch, while a flush came over Jane's cheek. She felt inclined to go away, and made a movement for that purpose. "Oh, do not go," said the General, in a voice gentle and kind — too fascinating, alas! for her; "let us converse for a little once more. You are preparing to leave us?" Jane replied in the affirmative. "You will visit the Duke of — ?" "Perhaps so." "You will then go to court, and will form a splendid *parti*?" "Oh, I care not where I go," said Jane, in a voice of suffering. "What should it signify to any human being but myself?" The General looked at her with that penetrating gaze whose deep, sad tenderness had first touched her. He saw her flitting colour and agitated bosom. *Could* there be in that emotion one thought of him? He had placed her previous dejection to the score of the remembrance of her bereavement, stirred by the thoughts of home; but what should mean this flitting hectic, which her hand, shading her face, and her drooping ringlets, only half concealed? Could it be? A thrill of strange pleasure quivered in his heart. "Jane," said he, "my cousin, my dearest friend, is there anything I can do to make your way easier, for however short a-time? Ah! I feel that I have too often sought your converse — your presence. But how should I presume to offer to you a shrine of withered hopes and affections? The heart which should unite itself to yours, ought to be as fresh as your own. It should never have felt, that if to cease to beat were the result of a wish, it should have possessed no strength to resist that wish of doom!" He looked at the lovely being before him with more intensity of suspense than he thought any earthly thing could have again inspired him with. No sound gave him intelligence or hope. Perhaps, if at that moment she had spurned him from her, Frederick Maitland would but have continued his earthly journey as he had done before, with heart often pained and weary, but with eye fixed upon heaven. He looked at his cousin during a few long seconds, whose measure his pulses *did* tell, while her face was yet more shaded, and her silken lashes were closed upon her cheek. So low was earthly hope within him, that it was already beginning to fade — the flitting fire was already passing away, and he had said to himself, "Courage; these pangs which I ought not to feel will soon be over," when Jane's timid glance, like the twilight of the summer heaven, met his own. It expressed pity, reproach, and love. In another moment she was clasped to his heart. And her tears, agonizingly repressed, found vent *there* — where she had least expected they should — on the bosom of her friend. Frederick, on his part, felt, almost with fearfulness, that elasticity of the human heart which springs back to its first freshness and vigour, like a bow bent, for however long a time.

"Ah!" said Jane, again timidly raising her eyes, while a smile beamed through her tears, "it is not in this way I would have chosen to answer you; but since my pride has been so humbled, I will not again take refuge in it." "No, no," said Frederick, as he drew her closer to his breast, "let us give pride to the winds; *take refuge here, beloved.*"

CHAPTER XX

"Herein the device of King Henry VII, was profound and admirable; in making farms and houses of husbandry of a standard — i.e., maintained with such proportions of land unto them as may breed a subject to live in convenient plenty. And no servile condition."
                                                                    BACON

It was on a glowing afternoon of high midsummer, that General Maitland and his young bride approached in a travelling carriage the stately domains which the lady hailed as her own hereditary possessions. And with joy mingled with profound emotion she pointed out to him a little rivulet running through the copse at the foot of a natural ha ha as the boundary of Chesterlee in that direction. To gratify her feelings, the General stood up to survey the prospect. He had none of that littleness which would depreciate the value of these new acquisitions lest he should seem to admit that *he* was enriched by them, nor did he at all suspect that Jane viewed them in that light. Where he loved, he trusted freely and fully. If suspicion of woman's nature had ever cast a shadow over his mind, it had vanished with the noon-day of the brighter affection which had burst so suddenly forth. The clear light of that love was now upon him — the spiritual smile and eye of his bride were there; and what, after all, were so many square miles of rich English land to these? At that moment he felt with thrilling intensity that were such miles multiplied by thousands, they could not form the paltriest measure for the measureless riches of a union like his. This feeling might have induced him to look with indifference on slope and field and copse; but that, in present circumstances, would have been selfish too; he therefore extolled with apparent, nay, with real, delight all that he passed. "What magnificent wood!" he exclaimed, as they came in sight of a noble slope of oaks which bordered some rich pasture-land, "I do not think there can be finer in England." "Ah!" said Jane, standing up likewise to gaze on that well-known friendly scene; "even you cannot know what I feel for those old giant oaks. How their great arms do fling themselves abroad as if in enjoyment of this glorious sun-light! If there was anything my dear, dear father used to be proud of besides his cottages and his poor little girl, it was these oak trees." Her husband perceived, as she spoke, that her cheek grew pale, and that she trembled. He took her arm in his, in order to lend her support. "*Thank God for this*" said she, as she accepted it, looking in his face with beaming gratitude. "Yes, dearest," he replied, "let us *thank God*; — while we hold all his gifts, even each other, as infinitely, oh how infinitely! inferior to himself!"

The beauties of the country through which they were passing opened up at every step more and more. Everything was in a condition of superb cultivation — everything most luxuriant in its kind — corn-fields, wood, and above all, abundant pasturage. The singularly fine cattle which reposed under the trees, or refreshed themselves by standing up to the middle in shady pools, added not a little to the picturesqueness of the scenery. But what struck General Maitland as most peculiar to the spot, was the number and aspect of the cottages. They were all built in the choicest nooks upon the slopes of the pasture-ground, beside the streams or rivulets, or under the shade of wood-crowned knolls. Each had its fragrant garden, and the larger ones their outhouses and court behind, seeming, from the sounds that issued from those within ear-distance, to be abundantly stocked with their appropriate feathered and four-footed species. The cottages themselves varying somewhat in architecture, in order to avoid a disagreeable sameness, seemed to possess all the accommodation necessary for comfort, though not for ostentation. Latticed windows, peeping through the ivied roofs, intimated that there were upper chambers, which left one apartment, at least, to be devoted to the enjoyment rather than to the necessities of life, and its window sometimes thrown up to admit the fresh breath of roses and honeysuckles, permitted the traveller to see, when close upon the road, that the hand of taste had not been unemployed within. The faces of sweet English girls, and of busy matrons, were occasionally seen through the shrubberies — the noisy play and laughter of happy children fell sweetly on the ear — the sound of which, however, frequently ceased as the carriage came into view; for it was at once surmised who it contained, and the quick flight of the romping boy or the light gliding figure of his half-grown sister, seemed to be on the errand of proclaiming breathlessly to the household and out-workers on the farm, that the *Lady* was passing by.

It had been the express wish of the latter that no *public* demonstration should be made on her arrival; but that it should be in all respects as private as possible. "I see," remarked General Maitland, "that there are no farm-houses of a superior class to those of which we have already passed so many!" "No, not a single one," replied Jane, "on the whole of our estate. These are the kind of tenantry whom my father said he could love, and who could love him in return. After all, it is a disagreeable intercourse (is it not?) which one would have with the high class farmers. We can scarcely visit them on terms of equality, and it would be ruinous to them if we did; so their pride is always on the alert, and the slight intercourse between us is constrained and unpleasant. How different it has always been here! Each of those farms, and even labourers' cottages, seems to me like a new home. And what an event it was when we used to call and partake of their fare! I cannot call it *humble* fare, for it was always the very best of its kind. As great a happiness it surely was for us as for them. The sons of our own tenants always had the first choice of the vacant farms, and in sending the other sons into the world, my father gave his advice, and if possible his assistance, so that the manor-house became the place of resort in all times of difficulty. My dear father said he was determined to banish pauperism and misery from at least one estate in old England!"

"Are there any manufactories in the neighbourhood?" inquired General Maitland. "Yes, several." "And did they not create pauperism?" "Not to any extent. My father made a point of visiting the manufacturers on terms of friendship. He said he did not know why any foolish pride of aristocracy should keep the two greatest national interests apart from each other. The proprietors he considered but the stewards of the national prosperity in one form, and the manufacturers in another, no less important. So you can scarce conceive what an influence he exerted over the minds of those gentlemen-manufacturers with whom he considered himself connected. I believe they have always exerted themselves sincerely for the comfort and respectability of their people in every department, and papa considered their vicinity a great blessing, because they furnished employment to the surplus labouring population. And our people had always the first offer of employment. Their happy homes were at hand, which was a kind of guarantee for good conduct." "Ah!" said General Maitland, "would that we had a nation of such legislators as Sir Arthur! I have been doing what I could with my people, but cannot show such external results, owing to the want of adequate wealth, which is surely a great blessing when husbanded for the good of our fellow-creatures." "My father," said Jane, "certainly did possess the vantage-ground of a sufficiency of wealth; and he constantly impressed my mind with the idea, that it was in no ways difficult to maintain an *accumulating* wealth without racking or burdening the tenantry. He bade me consider the first symptoms of embarrassment in the rent-payers as the commencement of my own embarrassments, and therefore to maintain their prosperity even at a temporary sacrifice. For that reason he took care that his displeasure *never* fell on misfortune, but always on careless or immoral conduct." "That maxim of the welfare of landlord and tenant being the same, is yet but half understood," said General Maitland, "although it has been hackneyed into selfishness; and on the selfish principle it never can be fully developed. Nevertheless, it is most true; for as the laws of the great Creator never contradict themselves, a true beneficence and a true policy mutually protect each other."

The massive turrets and balconies of the manor house at this moment became visible, outlined as they seemed against a gorgeous tapestry of clouds amidst which the sun was sinking with broad red disc. It was a residence truly baronial, of which each succeeding baron, as he held his mortal tenure of it, in the course of past centuries, had added screen or court, tower or balcony, as his convenience or fancy directed; and sometimes, as it might be, at the suggestion of the high and courtly dames who had been led hither to their bridal home. The lawns, gardens, and deer park, were disposed so as to have the most imposing effect from the windows of the mansion, and the avenue into which the carriage of its possessors now entered might have vied, in the beauty of its ancient trees, with that of royal Windsor. In a state of half-sad, half-delighted repose, the lady of the manor was reclining over the side of her carriage, recalling the far distant time when these very trees had first awakened a sense of the beautiful in her mind, and the many times since that, in company with her beloved father, she had seen them pass thus in review between her and the clear heaven in all their varied forms of grace and magnificence, — when she became aware that a small group of her tenantry and pensioners in the more immediate neighbourhood had assembled, notwithstanding the orders of the steward, to greet her arrival. Giving three hearty cheers on the approach of the carriage, they were about to depart, as if uncertain how the intrusion might be taken, when Jane, rising hastily, begged the coachman to stop. The familiar faces of her people had awakened still warmer emotions in her heart than those of the old trees. "I must speak," she said "to my friends. Thank heaven, I am not a queen, to pass through my dominions in solemn state."

No sooner was it perceived that General Maitland had stepped from the carriage, and had offered his hand to assist his lovely bride, never so lovely as when following the warm impulses of her heart, than a cheer of more than the old English heartiness once more awakened all the echoes around the ancient barony, and made the high arches overhead quiver as if to the rushing breeze. Jane walked up to the group leaning on her husband's arm, and addressed to them a few kind words in that sweet thrilling voice whose tone could have commanded silence from a much ruder audience. "I could not pass you, my old friends," said she, "without just asking how you were, and how it was all with you." "It is exactly like your Ladyship — God bless your sweet face; it is the sweetest sight we have seen since you went away; and God bless your noble husband!" were the exclamations which burst from many voices. "And you are here Mrs. Field, and have brought your family with you," said Jane, patting the head of a rosy boy, who looked up with awe and wonder in her face. "Only the two youngest, my Lady," said the woman; "they were born since you went away." "What! this baby in your arms, and that stout little fellow running by your side? Ah, these are the chronicles of time. And Dame Jones, how have you been?" "But tolerably," said an old woman, who strove to hide her tears with the corner of her shawl "I have buried my sweet daughter as was ages with yourself, and was called after your blessed mother. But I'll tell you all about it when you come to see my poor cottage; which I hope you will, as in the old times." "Indeed I will," said the lady, and then we shall have a talk, as of yore. I am sorry it should be about the death of Lucy Jones, the sweetest girl in all the country round. And you, farmer Thomas, I am glad to see you looking so well." "Why not speak up Joe!" said a dark-eyed lively help-meet, looking in the goodman's face, now suffused with an honest blush, but not the less of pleasure. "There is he, quite dumb, ma'am, who has said every night for the last year and a-half, that the sun didn't shine as it used to do, and that the manor-house looked so dead-like, it made him sigh as he followed his plough." "Well, my little fellow," said Jane, addressing a very fine boy of ten years old, "you shall be my assistant-steward, and shall help to invite all these good people, and as many more as you please, to dine this day-week on the lawn before the manor;" and with smiles and kindly greetings, General Maitland and his lady took farewell of the party; and having re-entered the carriage amid cheers and blessings, in a few seconds more they reached their home.

The hall door stood open, and the housekeeper, an elderly woman, of tall and lady-like appearance, waited to receive them. She had acquired a considerable degree of stateliness, amounting to formality, during the long period of her matronship and absolute superintendence over the household affaire of the manor. Not so the old butler, who had held his post for even a longer term. A kind soft-hearted old man was he, who came forward to welcome his lady as fast as his not very active limbs would permit him; nor would he allow any hand but his own to put down the steps of the carriage. "Our good old servant, Philips," said Jane, holding out her hand to the faithful creature, as her heart swelled with the recollection that he only was there to meet her as the representative of her ancient house. The servants were drawn up in line in the hall, to receive their lady and the new master. They had all been in the house at Sir Arthur's death, and Jane had a word of remembrance for each. But as a footman and a page were about to precede them, in order to usher them into the best drawing-room, which Mrs. Wilks had carefully decorated for the occasion, Jane called them back. "Philips will attend us to-day," she said, — "to the western gallery." Philips, with a look of gratitude, which silently thanked his mistress for the kind distinction, led the way, and with a fervent blessing, uttered with hands clasped together, he returned down stairs, while the heiress once more trod the long gallery, which contained the portraits of her ancestors, with the husband in whom now centred all her earthly hopes and wishes; and led him, not without some pardonable pride seated on her beautiful brow, through the array of noble knights and ladies, who looked down upon their latest descendant — to the great western window, which opened on a prospect celebrated for its magnificence, and gazing upon which, no association with human misery, in so far as man can prevent it, saddened the hearts of those who knew it best.

"Well" said Mrs. Wilks, addressing Philips, as he re-entered the hall, "if my misses had married any way beneath her — as indeed she might, marrying so far out of the way as Scotland is, which nobody knows — *I* was determined to have taken my leave." "Ah, Mrs. Wilks," replied Philips, "*I* wouldn't have done that. If she had married any how, so as to occasion her a sore heart, she'd have had all the more need of her old servants to comfort her. Sure you wouldn't act so by your own daughter, Mrs. Wilks?" Mrs. Wilks drew herself up, as if she were not sure; but it was a sign which Philips did not understand. "And how should you be less considerate," he continued, "for our lady?" "Oh ho!" said Tom the groom, who had been in the house first as stable-boy, then as groom, for the last fifteen years, but who was nevertheless still a young as well as handsome man, "I know'd my lady better than to suppose she'd ever do such a thing as marry below herself. Yon gemman, if he aint a duke or earl now, will be, I'm sure, one of these days. Didn't I teach her to sit a horse, and was acquainted with her spirit? Bless you, there was'nt a bit of blood in the stable but know'd her hand afore she was ten years old. I wanted to say something of the bay I've been a-breaking in for her, but I hadn't courage. I'll show off his paces this evening, when maybe my lord and she'll come to look about a bit. *I* never feared she'd marry a rush-light or a farthing candle!"

How suddenly, in this world of many-coloured events, possibilities lightly spoken of to-day, and viewed through the haze of distance, may become realities to-morrow! The next morning brought a funeral letter, sealed with a coronet, to Chesterlee, and a few words of grief from Lady Grace Maitland to her uncle. The Honourable General Maitland was Earl of Lentraethen — his beautiful bride already a countess. In Edinburgh, in the home they had left, the rites of a funeral were to follow the festivities of a marriage, at which poor Philip Maitland, the deceased earl, had assisted with unfeigned delight. He was aware of the advantages brought into his family — a vast increase of wealth, and a probability of preventing the title from passing to a stranger, then a remote prospect for him. Alas! he little thought how soon his title, and his estates, and his home, should know him no more. With his friends he left the remembrance of a good-natured smile and a kindly word — not ineffaceable, because they found but few things to recall them; with his tenantry, the memory of sundry good-natured actions, to be enhanced or forgotten according to the nature of the succeeding reign; and with his family a grief, sincere for the time, but not long, deep, or inconsolable. Men must lay hold on more than one element of our natures, in order that their hold shall be permanent.

"I have news, Jane." said the new earl, entering his young wife's dressing-room early on the morning after their arrival — "news which I know will occasion you sorrow. You are already Countess of Lentraethen; my brother is no more; here are a few lines from poor Grace." This seemed more overpoweringly painful to Jane than even her husband had contemplated. She became pale, and appeared ready to faint. "What!" said she, "he who gave me to you with so much parental kindness but so lately?" "Yes," replied Frederick, as he mingled his tears freely with hers, " my ever kind and generous brother. Ah! Jane, do not these titles sound like records of death, rather than records of honour? Other men, who win their way to honourable fame, drop down, one here and one there, and leave upon their tombstones only their own names; but the long line of family honours seems strewed with the bodies of the dead." "To which we," said Jane, "are soon to add our own; yet," she continued after a pause, "we may brighten even this short span of years, with a life for God and our fellow-creatures." "I may be wrong" said her husband; "but I do not feel as if a title would aid us much in that way. I should almost consider this accession as unmixed evil, were it not that the estates are not entailed, and that I think my brother's family will not suffer pecuniary loss. I must leave you, dearest, it may be for a fortnight, that I may look after the funeral of poor Philip, and do what I can for your cousins, whom I know you love. You will not grudge me that time?" "You know," said Jane, fresh tears starting, "that I shall not be the happier without you; but I should be selfish indeed to wish to detain you from such duties."

The travelling carriage was again ordered, with fresh horses, which were, however, only to proceed to the nearest post town, whence the Earl meant to go on by the mail, as the speediest conveyance. Jane busied herself in writing letters of tender sympathy to her cousins, perhaps without adverting to the circumstance, that their grief might be less poignant than her own, when she had experienced a similar bereavement. She thus found a stimulus and a vent for those feelings which her home-coming had so deeply stirred. She prepared likewise little presents for Julia, whom she begged her husband to bring back with him on his return. "What happiness," said she, "would it be for me now to have her with me in your absence!" This, however, he gently declined, saying, that till they became more settled, he considered her better in her accustomed residence with her bonne. And now, as the sound of the carriage wheels approached, Jane felt an anguish not to be accounted for solely by the primary cause of their grief. She considered the absence, for even so short a time, of the husband in whose being she began too much to live, as in itself too dear a price to pay for a coronet. But even hereby was she reminded of the attraction of the heart to creature-worship. *Self*-worship she had long renounced in sincerity, at least, if not in perfection; for who of fallen man can say that he is absolutely purified from that primary and most subtle evil of the human heart, which appals, by its vigorous life, when it had been thought long withered at the root! But creature-worship! still base, if not so degrading! This was the thought which penetrated the young Countess, as the sound of the wheels died away upon her ear. "0 God." said she, with clasped hands, as she retired to the privacy of her own closet, "how seldom is that highest and holiest act of the soul rendered to thee, with that involuntary fervour with which we render it to a fellow-being! Give me, oh! give me, that humbling yet most exalting worship of thee, in the inward life of my spirit, which cannot feel that solitude where thou art. Draw me, draw me to thyself; for thou only art my eternal home!"

As for the Earl, he stepped into his carriage with feelings certainly of no great elation. His absence from his beloved wife now, when he knew how much she needed his presence, was not what he would have desired. And the dead body of an affectionate brother awaited him at the termination of his journey. But it was not a new thing for him to find that the world was not his resting-place, and he had not even yet forgotten it. Perhaps no small share of the feelings of exultation excited by the accession of honour which had already begun to be whispered among the domestics, were concentrated within the heart of Tom the ostler, as he rode the leader, very much as if a coronet had just fallen on *his* brows. The proudest day of Tom's life was certainly that in which he put up the *Earl's* carriage in the stable-yard of the inn at — , until he himself had had his gossip, and the horses their feed. That which, of all things else, he took credit for to himself, was his prediction of the previous day. "He wasn't an earl yesterday," said he to his audience, "and yet I seed it writ on his brow, as soon as ever he stept across the hall door. Bless your hearts, he had all the marks on 'em. A step such as you observed — remarkable fine teeth (Tom was an adept in teeth, from his experience in horses') — a smile to draw one, and an eye to keep one at a distance. Though, to be sure," continued Tom, lowering his voice, as if making a humiliating concession, for he was a great stickler for blood in men as well as horses, "I have seen some of 'em lords, as I'd have made a better one myself — if I'd been bred to the profession, I mean, of course."

CHAPTER XXI

"It is a poor centre of a man's actions, himself; it is right earth."
BACON

Our young Countess, however, determined not to yield herself up to the indolence of sentiment. Much as she longed for the restoration of that communion — that fusion of self into the being of another — longed for too often, alas! in vain, by all sensitive hearts, as the true elixir of life — for it is, indeed, the shadowing forth of the spirit's immortal destiny — she remembered, and the absence of her lord served to recall the lesson — that, after all, the staple happiness of existence must consist in active usefulness — in the forwarding, in some measure or other, of a great and good end. Of all ends, she imagined she had found the greatest and the best, and she determined that, with the divine aid, she would not let it slip. This she felt was a critical time, and she even thanked God for that separation which recalled her to her nobler destiny; for she became aware that the most seducing temptation to self-ministering comes to a heart like hers through some of its best and holiest affections — affections not assuredly to be renounced, but as surely to be guarded against as the *summum bonum* of existence.

Besides all this, she began to feel a considerable accession of uneasiness with regard to her tenants, as to how much they might have actually felt the loss of the fostering hand to which they had been accustomed, and as to the manner in which the person, hastily selected in a moment of distress, as land-steward, might have fulfilled his duties. It was then with some anxiety that, having ordered a pony phaeton, she set out, before inspecting her own grounds, to pay a series of forenoon visits to her tenants. Everywhere she was received with an enthusiasm which knew no bounds. There had, indeed, she found, arisen many misunderstandings in her absence, and some harshnesses, too, which grieved her deeply; but these were related more in joy than sorrow, for the sight of her face, as was truly said, already half removed every heart-burning. "The dear young creature, and I must call her so, countess though she be," said a young farmer to his wife, as the phaeton drove away from his door, "she has grown taller, as well as handsomer, since she went away." He drew, as he spoke, a fair-haired girl closer to his knee, caressing her more than his wont, as if the visit of the lady had rendered even his children dearer to him. "Yes, John," said his wife, with the reflection of the same delight in her face, "and you know she very well may, for she wasn't eighteen when she left — that is just the age I was when I married you, and you know I grew a great bit afterwards." "I know that, Ellen, well enough — you grew after your first baby; but aint our lady much older like too, for all she is handsomer? Yet it aint years of age, but of thought, she has got added to her somehow, dear creature. Perhaps the lessons that her father gave her, and that she had to learn by rote, have got into her nature!"

What do not our selfish land-owners — they who herd together in large towns, that they may rival each other in folly and vice — what do they not lose? The showers that first ascend to heaven, from lake, and sea, and stream, return again to make the earth verdant; but the draughts which great men make on their country's resources, return not to foster the land and its inhabitants. They are lost in the desert wastes of fashion and folly, or they fall on the barren, stony places of self-ministry. Such wealth ought to be made by machinery which not a human hand should touch! Grind, grind, grind with its iron teeth! What then? All human beings but *the few* should die of extinction! Men should not be crushed into worms! A thousand victims need not be made, that one miserable man might offer himself up at the shrine of his own depravity!

Yet, notwithstanding the fulfilment of her temporal duties, something else there was which pressed from day to day on the spirits of our young Countess, and brought a shade on her brow, as she renewed her intercourse with her old tenantry. Health, happiness, and blessings saluted her. The grievances which she met with were easily redressed; everywhere she found blooming gardens, flourishing fields, and pleasant faces; yet it was even these which spoke sadness to her, as ever and anon the words came, ringing in her ear: *"Man shall not live by bread alone, but by every word that proceedeth out of the mouth of God."* Here was the life by bread in its perfection and fulness; here was the life, too, by many of the sweetnesses of humanity; but where was the higher life, enkindled by the Divine Spirit, drawing its nourishment from the Divine Word? She had begun to hope that it glowed, however feebly, within her own breast; but around her she felt it not — she found it not; and she feared that the light was darkness. Often did her thoughts return to the hut on the Highland mountain, where, kneeling on the earthen floor beside the bed of the dying, she had heard old Samuel pour his sublime prayer into the ear of the Omnipotent, and where she had become first conscious, for a time, of the sweetness of approaching Deity, through the divine way, the lovely humanity of a Saviour. There had she first seen communion with God in purity, without the interposition of man, under any form or pretext, between man's spirit and the Father of life. And as she contrasted the poverty, the all that contributed to the self-negation, of those distant peasantry with the rich Epicureanism around her — she felt how much she loved the heavenly light which illuminated their bleak mountain-tops, and that could all her wealth have purchased it for her people, she would have thought it but a feather's weight in the balance; — yet well she knew that it was vouchsafed only to the prayer of the humble and contrite heart.

It was on the fifth day after her return home, that, having taken an early breakfast, the beauty of the morning tempted her to take a stroll by the deer-park, where for some time she watched with pleasure the graceful herd trooping from place to place, or the young reposing by the sides of their mothers in the sunlight — their shadows pictured on the soft sward beside them. A shaded rivulet ran close by, humming its grateful murmur; and our young Countess thought of tracking its course, as she had many a time done in days of yore, as far as the pauper village, close by which it took its course. This village was not *called* pauper, inasmuch as there were no marks of pauperism in or about it; it was simply termed Leetown, and was in truth one of the loveliest spots in the whole neighbourhood.

When, after a walk of about a mile beneath the nut trees and shrubbery which almost concealed the little bubbling stream, Jane came again into the sunlight, and stood upon the rustic bridge, on the other side of which the village lay in its bright seclusion, she stopped for a few minutes to contemplate it, while a gush of that peculiar love came over her heart, which a parent feels for the most impotent or helpless of his offspring, who receives as a blessed compensation for his helplessness an additional supply of sympathy from its parent's bosom with the additional succour it requires. Leetown was a little pet spot, like the pleasant suburb of some larger place. It consisted of a single long street of dwarf cottages, of two apartments each, with small flower-plots in front, and patches of vegetable ground behind; and sweeter flowers or more luxuriant creepers there bloomed not in the whole country than those within the trellis-work of these tiny flower-beds, and around these humble porches. And then there were the great sheltering trees at the back, which formed a kind of awning from heat or shower, peopled by a busy and noisy tribe of rooks, without whom the village would seem to have lost half its population. At the farther extremity there was a gentle wooded eminence, full of rustic benches, with here and there an arbour, the little memorials which invalids had formed for themselves from time to time; all which made a spot more delightful for the aged and sick to repose in, and forget their sorrows, than the perfumed and cushioned chambers of the suffering great.

And what a history this village had in all its shifting personalia! Ah, it was a living book for young high hearts in mansion and hall to come and study out of, and draw the blessed life of sympathy and gentle thoughts from, as Jane herself had done. There, in that cottage, with a peculiar breed of doves hovering about the roof, was the old widow who had outlived all her family, and who took charge of the idiot boy. And he, in his turn, took charge of the little orphaned child who lived next door with its aged grandmother. There he was even now romping with it, in rude and yet tender gambols, in the avenue behind the gardens — now laying it down on the soft sward among the daisies and buttercups, and now tossing it up towards the rooks' nests in the high trees, to which it stretched its arms and lisped out its little speech, and the rooks answered in their noisy gibberish; while the idiot leapt and frisked almost like the uncouth young of some kindly-natured animal that has a glimmer of reason in it. Then out before their cottage doors, seated in their arm-chairs, were many invalids inhaling the breath of the flowers and the fragrance of the morning. These mostly came from the neighbouring factories, and consisted of such as had lost their relatives; for if the homes of kindred had been open to them, they would naturally have preferred their love to the care of strangers. But they wanted for little, unless those wants were of the heart. The poor are proverbially kind to each other, if their feelings are not blunted by vice; and here were many growing boys and girls, orphaned from various causes, who were both able and willing to render active assistance.

It had been the practice of Sir Arthur, right or wrong, a practice firmly pursued by him, to treat those parents who indulged in degrading vices as having forfeited the rights of nature, and to do all in his power to separate them from their families, by depriving them of employment on his estate; — at the same time providing for the children, and for the mother if she remained virtuous. The father, if he did not choose to wander into some town to earn his subsistence by begging, was sent to a workhouse at some distance, where he was subjected to hard labour; and if reformed, as some times was the case, he was permitted to regain his station only by commencing with the humblest kind of manual employment. And every man, cursed with a wife whose intemperance he could prove, was not only permitted, but encouraged, to send her to the same work-house. Work-houses may be blessings, as Sir Arthur remarked, when provided for the restraint of idleness and vice; but work-houses for the *unfortunate* are nurseries of pauperism and crime. It was seldom that a whole family emigrated from the estate together; the mother seldom failed to avail herself of the advantages of Sir Arthur's protection; and, generally speaking, the separation system acted most favourably for the morality of the tenantry. Such cases were of rare occurrence, and could not fail to leave in the neighbourhood the stamp of disgrace. It is for those already lost that the blight of character and affection has no terror. Sir Arthur was, besides, somewhat austere with regard to the beggary which he said belonged to other people. He provided, indeed, a place where all wanderers might have a night's lodging; for he pitied the wretchedness which had no natural protector. But this caravansary was not in the village, for he feared to infect his own comparatively virtuous poor with those plagues and leprosies which stalk the country in rags; it was at a solitary place near the high-way: and his tenantry, who were thoroughly acquainted with his sentiments on political economy, knew well his antipathy to harbouring vagrants more than a night on his property. However, we digress.

When our friend had satisfied herself with looking on the scene we have described — the little leaf in the daily history of that quiet place — she stepped into the nearest cottage, the door of which stood ajar. It was tenanted by an old woman, whom she thought she remembered as being of somewhat eccentric manners. The doors of both the inner apartments were now shut, and she hesitated whether she should raise the latch. She did so softly, but again softly closed it — for a single glance had been sufficient to show her what was passing within. The old widow, already in her house and person scrupulously clean, was kneeling at a chair, while a large volume lay open on the table beside her. It was evident that she was in solitude maintaining the form of family devotion. Jane's heart beat quicker within her bosom. Even *here* there was one, taught of God himself to worship him in spirit and in truth. Here she might find sympathy. Here was one ray from heaven struggling through the darkness. As she stood she heard a low murmuring voice breaking the silence, and then all was hushed again. At length a movement told her that the widow had finished her morning devotion — that which she had probably once held with those who were gone for ever, but which even in solitude was not deprived of its essential sweetness.

Jane now advanced and accosted the widow, who received her with some surprise, but with that mixture of humility and true dignity which ever *ought* to belong to the Christian character. It is, however, more frequently met with in the humbler walks of life than in other spheres, because *there* fewer points of contact exist between the believer and those around him; his enjoyments are more exclusive, owing to that refinement of taste which Christianity imparts; and thus the outward expression of the inner life is less apt to be rubbed off by intercourse with the world. When the first salutations were over, and Jane had seated herself in the old-fashioned arm-chair, she began to wonder as she looked around her, how it was that she had been in that room so very seldom — scarce, at all for the last seven or eight years. This wonder, she expressed with a regret, that she had seen so little of one who made *that book* — she pointed to the Bible — her companion. The widow's face became lighted up with a smile of uncommon brightness. It was all of unfaded beauty that was left to one who must have possessed in her day an uncommonly fine person. "Yes, my lady," she replied, "I have few other friends left. But, blessed be God, that as the world grows darker, *that book* gets all the brighter; and as the love of others leaves us, the love of Jesus gets warmer and warmer. Sometimes," she continued, "when I bruise some of my garden herbs, and feel the odour that comes out from them, I think that *it needs* affliction to bring out all the hidden sweetness that is in the Word of God." This figure had been often used poetically, as applied to the human heart, though Mary Vans was too devoid of spiritual pride to use it in that sense, and certainly her own similitude was the truest and the best. In all probability, she was ignorant that it had ever been used at all; but there is no one acquainted with the developments of true Christianity, in even the humblest stations, who has not observed how much it is of its essence to develop the elements of poetry and the powers of thought.

Jane replied to the widow's remarks, by expressing a fear that she had had much to suffer. "I have indeed been," said she, "what the world calls very unfortunate; but I sometimes think it is only in heaven that we can truly know *who* has been fortunate or unfortunate in this world. My husband brought me from a neighbouring town, where I was employed in a manufactory, and lived with my aged mother. We took her with us to your farm at Holly Green, where we lived happily for many years. I had there four sons and a daughter; and it used to please me in my vanity to hear it said, that there was scarce such a handsome family in the whole country round. As my boys grew up, every one of them in turn went to sea. Nothing could avail to keep them back; yet they were dutiful, steady boys, and began to rise fast in the navy and merchant service. But within two years tidings came that one and another was taken away, till all were gone. Two died of fever, one was drowned while bathing in an African river, and my oldest" — here the widow shuddered —"was murdered in a dance by a Portuguese sailor, on the coast of South America. As the account was told me by a shipmate, he had taken a girl to dance to whom another man was attached, and without a moment's warning, even in the midst of the revel, the knife entered his back and pierced his heart.

I became stupified; but my husband, who was naturally of a delicate consumptive tendency, sank fast under so many trials. It was strange, that with the news of that cruel murder of our first-born, there should have arrived the sea-chest of the youngest, our fair-haired William; and in that chest, carefully wrapped up in a silk handkerchief, was a Bible, with these words written on it, 'To my mother.' Here it is," continued the widow, taking a common clasp Bible out of a drawer, while her tears began silently to flow. "You may see, dear lady, it is full of pencil marks. I didn't give it him. No, God forgive me! No; I put no Bible in any of my boys' trunks. There was no comfort I could think of forgotten, but that of which they were to have the *real need* — that was never thought of. But God put this Bible into my little William's way. He was but fourteen when he died. Do you see this passage, dear lady, how it is marked in the 3d chapter of Ephesians? 'That you may be able to comprehend with all saints, what is the breadth, and length, and depth, and height, and to *know* the love of Christ which *passeth knowledge*.' The last two words, you see, are lined under. I felt glad that my sweet boy had found enjoyment in the Bible; but it was more because he had some comfort in his last moments, when I was not by to soothe him, than because his soul might, in God's infinite mercy, have been saved. Then the fate of his elder brother would come across me, with some glimmering awful sense of eternity, and ever my troubled mind would return to William's Bible, and the passage marked, till I began to have a restless anxious sense that *there* only I could have peace. I often afterwards pondered on the words, 'The love of Christ which passeth knowledge;' but it seemed to me a strange love that deprived me of all my earthly blessings."

"Blessed be God, I understand it now! My husband, too, would often have me to read out of William's Bible; and he often read out of it himself. He was not a man of many words, but I do think the truth began to shine into his heart. The last words he ever looked at were just these, '*The love of Christ which passeth knowledge*,' and his finger was upon them when he fell into the sleep from which he never awoke. Your noble father proposed that I and my girl, my pretty Alice, should then come here and teach a school, which he thought might be an advantage to the orphan children. We did so, and the school prospered greatly for a time, till Alice began to show signs of her father's disease, and I, in terror and despair, took her away to the town where I was born, to put her under the care of a doctor I had heard highly spoken of there. I spent all the money we had ever saved, and after all returned here, that Alice might linger out a little longer, and then die. It is strange to me that her death should have seemed to come so sudden at last. I was so taken up with tending her, cooking her little food, and helping her to walk out a step, when she could, that I seemed to think all *that*, though it was so sad, was to last for ever. Once, it happened that a minister, I know not of what People — our own Church, a Wesleyan, or Baptist — came in and prayed by her when she was very low. He asked, in passing through the village, whether there were any sick in it; and we never knew his name, but his visit was like that of an angel of mercy to us. I think ever after Alice's soul was more in heaven. Often, when she was able to be out of bed, when we had read together out of William's Bible, she would kneel down on this very spot, and pray aloud with such humility, and such a sense of sinfulness, as seemed wonderful to me, who could see no sin in her; — but who can see God's purity and see *himself* pure! She made me pray by her, too, when I was but like an infant, and did not know the meaning of the words I said. Well, I had to follow my last and best to her grave; and as I heard the stones rattle on her coffin-lid, the words again sounded strangely in my heart, '*The love of Christ which passeth knowledge*;' but I hurried away from that love as if I didn't want it — it grew dark within me."

"I still liked to go every Sabbath morning to the parish church; and I thought that joining in the prayers brought me some ease for the time, and I came away always with a more humble mind, but I didn't get much light from the sermon or the Word of God. It happened that there were some Wesleyans who hired a house at a little distance, and preached in it every Sunday. Your papa didn't hinder them; for he said he never would stand in any one's way who tried to make his fellow-creatures better. I went to this meeting-house, and what do you think the text should be? Why, just the very words which so troubled me, '*The love of Christ which passeth knowledge.*' A great light shone into my understanding as the preacher went on to show what that love was, and how it had been shown; and that trials did not serve to throw any doubt upon it, for that the Captain of Salvation himself having been made perfect through sufferings, much more did his followers need to be perfected by the same means. Ever since that time I have been led on my way rejoicing. Until lately, I have not given up attending at our own church; but oh! I love fellowship with all those who love the Lord Jesus Christ! *That* makes the true Church; for, lady, it is bad to be held by a name. God is a spirit, and it is the *spiritual nature* he looks upon, and not on the differences that men have made."

Jane had listened to the widow's narrative with attention and much sympathy. "How is it, Mary," asked she, "that I have not known you better? How long is it since all this happened?" "Ah," said Mary, "it was when you were no more than a child. You did come two or three times with your noble father to see me, but I fancy he didn't mind much about your coming often; though, I think, if he had lived he would have changed his mind." "What makes you think so, Mary?" asked the Countess. "Because he came by himself pretty often for the quarter before he was taken from us, and he used to want me to speak about religion, and to tell him how the Lord had dealt with me." "And do you think," said Jane, with an emotion which thrilled her heart, "that he *believed* what you said to him?" She fixed her eyes on the widow's face, to scrutinize it earnestly as she replied. "I think, dear lady, that he did not *disbelieve* it," said Mary, after a moment's consideration, as if she were anxious to unite strict truth with what she could of charity and hope. "I think," she continued, "he pondered it deeply in his heart. Often he would leave me with a sigh which would send me to God in prayer. Many a livelong night, when no sleep has come near my eyes, I have spent in prayer for him, and for you too, dear lady. He is now in the hands of Him who cannot err. And *how is it with you?*" The latter query was pronounced in a tone of sober, serious inquiry, and Jane hesitated for a moment before she replied to it. At length, in a low and very humble, but earnest tone, she said, "For me, I hope God has been leading me. I hope he has been teaching me. I see, at least, the necessity of his teaching. Ah, Mary, the world, our own hearts, are repugnant to pure devotion — simple faith. How, then, should that divine light" — she pointed to the Word of God — "burn without a divine power to guard its life within?" Mary covered her eyes with her hand, as if she were offering a silent thanksgiving to the GIVER OF LIFE.

"You said," continued the Countess, "that you have attended the parish church *till lately*. Have you, then, now given up going?" "Yes, my lady," said Mary, composedly. "And why so?" "Because, although I cannot say I had much benefit from the preaching of our last rector, I got no harm from it; but the young man who has come since your ladyship went away, has brought in new customs which make our church look like a *Popish* chapel; and there is a difference in the preaching too, more than I can altogether explain. We didn't hear much about Christ before, but now there is something else put in his place that they call '*The Church*,' which is always put forward instead of the Word of God. '*The servant is not above his Lord*' and when he is, there must be something wrong." The Countess made no reply. She rose, took an affectionate leave of the old woman, who, it touched her to think, had been offering supplications for her immortal welfare, unknown and alone, when no other being had cared for it under a like aspect; and, as she took her way home, she pondered much on the widow's story, and on what she had heard respecting her beloved father. The other information, too, communicated by the old woman, which had not reached her before, required her most serious consideration. Upon the death of the last incumbent, which took place in her absence, the living had been sold, contrary to all former practice with regard to it. It had been long the boast of the lords of the manor that their church-patronage had been unsullied by purchase; but the land-steward, perhaps ignorant of former customs with regard to it, had sold it to the highest bidder, without consulting his lady on the subject.

It was not without extreme pain that the Countess had viewed, during her sojourn in Scotland, that return of her native Church to Popery, which had so rapidly developed itself within that period. Her own religious sentiments had been germinating in precisely an opposite direction; and between the Christianity whose essential nature is an apprehension of sublime and eternal truth, and that other Christianity, or rather semblance of it, consisting chiefly in form and usage — perishable because material — there is an entire antithesis and native antipathy. The young Countess' dislike to Popery was, besides, hereditary. Her father, who was thoroughly conversant with its history, and who had spent much of his early life in close contact with it abroad, invariably expressed his unqualified detestation of it in its every phase; and when asked why he, who was so liberal towards all other forms and sects, should be so intolerant of that, he replied, "simply because he could not tolerate intolerance. There could be no parleying with despotism, but as a preparation for submitting to it." No country, he alleged, could flourish in connection with Rome, either politically or morally. He constantly avowed his opinion that she was the most monstrous anomaly which still flourished on the face of the earth; that she had within her a race of enslaved and degraded priests, reared for the purpose of enslaving and degrading mankind; and that the mainspring of the power which should destroy her might ultimately be found even among those very bondslaves. With these sentiments he had taken pains to imbue the mind of his daughter, and had conveyed to her far more than the general hearsay knowledge of the true character of the Papacy — its crafty duplicity when weak, its exterminating ruthlessness when strong; so that she, when the wolf had entered her fold, albeit in sheep's clothing, felt the necessity of acting with prudence and decision.

  The day following was the Sabbath. As old Philips cleared away the breakfast things, he inquired whether it were her ladyship's pleasure that the carriage should be ordered for church. Jane replied in the affirmative. "There are strange changes there," said Philips lingering, as he was leaving the room; "I don't know that your ladyship will quite like them." "I don't know that I shall, Philips," replied the Countess; "but we shall go and see." The parish church was about three quarters of a mile distant from the manor-house, situated in a spot whose shady retirement was, during the week, scarcely ever disturbed. Its grey walls were mantled with ivy, and, where exposed, were covered with moss and lichen of many a varied shade. The trees around the church-yard were doddered and bent with age, and the tombstones were, many of them, almost buried beneath grass and wild flowers. The morning of this day had been showery, with alternating gleams of sunshine, and the bright herbage and clustering foliage sparkled to the light. As the carriage drove up, colonies of birds innumerable rushed into deeper hiding, scattering the rain-drops in their flight, as if they had been a set of usurpers, instead of the lawful inhabitants of the place, and were now fearful of a surly summons to quit. The young Countess gazed with a yearning interest at the well-remembered windows, with the swallows twittering in their lintels; — their laurets and trefoils had been recently stained in red, and brown, and blue; in the oriel, a mass of cloud was besprinkled over with bright yellow stars. She could not help feeling some contempt for this as a piece of taste. It looked like the garish art of man, introduced into the chaste, still sanctuary of nature. And in the interior of the church things were still more changed. Jane scarce recognised any part of it but her own pew, which, with its old escutcheons and hangings of crimson and gold, still remained, as she had last sat there in the deep distress of recent bereavement. And now, with spirit changed and awakened, she knelt on the spot where her father had used to kneel, and vowed, amid her falling tears, that she would, by the grace of God, tread in that dear father's footsteps, so far as they had followed the *Sacred Word*; and that as more light on that Word was given her, she would follow it as the symbol of the divine presence, if it led into the paths of holiness and peace.

The voice of the clergyman broke upon her ear: "*The sacrifices of God are a broken and a contrite spirit; a broken and a contrite heart, O God, thou wilt not despise*" Here, at least, were the accents of her Father in heaven; and they fell gratefully on her heart, as she still kept kneeling, her face buried on the pew. But the spell was broken. The organ gave its first peel, and she stood up to join in the psalm. The people were but thinly scattered. They had ceased to take any part in the "grave, sweet melody" of the sanctuary, and there was an utter want of sacred feeling — almost of propriety — in the shouting of the half-dozen chorister boys who chanted the service, making occasional wry faces to each other; while the organ, fine as were its tones, seemed but a soulless thing. And now, when forced unwillingly to break the sweet, short communion she had just held with her God, the figments of Popery below met the Countess' gaze with a double repulsion. Above the altar, there was a copy of the Transfiguration; on the one side, a copy of Guido's "Christ," with the crown of thorns; and on the other, a beautiful Murillo. There had been no picture there formerly — not even an altar-piece. Sir Arthur had not permitted it. And the *rationale* of this Protestant dislike to representation became more than ever strongly apparent to the Countess' mind. "Why be thus compelled," she thought, "to represent to myself my Saviour after the imagination of Guido, or any other which the presence of these pictures almost necessitates? Is it not an adoration paid to the *fancy of the painter*? Or why be compelled, especially in the act of worship, to materialize the divine PRESENCE, of which we can form no conception? 'Blessed are they who, having not seen me, yet believe' — 'Though we have known Christ after the flesh, henceforth know we him no more.' "

With increased pain, as she cast her eye downwards, she perceived innovations still more approximating to the grossness of Romanism. All tended to materialize the heavenly, instead of elevating towards the heavenly the things of sense. Wax tapers yet unlighted, stood on the altar, which she well knew, according to the language borrowed from Rome, were meant to denote the light of divine truth. Wax tapers setting forth the light of divine truth! What a demonstration! "But did not the glorified Redeemer himself," it occurred to the mind of the Countess, "symbolize his Churches by golden candlesticks, in the midst of which he walked?" After a few moments' reflection, however, there appeared to her in *that* figure the same poetical justness so conspicuous in the whole of the sacred symbolical writings. The sun-dweller may characterize the reflected ray of the far distant planet as correspondent to the smallest beam which issues from his own glorious orb; but shall the wanderer through night and chaos so represent the source of light, when it bursts full upon his view? So may the Infinite Truth symbolize the truth which his Churches feebly reflect, by tapers rendered noticeable only by his presence — does it become *them* in like manner to characterize the Infinite? While these reflections occupied the mind of the Countess, the clergyman, with many changes of posture — now standing, now kneeling, now with back turned to the people, now with face — was performing the morning service. And when it was ended, he ascended the pulpit in white surplice, to give a short harangue upon some tradition of the

Church. *The Church* was reiterated at the beginning of almost every sentence — the HEAD of the Church was not appealed to once. How many efforts does man make to avoid the purity of the Eternal Light! How many wiles has the destroyer to keep from his fallen heart the influences of divine grace! Even that white surplice was a false symbol, suggesting falsehood. A priesthood sanctioned by divine authority? No; — in reality self-constituted — attempting to pluck, with daring robbery, the priestly garniture from that divine ONE, in whom are centred all the attributes of kingly priesthood for ever!

With a heavy heart Lady Lentraethen turned from the door of that old familiar parish church, determined that, until a purer gospel were preached in it, she should never enter its walls again. She did not think of separating from the Church of her fathers, because, consistently with its standards and government, she thought the Word of God might be carried into doctrinal and practical effect; but if the plague-spot of Popery spread from pulpit to pulpit throughout its domains, she resolved that she, at least, should lend her aid in forming a purer CHURCH OF ENGLAND, unfettered by State support; which latter, although most desirable, she considered in noways essential to the constitution of a true Church. Both she and Lord Lentraethen were too rational to wish unnecessarily to root up any form of government which had entwined itself with the affections and habits of a great people. But the formation a *Free Church of England* they considered most desirable; inasmuch as, at such a crisis many impurities, not of recent introduction, might be shaken off, which clogged the vital energies, and destroyed the usefulness of the Church in its present condition. The entire abolition of patronage was one of these desirable ends; a greater equalization of income was another. And last, not least — without which, all other changes are unimportant — must come the grand doctrine, that Christ alone is KING of his Church, wherever that Church may be located, or however it may be governed. Only and solely by the necessity which God seemed about to create for the pure in heart to come out of the State-endowed communion, could these things be accomplished — then only could a Church be consolidated, such as God and the nation would one day infallibly require. And it seemed no absurd imagination, but rather a hope, sanctioned equally by faith and reason, that a purified *Church* should be one day adopted by a regenerated *State* as her true help-mate, in the work of earnest application, to the furtherance of the nation's well-being.

On the day after the visit of the Countess to the parish church, the card of the Rev. Edward Clayton, vicar of the parish, was sent up to her. She sighed in contemplating it. From this source she thought she might have derived comfort and support in her arduous duties, but God had willed it otherwise. "Tell Mr. Clayton," she said to the page, "that I shall have pleasure in seeing him when Lord Lentraethen returns; at present, I receive few visitors." That same evening she went out alone to visit one or two of her villagers. A young man, far gone in a decline, was not expected to live many days; and she was going to see how his sufferings might he alleviated. As she was about to enter upon the narrow pathway which skirted the stream, a figure emerged from the wood, and stood directly in her path. She knew it to be that of the vicar by his dress, which was fashioned according to the strictest letter of the rubric, more than from any impression which he himself had made on her memory. She had looked upon him as the mere puppet of a service, and had scanned his features but indifferently; now, in an attitude of extreme deference, of marked humility, the young vicar, who might number some five-and-twenty summers, stood before her. His figure was slight and juvenile, his face pale and fair, and a deep melancholy blue eye was turned upon her with a look almost of deprecating entreaty. "Will the Countess of Lentraethen forgive me," he said in a low voice, "that I thus presume to introduce myself to her unbidden?" Jane bowed with some haughtiness; and saying, "When my lord returns I hope to become better acquainted with Mr. Clayton," she would have passed on; but the young man again hesitatingly addressed her. "Your ladyship is going to the village to visit the dying; I have been there even now." "Indeed!" rejoined the Countess. "May I then venture to ask what consolation you have offered?" "The consolations of the Church," said the young vicar with bended head. "Since you compel me to it, Mr. Clayton," said the Countess with the same mild, but distant manner, "I will say now what I would rather have deferred saying till another time, that with such visitations I can have little sympathy. You draw your consolations from the Church; I see no source of comfort for the dying in aught but the *Word of God*." The lady stepped on, and the vicar walked unbidden by her side. "And have you then, lady, renounced the authority of your Church?" he asked, with higher firmness, as though, losing that sense of humility with which at first he seemed oppressed, he felt himself rising into the *priest*. "I have not renounced my attachment to my Church," replied the Countess, "though if it continue to improve as it is doing," she added with some feeling of bitterness, "under the auspices of Rome, I fear that my attachment will not continue to strengthen in like proportion."

"You have been in Presbyterian Scotland, my lady," said the vicar, "which has no Church, and I fear you have learned to look with favour on Puritanism." He laid his hand on his heart, and looking with interest in her face, he added, "Would that I could rescue you from that great snare!" The Countess made a sudden stop; and casting up her eyes to the gorgeous evening clouds that hung behind the tracery of foliage above, the rich blood mantled to her cheek. She had never before thought of giving a name to those religious feelings which had been kindled within her, or to that religious system which she had imbibed. "*Puritanism!*" she slowly repeated, "I know not what you call *Puritanism*! but my soul has drank, God be thanked for it, from the *pure waters of the living Word!*" "Without the parental guidance of any Church," rejoined the vicar, "or of that misnamed a Church, which cares so little for its most sacred functions as to give them into the hands of the laity, yielding to the unworthy influences of democracy." "What sacred functions?" inquired the Countess. "The rite of ordination," said the young man, "which, although it must rest on a lower level, where there is no legitimate right to the performance of it at all, ought still to be held sacred by those pretending to exercise it."

"I never heard," replied the Countess, "that those you denominate the *laity* in Scotland have ever conferred ordination, or that it is performed there by any others than those who have been themselves ordained." "But," rejoined the vicar, "it is given at the bidding of the mob, at the mere good pleasure of the multitude." "I think, sir," rejoined the Countess, "that some little confusion must obtain in your mind from an ignorance of ecclesiastical affairs in the country you speak of. What is analogous to *ordination* here, is there, too, retained strictly by the clergy; who, I fancy, would sacrifice as much as you would do, ere they yielded it into other hands. It is the mere allocation of clerical labour — the formation of the tie between one who has been already ordained, in your sense of the term, and the Christian people, in which the Church of Scotland asserts that the latter have a right to be consulted. That profanation was certainly not committed in your appointment to Chesterlee; may I ask what was the more sacred and rubrical substitute?" The face of Clayton became crimsoned with a flush as if of anger, and then the blood as suddenly retreating, left his face pale and his lips livid. "*I* had no hand in procuring it," he said, in a husky voice. "But it was *bought* — purchased for you with money — I do not ask whose," continued the Countess. "My steward has accounted to me for the living, among other business transactions. He disposed of it wholly without my knowledge; for the disgrace of receiving such money has never, so far as can be shown, stained the treasuries of the barons of Chesterlee. As I cannot but deem it a robbery of my people in the highest sense, I shall, of course, employ it in the way which shall best make them restitution for the wrong done them." "Lady," said the young man slowly and solemnly, "as God lives, I had nothing to do with the procuring of this living." "I do not blame you, even if you had," replied the Countess, "so much as that wretched system of traffic in holy things, which has so long polluted our Church. I believe the eyes of some of our worthiest men are not yet opened to its enormity. But now, when you have discovered that it is that very thing which is *here* held so lightly as to be bartered — trafficked for — sold to the highest bidder — which in Scotland is sought to be made purely available for the good of the Christian people, I must be permitted to request, that you will judge less harshly of other Christian communities, until you know them better. Perhaps your information on other points, likewise, may be deficient."

As Lady Lentraethen cast her eye on her companion, she saw that his head drooped with a painful feeling, which was now more real than apparent — that his step was less firm, and that his compressed lips and agitated colour showed considerable marks of internal emotion. Her heart was formed to relent at the sight of suffering; and she addressed to the young man, in whom she could not but feel a lively interest, some words of greater kindness than she had hitherto done. It was not difficult for her, at the same time, to make him understand that, as the village was now in sight, she would prefer entering it alone; and, with a bow profound, but expressive of a different sort of humility from that with which he had at first accosted her, the vicar struck into another pathway.

CHAPTER XXII

"There is an exquisite subtilty, and the same is unjust."
ECCLES

From EDWARD CLAYTON to Dr. BREMNER

My Dear Bremner, — Will you still allow me to address you in my difficulties and distresses? My friends are few — did I say *few*? There is a sense in which I have no friend. Great God! it is a fearful thing for man's heart to find itself alone in the universe! But you well know that I have vowed mine to a mistress who brooks no rival. Well, it is done! I cannot now put the question — Was it *well* done? That dark shadow of crime yet haunts my spirit. I need not stain my paper with that which can never cease to steep my soul in guilt — for you know it well. You know that I, who in England had been bred without a religion, in that moment of agony, in mighty Rome, flew to find peace in the bosom of a confessor. You know his verdict — that a high and special absolution, and a life-devotion to the interests of Holy Church, could alone atone for my sin. I became a priest of the order of Jesus. Furthermore, I am sent to fill a pulpit of the Church of England, that, with other members of the same order, I may take advantage of the rising tide to draw this erring Church back into the bosom of her mighty mother. But it was anguish, remorse, that lent intensity to my belief. I know not whether it was wise to send me *here*. The unveiled Protestantism of England glares unpleasantly upon me. Yet to *my* Church, what signifies it? Ha! she has my secret! What am *I*? — and the fearful oath by which she binds her priesthood! Should I be *doubly* guilty? In vain I gnaw my chain. Heaven of heavens! a vision sometimes scowls upon me in the intensity of despair with which I rend fruitlessly the adamantine bonds which are upon my spirit, that Rome's *priests* — yes they, her bond children, her sworn and chosen ones, may yet, when despair has risen into frenzy, turn upon their mother and *burn her with the fire* of their despair. Are there not thousands of souls in prison among these wretched priests? can she altogether press out of men the better nature? Ah! not even crime, the most tremendous pressure which that nature can sustain, is capable of this. In spite of all, goodness! thou divine shape, I love thee! My natural candour revolts at this double-dealing — this seeming to be one thing, while I am in reality another.

But I rave. *Your* soul dwells at ease — you know not the agony of mine; I want, however, to be fortified, supported by your cool, sagacious judgment. What, in reality, do you think of Rome's maxim, that the end justifies the means? One thing my mind has grasped at — it is the state of the poor in this rich, teeming, fertile country. God of mercy! it is deplorable — it is daily, becoming worse; misery is the hydraulic pressure which crushes nature out of *them*. By what right did the rich aristocracy of this country appropriate those revenues which were, in great part at least, devoted to the relief of misery, without making the poor — as legitimate children of the soil as they — any adequate compensation? For the poor law in its present working is not such. It were surely better that the hierarchy of Rome still possessed the stewardship of their once rich domains than that they should feed the ever-devouring maw of hungry wealth! Here, however, I have not the poor *salco* which the sight of poverty affords; the barons of Chesterlee have understood their duty. Here there is no individual without a home, and flourishing homes are as numerous as the soil will support. The hereditary heiress, now Countess of Lentraethen, is, besides, strongly Protestant in sentiment. She is determined to use her influence — which is unbounded — to the utmost in opposing any innovation. Young, extremely beautiful, full of soul — her inner life seems to be wholly Protestantized.

They err, who say that Romanism only possesses any advantage of sentiment. Here is, I think, the true distinction; to Rome belongs most properly that sentiment which is associative, to Protestantism that which is contemplative. And thus, as memory and the senses belong to all, while the inner faculty is the gift of the few, Rome influences more widely the minds of the masses; Protestantism entrenches itself more strongly in the feelings of its real disciples. Their hearts are captive to a visionary Saviour, their souls to an infinite God, and their convictions to human reason and their own consciences. Protestant *forms* are nothing. In the masses they are ill-digested prejudices, and can ill contest with our majestic ritual; but give to the *vitalities* of Protestantism the strength of numbers, and we on our part could not maintain our ground.

I write to you my thoughts as they arise — that which few of my order dare to do; but I know that I am safe. *You, too, have a secret in Rome's keeping*; we are bound together by ties stronger than friendship itself — those of eternal destiny. How does she lead us captive! You, who might have aspired to the highest honours of the Papacy, and who have listened favourably to the maxims and policy of Rome, are a member of a humble Church, without a hierarchy, with scarce any scope for ambition. I, on the other hand, a sympathizer, almost a universalist, without having ever attained to earnest belief of any kind, am doomed to work for, to annihilate myself in, the most despotic religion the world has ever known!

To conclude — my present condition is so especially painful that I mean to implore the Vatican, either that I may be recalled abroad, or at least located where I can accomplish more. — Yours unalterably,

EDWARD CLAYTON.

———

From Dr. BREMNER to the Rev. EDWARD CLAYTON

Dear Clayton, — Most willingly should I be your counsellor, if I imagined that my counsel would be of service; but, my dear friend, I fear much that what you need is what I cannot supply; and that is, a different conformation of mind. When will you learn to reflect, or to be influenced by the reflection, that this sublunary state is, and I fear must continue to be, a state of imperfection; and that our desires and our efforts must, therefore, be directed to the possible, and not to the impracticable? That which we can perform must always be coincident with the sphere which our destiny has appointed us; and I am satisfied that in that sphere only can we best perform the duty imposed on us by the conditions of humanity. To do justly, to love mercy, and to walk humbly with our God, are duties which can be performed equally in all spheres, and under all forms of being; and what more does the Almighty require of his creatures? The fanaticism of impossibility I must ever endeavour to suppress, as a crime against the happiness of the species. Here it rages as an epidemic. Even your own Church has not been always preserved from it. Inflated by the oxygen of spiritualism, too subtile for the human mind to inhale, the Jansenists might have ruined your Church from within, if it had not been assailed by the rude hammers of the Reformers from without.

In reply to your question, I think that, to a modified extent, it must appear evident to all that *the end justifies the means*; because, *practically*, we all, in some degree, avail ourselves of the maxim. It is a doctrine, not of morality, but of necessity. Yet I do not give my approbation to the present policy of Rome, in introducing her ministers into the Church of England, because I disown proselytizing in every one of its aspects. If England, of her own accord, return to Romanism, why restrain her choice? But, for my own part, I should say, let that choice be entirely voluntary. However, as to the policy of Rome, you, as its sworn minister, are not to judge, but to obey. If you can further it better by a transference to some other locality, by all means endeavour to procure such. You, I would say, are not the man to deal with sincerity in any of its forms. For myself — many years older than you — I have learned to look upon life with a colder eye. To live easily I owe to myself; to further the suavities and amenitiesof social life — to promote the sanity, moral and physical, of the circle in which I exercise some influence, is the duty I owe to the State, which, in return, provides for my personal comforts. Strive, my dear friend, in spite of an afflictive accident, in which fate alone was guilty, to acquire this composure of mind so indispensable to tranquillity, while you retain your anxiety to ameliorate the condition of humanity by those means which destiny leaves at your disposal. *It is all we can.*—Yours, most sincerely,

GAVIN BREMNER.

CHAPTER XXIII

"I pity him, who'er he be, who fills my father's room;
For he that acts the traitor's part must meet the traitor's doom.
Ah! Better far to view the grass grow o'er my father's grave,
Than see him shepherd of Christ's flock — the State's dishonour'd slave.

"Father, they call thee rebel now; but this I wis is true,
My country's foes ne'er better fared that I was taught by you.
Farewell, my boyhood's gladsome home — thou art no home of mine;
I could not love thee now as I have loved in "auld langsyne!"

Written by an officer of her Majesty's — th,
lately returned from India.

It is the 18th of May, in the year 1843. What stirs the pulse of old Scotland, usually so healthful and so steady? Not since the day when the last of her martyrs stood beside the gallows that frowned in the Grassmarket, high above the mute and awestruck crowd, bidding farewell, for the sake of Christ, to sun, moon, and stars, and all earthly delights — not since that day has her life-blood throbbed so vehemently. The morning dawns over the city of Edinburgh, calm, close, and sultry. The huge masses of building, irregular and picturesque, that bestride the back of that ridge which terminates abruptly in the Castle-rock, loom gloomily and silently against the early summer sky. Old St. Giles still rears his coronet above them — he has looked down on many a strange scene; but the HEART OF MID-LOTHIAN is not there to-day. There is the classic Calton with its proud monuments, girt around with the leafy honours of young May, gleaming nobly forth in the breaking sunshine; — all is yet silent there. We pass forward to yonder city of palaces, which stretches its spacious streets lengthways and crossways to the four cardinal points of the compass. Near the centre, there stands a church, with pointed spire and pillared colonnade. The morning hour of six has not yet struck, but a dense and anxious throng — yet no vulgar throng — are blocking up the street, and pressing forward towards the unlocked gates. It is said, too, that there are watchers within who have sat there the live-long night, in restless expectation of what the morrow should bring forth. Five long hours will yet elapse ere these gates are unbarred. What can have made the dwellers in this stately city, whose cheeks have pressed downy pillows, who might still have been drowned in soft slumbers, who might awake to luxury and mirth — what can have led them to keep watch and ward here so long! Ah! the strong heart of Scotland is *here*. This day is pregnant with the fate of her well-beloved Church.

Noon-day blazes forth, and the buzzing streets, with their swarming thousands, tell of some great expected drama. St. Andrew's groans with its half-suffocating crowd. St. Giles' is full to overflowing; and, in another quarter, a large rude building, which may contain 3,000 people, is full of anxious expectant faces. What should they expect to see there? The Calton is now alive with overhanging multitudes. The long street which stretches upwards from the royal palace of Holyrood to St. Giles' is densely peopled, and every window, pinnacle, and bartizan has its knots of busy yet patient lookers-on. Twelve o'clock at length strikes, and a line of dragoons, on prancing steeds, with helmets glittering in the sun, open up the crowd with difficulty to make way for the representative of majesty — the Lord High Commissioner. He is coming with pomp and pageant, according to use and wont, to hear sermon in old St. Giles'. The city dignitaries precede him; and a long line of coaches, with fantastic and party-coloured trappings, proceed slowly up the ancient picturesque street. The children wonder and admire — but to *men* in Scotland the age of gingerbread state is over! Their hearts beat for something else to-day!

Another hour passes, and again a long procession emerges from St. Giles'; but it has neither pomp nor glitter. Scotland's pastors, from her secluded hills and valleys, her quiet manses, sheltered amid their shady bowers and alleys, are there; — men, to whose truthfulness, and piety, and anxious fostering care, her sons have owed all that they have been, and are still, at home and abroad. These men, in their simple dress of black, wear serious, deliberative, care-worn faces. Pageant is little for them, and yet upon them all men's eyes are fixed. Will they, for the sake of their dear homes, abandon Scotland to the mercy of the civil power to-day? dethrone God's Word, and set up over her the sword of the State? Will they consent, at the bidding of a law-court, to obtrude the unholy and unwelcomed pastor — at the bayonet's point if needs be — into her dearest sanctuaries? There are men among them who will do all that; but with them we do not now meddle.

The Commissioner enters St. Andrew's — the last representative of majesty in the Free Assembly of any Protestant Church. The representative of the Church of Scotland enters likewise — her elected moderator. The ceremonies of recognition between these two estates, the sole visible relics of the ancient independence of the country, take place. The multitude arise, and the moderator offers up a solemn prayer. Then there is a pause, and all hearts beat high. The moderator* looks around; in a voice not imperious, — low, calm, subdued, — he tells the house, in a few words, that the independence of the Assembly has been infringed upon — her voice, expressed by the majority of her members, disregarded — the constitution of the country violated. They cannot now proceed to constitute here another Free Assembly. He lays down upon the table a statement of the grounds and details on which these assertions are made — once more he bows to the Lord Commissioner, and with step firm, composed, and dignified, withdraws. Chalmers follows. Then one by one, nearly five hundred men. Are they led on by CHALMERS? — by the MODERATOR? For them, great and good as they are, do five hundred pastors thus sever themselves at one step from those retreats where, sheltered from the storms and conflicts of life, some of them have ministered for twenty, thirty, ay, it may be *fifty* years? Oh, how much more peaceful, how much more holy, than were ever cloistered walls! Has there been a room in those familiar households, a shrub or tree in those sweet gardens, that has not been consecrated, by blessed memories of earth and heaven? Their anxieties hitherto have not been of this world; — yet now they cast themselves on the world again, as their places are left vacant in that Assembly on that day. They see

---

* *The friend and biographer of Dr. Thomas Brown, one of the finest intellects of Scotland.*

not Chalmers — they scarce hear the long-drawn sigh, more a sob, a cry, than a cheer, which echoes around the church as they depart. The sounds of sympathy which burst from the multitudes without — the sea of waving hats and handkerchiefs, as if to hail a triumph — the respectful opening, without bayonet or spear, of the deep lanes of human beings that meet their progress; — these pass all but unheeded. For them this is an hour of fiery trial. Far other scenes flit before their vision — far other voices greet their ears, and grim shadows of persecution, of cold and weariness, and pinching poverty, hover in their path.* Applause avails them not. No man's virtue, no man's fame supports them in this hour. But HE who has been with them in the temptation and the struggle — in the sanctuary of their closets — in by-gone times of anguish, when, as they walked forth, often it might be, in the evening twilight, the dim stars shining down upon their trouble and perplexity, truth beamed forth clearer and brighter, and the GLORY OF GOD became to them a shining light more luminous to guide their path than the sun at noon, — HE who was with them then is with them now. One like unto the Son of Man walks with them. HE alone is their leader — CHRIST THE KING, the CAPTAIN OF SALVATION.

Again the voice of prayer is heard. In the hall, where three thousand people wait to welcome the pastors of their Free Church, the moderator pours out a fervent thanksgiving, a deep and solemn expression of gratitude to God for strength vouchsafed to vindicate the great duty of allegiance to Christ, their only KING and HEAD. And now, for the first time, before God and not before men, there is an outpouring of full hearts, and overcharged bosoms swell, and down manly faces unwonted tears find course. And the whole Assembly stand up and sing together, in the words of inspiration, a strain of deep-toned melody, praising God, while they beseech him for farther light and guidance,

> *"O send thy light forth and thy truth;*
> *Let them be guides to me,*
> *And lead me to thine holy hill,*
> *Ev'n where thy dwellings be."*

---

* *Some of those men have since died through the cruelty of proprietors in refusing them any dwelling-place.*

At this moment the sun, beclouded for a time; streams in with unusual brightness, and illuminates the open Bibles.

Dr. Welsh then moves, that he concede the honours of the moderatorship in favour of another, who, on such a momentous occasion, will, with the greatest propriety, fill this place of dignity.

The motion is carried with one voice, and CHALMERS takes the chair as moderator of the first Free Assembly of the Church of Scotland dissevered from the State. No Commissioner is there with gallant uniform, with throne and quartered arms, with pages, pursebearer, and mace.

But all men feel that there needs no more to adorn the head of Chalmers than that bright halo of honours with which his Creator has encircled it for so many long years. All feel, too, that another THRONE than that of the Lord Commissioner has been established here.

CHAPTER XXIV

"I am contented here; I ne'er have seen
A vale more fertile, or a hill more green;
Oh! Would to Heaven th' alternative were mine
Abroad to thrive, or here in want to pine;
Soon would I choose."
HON. HENRY ERSKINE

In the spring of the year following that in which the Earl and Countess of Lentraethen took up their residence in England, the intelligence reached Chesterlee of the death of Sir Duncan Ross. He had been assassinated in the streets of Rome, at midnight, by a disappointed rival. Wonderful to say, however, he had left a *will*, whereby he left his estate of Rosemount, with a modicum of debt, equal to two-thirds of its value, to his niece, Miss Hamilton Legh, now Countess of Lentraethen. The will had been drawn out on his separation from her nearly two years before, and was accompanied by a letter of the same date, in which he described his motives for making it at so early a period of his life, as arising from a consciousness of the precarious life he led. At the same time he expressed his gratification, that in leaving his estate to so near a relative, and one so able to clear away all its embarrassments, he could inscribe on his gift that which had been inscribed on the apple of discord, though he hoped with very different intentions, "To the fairest." "I have a pleasure in thinking," he wrote, "that my distant Highland home will be sometimes visited, and brightened by the smiles of living beauty, as it is adorned by the lovely creations of fancy which enrich its walls."

Lord and Lady Lentraethen prepared, therefore, to pay a visit to the Highlands in the course of the summer, taking care to leave Chesterlee without anxiety for the welfare of their people. Clayton had effected the exchange for which he so much wished, and by paying treble what had been received for the living, it was redeemed, and a man of truly Christian character and principles settled in the vicarage. Another church was in process of building on the more distant boundary of the estate, and missionaries were at work under the superintendence of the vicar. The management of the estate was left with the most experienced of the tenants, a man of great intelligence and probity, who would deviate in no respect in his dealings from the line chalked out by Sir Arthur and his heiress, and who possessed the fullest confidence of the tenantry.

It was about the same time of year as that when the young Countess had first accompanied her husband to her beloved home, that she again found herself journeying with him towards another home, not less beautiful in its way, in the far distant Highlands. They had visited their cousins in Edinburgh, and had taken the steamer from thence to Inverness, where, in order that they might the better enjoy the scenery and weather, they procured a double-seated pony phaeton, in which they drove round the head of the Beauly Frith, and after an exquisite ride, found themselves within sight of the lofty mountains, now robed in their most gorgeous attire of summer blue, which towered behind Rosemount. May Morrison occupied the back of the phaeton, and the Earl's valet accompanied them on horseback. There was a piece of moorland about three quarters of a mile in extent, situated on the nearest verge of the Rosemount estate, and there they found nearly the whole population of the adjacent country poured down to receive them. The women and children, dressed in holiday attire, kept in the back-ground, clustering upon the knolls and eminences which afforded them any vantage-ground of sight; while the young men — bonneted and plaided, with bunches of heather disposed as nosegays or cockades — lined the carriage-way, and rent the air with acclamations. About twenty of the handsomest and most robust, who had been stationed at a certain point for the purpose, came forward to unharness the horses, and substitute their own services in drawing the vehicle; but Lord Lentraethen, addressing to them a few words of thanks, forbade this demonstration of respect, urging that it might prove disagreeable to his lady in so slight a conveyance.

Never had the Countess looked more beautiful than now, as robed in white, with a white crape bonnet wreathed with roses, in which she had entwined on their way some branches of the mountain heather, she beamed smiles and glances of radiant goodness upon those who were already her friends and children. And when, by way of making up for the disappointment occasioned to the youthful band who had held themselves in readiness to draw their conveyance, she stood up and showered among them the buds of a bouquet which she held in her hand, the enthusiasm knew no bounds—the shouts were caught up by the most distant of the stragglers on the rising ground, and the moor became one sea of waving handkerchiefs and caps tossed into the air. The lofty background of mountains, whose summits pierced the clear heavens, and whose sides, clothed with purple heather, glowed intensely to the sunlight; the dark fringe of pine on the lower slopes, that gave place in turn to rich corn fields, whose verdure the first tinge of autumn had not yet invaded; the brown moor, covered with a picturesque population full of motion and enthusiasm; and the noble figures of the Earl and Countess, as they stood in the midst responding to the warm-hearted greetings with which they were welcomed, altogether formed a scene as animated as it was in reality touching and beautiful.

Lady Lentraethen looked delightedly at May, as if expecting from her a sympathizing glance; but, to her surprise, she saw the girl pale and trembling, looking tearfully over the crowd for some one whom she did not discover, until her eye rested on a spot on the moor, on which it seemed to dilate with a kind of timid fascination. Lady Lentraethen, too, looked narrowly at this spot as they approached it, and saw the marks of a cottage and its garden — some stones of the walls and enclosure lying scattered on the moor. One black spot seemed to mark where the hearth had been, and a sort of attempt at stunted verdure for some distance around suggested the idea that a part of the ground had been brought under cultivation for the use of the inmates. But what surprised Lady Lentraethen was, that the same tokens were repeated at intervals, appearing to indicate that there had been several cottages in the neighbourhood of each other, now razed to the ground. In one place some gooseberry bushes still held their places, and the remains of an arbour in one corner, and of an arched gateway in another, showed that upon this little garden some pains had been bestowed.

"Do you remember these cottages, May?" asked Lady Lentraethen. May answered, with a sob and a burst of tears. "That" said she, with an endeavour to compose herself, and pointing to the garden with the arbour, "belonged to John Gray, the carpenter. How proud he used to be of his garden! That other was poor Matthew Ross', the shoemaker, who had the deaf and dumb boy." And May enumerated the former tenants of the cottages, with the exception of one which had belonged to the father of young Kenneth Ore, whose figure she had vainly sought in the joyful crowd, and the desolation of whose homestead had struck her with terror and dismay. "What does this mean?" said the lady to her husband, with a darkened countenance and an anxious eye. She was answered by a melancholy shake of the head. "Such things are too common, Jane," said he; "although, thank God, we in our experience have known nothing of them. The landlord or his factor has got tired of his small tenantry, has had some scheme of improvement in his head, and has razed their cottages." "And *where are the people?*" said the Countess, in a still more anxious voice. "Turned adrift into the world, my love, probably," said her husband, in a half sarcastic, half melancholy tone. "God of heaven!" said Jane, "can such things be? *Where is the chieftan's heart?*" She was responded to only by another sad shake of the head.

When they reached the village near Rosemount, they found it gay with all the flowers which the cottage gardens could supply, while a triumphal arch had been erected over the bridge. The principal roadway was so thronged that the progress of the new proprietors, to whom those eager multitudes looked with hearts beating high with hope, was necessarily at this point slow. One there was, however, whose eye already dim, grew still dimmer as it looked upon the pageant, and whose heart fluttered with other feelings than those of happiness, as the phaeton, drawn by two cream-coloured ponies, showing to advantage the noble figures of the Earl and Countess, drew near. In an unenclosed court, before the door of a long low house, beside the bridge, which showed the doorway of a shop at one end and that of a dwelling-house at the other, there sat, supported by cushions, the emaciated figure of a young and very handsome lad, whose temples leaned painfully on his wasted hand. May Morrison started up involuntarily, as she beheld this spectacle, exclaiming, in a low voice, "My lady, there is Evan Munro. Oh, how ill he looks! What a change!" Lady Lentraethen looked steadily at the young man for a few moments, and then bowed with marked kindness. A crimson flush rose to Evan's brow. He made a sudden attempt to rise, as if to return the salutation, but, after a fruitless effort, he sank back powerless on his pillow. "Poor fellow," said Lady Lentraethen; "what a sad change! And the hope, too, of his family! Heaven help us!" and, amid renewed cheering, they passed on, to enter the grounds, at the gateway of which the throng ceased — to forget for a while, amid the luxurious beauties of Rosemount, that there were ills in the world beyond.

It was not so, however, with May. Her world did not lie here, and, with an anxious and trembling step, at the first moment she could escape, she directed her way towards the dwelling of Evan Munro — not for his sake alone, but that she might gain tidings of those who were still more dear to her. When she entered the cottage, she found the doors on either side of the landing-place standing open, but saw no one. As she stood, she heard the old clock tick, just as if she had heard it last but a few seconds before — as if in measuring time it felt no time, and lived exactly the same moments over and over again. May felt impatient at the monotonous sounds, as if *they* ought to have told her of the changes that had happened. She went in to look the clock in the face; but there it was, inveterately grave and mysterious, and everything else in the room was as stationary as itself. The tortoise-shell cat lay sleeping on the hearth, as if it had never opened its eyes for the last three years — the old bureau frowned in its heavy blackness as it used to do, and the very ornaments on the mantel-piece were there as if no hand had touched them; only May thought that every thing looked smaller and more humble than formerly, for this was a house she had been accustomed to look up to in her childish days. By-and-by she imagined she heard the low murmur of a voice proceeding from the adjacent room, and thither she softly stole, as if afraid of disturbing the silent order and of introducing some awful and unknown change which was about to fall upon *her*. She looked into the opposite room, and there, reclining on the bed, was Evan, still undressed, his head supported by pillows, which kept him in a half-sitting posture. His eyes were closed, and his face seemed more wan and hollow than it had done before. May drew stealthily near, and sitting down, ventured to place her hand on that emaciated half-skeleton wrist which lay over the side of the couch.

Evan opened his eyes, and stared in half-bewildered

surprise, as if he had been in a light slumber. " It's only me, Evan," said May gently, "oh! dear, how are you in this way?" Evan's head sank again on its pillow, as he took the girl's hand in his own and pressed it with a heavy sigh. "I am changed, May, am I?" said he, looking at her with a faint inquiring smile, as if almost unconscious of the extent of the change which had passed over himself, and wishful to ascertain it. May shook her head and cast down her eyes, unable to tell the truth as she felt it. "I know it, May," said he; "I know it — but it is no matter; it is best. It is not a hard thing to die," he added after a short pause. "Oh! Evan, don't speak so," said May deprecatingly. "To you it would be," said Evan in a quiet voice. "Life to you is full of hope; it has lost its charms for me; but thank God, thank God," he added with energy, "heaven has acquired many." "Oh! May," he said, clasping his hands and raising himself, as he looked her full in the face, "till now my Saviour was never truly dear to me." "You were well brought up," said May in a hesitating voice. "I was," replied Evan, "and I believe my conduct was irreproachable; but, May, there is a heart where everything, anything, may dwell but God. I never could say till now, with any truth, 'He is *all* my salvation and *all* my desire' I did not disbelieve the things of eternity — that is, in the infidel sense — *but I did not believe them*. Heaven was an easy dream — hell a dark shadow. *This world's future* was my only reality. I have of late felt within me more of heaven — more of hell, than once I thought to exist beyond the grave. The fancies that lured me on, as if they were all of good that God could give me, proved but fuel, that one breath of his anger might kindle into the fire that never should be quenched." Evan, sinking back, closed his eyes, as if exhausted by the exertion of speaking, and the feelings which had prompted it. His words echoed in May's heart. For a time they awed her into silence, so that she felt scarce the inclination to ask regarding what had, till then, so filled her mind; but as the rapid breathing of her friend subsided, her thoughts recurred to the subject. "This world's future had been *his* only reality!" — these words rung in her ears. "But it is a reality," thought she, "though not so important a one, and God does not forbid us to take an interest in it."

With this feeling uppermost, she imagined that she could make her inquiries with greater calmness. Still, as the words —

"And what is become of the catechist — and — and Kenneth Ore's — father?" trembled out, her heart palpitated, and her brain swam. "Away over seas," said Evan, in an exhausted voice. It was the fulfilment of Kenneth's prophecy, which at that moment she again seemed to hear. Dismay, anguish, tugged at her bosom. There was a long silence, disturbed only by the breathings of the sufferer. "Tell her—tell her," said Evan to his mother, who at that instant came in and grasped May's hand warmly, though her eyes became sufused with tears, and she shook her head mournfully as she glanced at the wasted form on the bed. "Tell her what, Evan?" she said. "About the folk over the seas," he answered languidly, as if further speaking were a burden to him. "I think ye're done out the day," said his mother. "Will you no take anything. It was too much for you, sitting out so long to see the show; — though our hearts were as happy as they could be in our great affliction, to see your bonny leddy come back wi' her ain, and till her ain. If she had but come sooner, there would hae been nae folk ower seas to speir after; — but, will ye no take anything, my son?" "No, no, mother — no, no," said Evan, somewhat impatiently. "Oh, ye're done out, Evan," repeated his mother — " it's quietness ye want. Come ben, May, and I'll tell you what ye canna but wish to know. Come ben, lassie, and dinna shake," she added, observing that May looked white, and that the hand of which she had possessed herself trembled; "dinna shake, ye ken there's naething hopeless but — the grave."

She spoke the last word in a lower tone, and with a heavy sigh. "Well, the catechist's away," she continued, as she placed May in the arm-chair by the fireside, "and oh! it was as sore a day for this parish as it ever saw, when he went. Since poor Geordie's set down in the manse yonder, ye may say that Samuel was the only minister in the twa parishes. He had much to do, for there was no death or sickness but what he was sent for. Indeed, indeed, it seemed to many as if the enemy was to be allowed to get a' his ain way here, when Samuel was ta'en away." "And how did it come about?" asked Mary, "and who went with him?" "0, as to the rest, that is, Angus M'Gillivray, Matthew Ross, Kenneth Ore, and his father, and a' the families on the moor, it was just that Jackson wished to get quit o' the sma' tenants, thinking that the bits o' waste land they had taken in to themselves might now be fit for pasturage, and that their wee bits o' hooses discredited the entrance to the estate. But for Samuel, it was a case of downright persecution. It's thought that Jackson was egged on by Geordie, for the croft and the bothie were taken from him, and he was refused a hole to put his head in, both by Jackson and by Davidson, and ye know that he and Sir Duncan had the hail twa parishes atween them. Samuel and his wife stoppit in this house for six weeks before they went away, and weel we have paid for it; our farm-rent was raised above our heads, and it's now more than the land is worth. The catechist thought that the finger of Providence clearly pointed him abroad, as the poor muir-folk had no other way to go, and him-sel' hunted out o' house and haddin, so that his duty lay in going wi' them to whatever desert spot they might light upon, that he might keep them in mind of ordinances and Sabbath-rests, till the Lord should send them the spiritual instruction that they will sorely feel the want o'. It's said that the hill-cotters, for two or three miles, are to be sent after them in a year or two; and that made a *by-ordinar* feeling at the coming of your lady, for it is known that she has a warm-side to poor folk, and doesna like to see them trampled on. Many a heart beat quicker this day at sight of her sweet face."

"And did the moor-folk feel no sorrow at leaving their own land?" asked May, recurring to the subject after which her heart still yearned. "Sorrow!" repeated the good woman — "ah, woman, sorrow is but a poor word to mention in regard to them. Who should feel sorrow at leaving his own fire-side, and the spot where himsel' and his forbears have lived time out o' mind, if it isna the poor man, and above a' the poor Highlander! I'm sure, if the poor folk dinna like their own homes, and the land o' their birth, it canna be the rich, that never stop at home, but prefer a' other airts that the wind can blaw. *They* canna hae the memory and the affection of the poor, that ken naething in the world out o' their ain parishes, and their ain bothies. But ah! and alas!" said the poor woman, wiping her eyes, and rocking to and fro with a sorrowful motion, "they'll turn the land into the land of the stranger and the sheep." — "And how did they go?" inquired May. "By the port of — ," said Mrs. Munro — "the ship took them up there. It was a dark day — the like hasna been here since the death of Dr. Blair. Half of the two parishes accompanied them some a few miles — some all the way to — . Before they took their journeys, they went into the churchyard, and threw themselves down on the graves of their people, lamenting till you might have heard the very hills sigh with the sound. I saw Kenneth Ore kissing the sod on the grave of old John Morrison, your grandfather, May. Samuel stood at the tombstone of Dr.Blair, his hands clasped together, and the tears rolling down his cheeks, and there, when he got composure, he poured out a prayer, such as was never heard from him before. Oh, how he besought the Almighty that *He* would go before them, and anoint a Bethel —a house of God for them with His presence and with his Spirit, on the wide sea and in the great Wilderness. And the many blessings he prayed for on those that were left behind! You couldna have seen a face. The men covered theirs with their bonnets, holding them up before them as they stood, and the women had their plaids and shawls drawn down over their heads; but ye might sometimes have heard a sob that couldna be keepit in, and seen many a young heart swelling as it would burst. God preserve us from such another day!"

On May's return to Rosemount, her pale face and ill-concealed tears betrayed her state of mind to her mistress, who sympathizingly inquired into the cause of her distress, at the same time expressing her surprise that the traces of grief alone should be visible in her countenance on her return to her native place. The girl repeated the narrative she had heard in the village, as well as a voice interrupted by sobs would permit. She became more calm, however, as she observed the glowing cheek and kindling eye of her young mistress — signs which she had now learned to interpret as promising speedy redress when a tale of grief was poured into her ear. "But we must not so lose our people," she said to May, when the latter had finished her story; "we must have them back again. Heaven is my witness, girl, that I would rather that corn and sheep were banished forever from my domains, if such a thing might be, than human beings. What are the green fields and pastures of a desolated estate, but like the luxuriant yet barren fig-tree which THE LORD cursed? I should expect home, and happiness, and plenty, to shrivel up in my own hands into things of nought, if I so made light of them with regard to my fellow-creatures."

These words, repeated by May, and circulated rapidly enough through the length and breadth of the parish, did, indeed, cause the well-springs of hope and joy to gush forth from many a bosom, mingled with a tide of blessings on the young heart that so well understood the feelings of the poor. Already, for her they would have sacrificed home, country, life itself — the very blessings she was so anxious to procure for them. So richly, so abundantly has God provided that the kindly fulfilment of duty by the GREAT, the worldly overseers of HIS flock, shall be re-paid!

As for May, she had only in hope and patience to wait till the glad tidings had crossed the great Atlantic, and to trust to her knowledge of the hearts of her countrymen that these tidings would be eagerly responded to. For winds, and waves, and all other accidents, she endeavoured calmly to place her trust in the God of providence.

It cannot be doubted that, under the fostering care of Lord and Lady Lentraethen, the Rosemount estate soon presented a new aspect. Smiling cottages arose on every hand, to which allotments of land were attached, sufficient to support the inhabitants in ease and plenty. Only two large farms were retained under the immediate oversight of the proprietors, that they might serve as models for the district, and support farming apparatus on a larger scale than the small-farm system pursued to its utmost limits will allow. The domestic habits of the poorer people, too, improved greatly with their improving prospects. It is the despair of accomplishing anything which in a great measure causes the improvidence of the poor. But the knowledge that character for cleanliness and industry would bring its own reward, and above all, a desire to receive well *"The lady of the light"* as she was poetically termed in the Celtic tongue by her people, when she came to brighten the poor man's dwelling, worked almost incredible wonders. One blot alone remained on the promising surface of things. It was the spot which of all others had once been the beloved of the people's hearts, — the parish manse. The change of seasons brought little change upon its desolate and neglected aspect. George Donaldson carried with him the ideas of domestic economy he had acquired in his father's house. The inner arrangements of his mansion were consigned to one slovenly domestic; while, without, things went on very much as they listed. The lawn was rank with unsightly weeds, the house out of repair in windows and doors, while around it the pathway had become a miry puddle, strewed over by chips of sticks, which were daily broken for firewood, to the great detriment of the trees in the neighbourhood. And the dear old garden? — it was a wilderness. Dogs and pigs straggled through it at their pleasure. The pathways of emerald grass, sown with daisies and buttercups, were now deformities; and the wimpling *burn*, with its sweet unceasing music, was choked with the nettles and stinking weeds that covered it from bank to bank.

George himself was altered considerably for the worse. Possessing a sort of coarse heartiness, which, had his parishioners been of the same stamp with himself, would have led him to place them on a free and easy footing, when he found himself received everywhere with cold civility or open dislike, he became sullen, morose, and even savage, treating his people as his enemies, and endeavouring to avenge on them his own unpleasant feelings by acts of petty tyranny. His rooms smelt strongly of tobacco and whisky, the public-house keeper and exciseman being his evening boon companions, with such of the same description as chance brought in the way. Since his settlement few besides had found their way to the fireside of the manse parlour, with the exception of Jackson, the factor, who came to consult over lists of obnoxious people to be exterminated, and Davidson, George's old patron, who frequently came to devise acts of mischief and revenge. A few times the voice of suffering despair made its appeal there — all in vain. Who may that strange haggard-looking female be, bowed with something more than age, who has acquired the quick, fierce, suspicious look of the savage, and who shows her bones, gaunt with famine, through her miserable rags? She has travelled down from the farthest heights, where the iron sway of Jackson is felt, and where cruelties are daily practised, unheard of in the more cultivated districts. In the latter, the people might be banished to another land; but they could not, in the light of day, be proscribed, hunted, denied food and shelter in their own. In the quick strong language of the Celt, this woman poured forth her wrongs. She had once lived, she said, in plenty, and her doors were never shut to the wandering poor. Her daughter, the pride of the heights, had, on a visit to the low country, attracted the notice of Jackson, who had himself, as was well known, sacrificed two of his children to the guilty wishes of his master. But *her* daughter, the sun-burnt girl of the black eye, with her strange tongue and her maiden snood, was more severely virtuous; and *that*, notwithstanding threats of the expulsion of her father from his sheep farm, which was almost a heritage, for his forefathers had dwelt there for many generations. These threats were not mere words. Before Annie returned to her home, her roof-tree had been fired — she found her house desolate. Happily, the father died under the weight of the sorrow, but the edict of proscription went forth against his wife and child. Food, fire, and shelter, were denied. Their nearest neighbours, under pain of similar treatment, dared not afford them; so they had burrowed a hole in the earth, and there they had lived — how, God only knows. But Annie's health had broken down, her mind was giving way, and the mother, made reckless by despair, determined to make an appeal against the great factor; as terrible to her as the Russian Autocrat to the forlorn exile of Siberia. She had heard that Mr. Donaldson was Jackson's friend. She had come to him. He might say something for her. Where else should she go, but to Christ's minister? George mused for a little. He then said a few words, harshly enough, to the woman, on the duty of submission to the powers that be; but he promised to speak to the factor; and the suppliant departed with a faint ray of hope shining in upon her.

Months passed away, and again she came. Nothing had been done for her relief. Her daughter's joints were stiff with rheumatism, and she feared — she feared — that the idiot's eye was coming into her head. But she herself would not cross the minister's threshold. She stood there pouring curses on him who should protect the sheep, and was in league with the wolf. But she cared not — she cared not. The "Lady of the light" had come, and she would go straightway to the mansion-house. The lady's blessed words had reached even to the mountain-tops, and touched them like the sun-rise. "God bless the *Sassenach*!" and she had never thought to bless the stranger, while she had reason to curse the people of her own land. George heard, and his cheek grew pale. "My good woman," he said, as he soothingly approached his unwelcome guest, "you'll not do so. You'll not take the kindness from the hand of the stranger, when it is ready to come to you from your own. As sure as the sun shines, I will speak to Jackson this night, and you will have a house over your head; and you will have the cows and sheep that were taken from you back again, with the pasture land. The woman spoke not; her heart for a moment was softened, and she wrung her hands. "But who will give me back the light of my child's eye?" she murmured, and without other reply or word of thanks she turned away. However, George, who went up to the topmost window of the house, to watch her proceedings, saw her stand above the road that led to the mansion-house, and seemingly speaking to herself, toss her arms wildly thitherward; but turning quickly, she took the path that led to the mountains. George instantly repaired to Jackson, who as quickly, on his part, sent to have the burrow-hole filled up, and justice done to the poor women, who, he wished, had made known their wants to himself sooner, and he would have been the man to right them.

Another day — it was in the depth of winter — an aged pauper, with grey unshaven beard and lank skinny hands, stood warming himself over the kitchen fire, while he kept entreating the maid, who, busied with some kitchen slopping, seemed to heed him but little, "to get a word for him of the minister." "What wad the likes o' you be doing wi' the minister" asked the damsel, sulkily. "I've been here many a time in the old times," replied the man with tremulous voice; "and never was refused a word o' *the Doctor*. Ay, ay; the last time, Miss Mary brought me a sup of milk and a plate of cakes with her own hands. My blessing be wi' you, lassie, speak to the minister." To be rid of the man's importunity, the wench at last shuffled away, and by-and-by the minister appeared following her, not as it would seem, in the most pleasant mood. "Is it you, Jacob?" said he, throwing himself on a kitchen chair by the fireside. "What is it you want, tormenting people this way in their own houses?" "Oh, sir, take pity!" said Jacob, clasping his miserable hands. "The wife is bed-rid, and *we have the silly boy*! We used to get half-a-crown in the month from the parish, and now we get but *the sixpence*." "You do not trouble the church, Jacob," said George, his eye gleaming luridly from under the locks which had not been adjusted that morning; "and your wife has Samuel the catechist, to read by her bed-side." "Oh yes, yer honour, Samuel reads a word by the wife's bed-side, and puts up a word of prayer." "Then tell your wife," said George, rising in a passion, and making a threatening motion with his fist at the man; "tell your wife that unless she puts away such quackers, and takes her minister, as the law binds her, the never a sixpence from the parish will she ever see. And come you to the church, Jacob, on the Sabbath-day," added he, turning with a scowl as he was about to leave the kitchen. "Come to the church, or it's the last sixpence" — he put his hand in his pocket and drew out a sixpence, which, half relenting, and half by way of bribe, he threw on the kitchen floor — "it's the last sixpence you'll ever see from me." Jacob stood looking at the coin, as if dubious whether, even in his beggarly poverty, he should pick it up; but reasoning with himself that it was the parish money, to which he had some dim consciousness of a right, he stooped for it, and then gathering his rags about him, and muttering something about the wife not being willing to sell her soul, he went out to face the pelting storm.

  The church, upon the Sundays, wore an aspect sufficiently bare. Jackson, to be sure, was there with his family, and filled one large pew well and regularly with flauntingly dressed women, and boys and girls of sundry ages; while the pew behind was occupied by such of the boors in his immediate service as he could command. But the *cortège*, proud and independent as it looked, and seeming to assert, as it bustled out and in, that it was quite enough to support any parish church, formed, in general, the whole of the congregation: neither cotte, peasant, nor farmer, would attend, notwithstanding threats of expulsion, which were oftentimes put in execution. The public-house keeper, and what party *he* could muster, came occasionally and placed themselves, in various pews, by way of making the audience assume as respectable an appearance in point of numbers, as possible; but though for the first few months these persons attained a new and exemplary regularity in their attendance, their old habits gradually resumed their power, and then they became less and less punctual, so that at length they could scarce be reckoned upon. Davidson, too, once in the month or so drove up in his carriage to the church door, by way of giving his marked and pointed countenance to young Donaldson; in general it needed all his efforts to keep up the congregation of the father, in whose parish he properly was.

  But it was at the communion season that George was most sorely put to it in the keeping up of appearances. "You'll appear at the Lord's table on the Sabbath-day?" said he, with an expression of countenance unusually devotional, to a cattle-dealer, a person of rather loose character, who was a relation of the public-house keeper's. The man stared at this unwonted mode of address. George repeated his words. "Sir," said the man emphatically, "that's a place I never was at, and I doubt I'm no fit for it." "How so, my good friend?" inquired George. " Because, sir, ye ken yoursel' well enough that I can tak' a glass or so o'er much at a time, and there's maybe ane or twa things besides unsuitable to a public profession." "But, my friend," said George, gravely, "your mentioning these things, and, in some sort, making confession of them, shows that you know them to be improper. Now you will take this token of admission at present, and, no doubt, you will repent of your sins afterwards." "I'm no sure o' that," said the man, musingly. "No doubt of it," said George, in a decided tone. "Na, na, maister George," said the man, turning away, "I'm no that ignorant but what I ken that repentance o' sin should come first, and a public profession o' religion afterwards; and I'm no going to add the sin of profaning the Lord's table to a' the rest. So good-day till ye." It was a singular circumstance, that this man became so alarmed at the nature of the sin which had been urged upon him, that he never afterwards went to hear George preach, but rather sought opportunities of hearing the truth truthfully delivered, when these presented themselves.

The news of THE DISRUPTION were received in Glenmore with thankfulness and joy. In the parishes of those 474 men who had quitted their livings, there were, indeed, mournings and lamentations. The Highlanders especially, who had not yet forgotten their habit of appealing to the sword in vindication of their wrongs, would have risen universally, were it not for the exertions of these pastors to suppress insurrections and inculcate submission. Some bloodless riots took place, but, on the whole, the fatal change from Blairs to the *Bremners* and *Donaldsons* was effected without other demonstrations then the calm and settled contempt of the people. While the men, who forsook their emoluments, constituted themselves into a FREE CHURCH, they did not forsake their corresponding duties. They seemed to receive anew the command of their Master — "Preach the gospel to every creature." Thus Glenmore and Aird, instead of being cast off, were again received into the bosom of their Church. Furthermore, they were permitted to choose, among its licentiates — those who had received the seal of approbation in life, doctrine, and talents — the pastor to whom their attachment most warmly cling. Need it be said *who* it was that received a united call from the people of Glenmore? It was the son of their former beloved pastor, — their own *Mr. Charles*. Oh! With what heartfelt joy was he not welcomed, and Barbara, and Mary too, and the good old lady, who seemed again to embrace her children. Not the gentle Emma; she had, ere now, gone to her rest. They could not indeed, re-inhabit the old manse, nor make its garden and its lawn and fields radiant with order and peace, as formerly. What of that? They lived in the hearts of their people; and, since the morning that their furniture-cart stood at the door, and the rooms in the manse had been robbed of their old companions, many another of the quiet manses of Scotland had been alike desolated — many mourners had gone forth — many chambers full of life-long memories had been visited in the anguish of everlasting farewell — many footsteps had traversed the beloved pathways, in garden and wildwood, for the last time — and the mourners had gone forth, and God's pillar had moved before them in the way.

Yet privations, sickness, death, and exile from their people, visited not a few. Many of the factors, and (shame to tell!) of the proprietors, practised every kind of persecution which the law permitted. While all denominations might come and go — rent houses or relinquish them with the freedom allowed to honest men — those whose lives had been devoted to the service of God and their country were treated as if they had been the common enemies of both. Why, then, should the Blairs complain, since they were not only permitted to breathe their native air, but possessed likewise a comfortable though humble residence in the midst of their beloved people? Jackson had at first refused them a dwelling-place; but they got one from a small farmer who had a perpetual feu, and their large congregation assembled for worship every Sabbath in that spot where formerly the Countess had been so impressed with the solemn beauty of the moonlight worship she had witnessed. This, for them, ere the winter storms set in was no hardship. Alas! for four bleak winters since, have the peasantry on some of Scotland's wildest heights been exposed to the driving blasts, the bitter frosts, and the chilling rains, while others have mingled the plaintive voice of their wild psalmody with the hoarse voice of the resounding sea, not daring to venture above the limits of its highest flood-mark.

It will readily be supposed that Lord Lentraethen, whose principles as a Christian and a patriot were wholly with the outgoing ministers, lent to Charles Blair his most strenuous support. His lady, too, who recognised in these principles nothing sectarian, but all that was great and universal — principles indispensable in all Churches and all States, for the complete Christian civilization of man — she, too, made a point of maintaining a close personal friendship with the Blairs, and of promoting, by every means in her power, their influence for good. "Ought not," she said, "the connection between a Christian proprietor and the missionaries on his estate closely to resemble the connection which ought to subsist between Church and State? While the *direct* object of the missionary is the moral and religious improvement of the people of his district, ought he not to feel himself supported, aided, and cherished, by the landowner, who has a species of power which he does not possess; while, on the other hand the landowner, in his efforts to place his tenants and estate in a condition of the utmost prosperity, will feel himself most powerfully aided by the high and ever-operative agency of the Christian minister?

With this sentiment Lord Lentraethen fully coincided; but with this qualification more fully brought out, that the missionaries who should *more especially* be countenanced by the proprietor, ought to have their principles tried by the standard of God's Word. While he considered that the proprietor had no right to suspend the toleration-laws in *any* case, he was, at the same time, responsible to God for lending his direct support only to teachers of religion whose principles were in accordance with Scripture light and truth. "To found our hopes," he urged, "of any advancement for our people, in enlightenment and prosperity, upon the success among them of the Christian religion, and, at the same time, to foster those who teach what Christ and his apostles never taught, would be an error at once dangerous and absurd. It is in vain to expect from the employment of such an agency, however plausible, aught but what will be ultimately subversive of the high ends of Christian philanthropy."

CHAPTER XXV

*"When Death proclaims th' irrevocable hour
Life's vain distinctions cease; th' eternal doom
all the sons of clay be equal in the tomb."*
                                        SOUTHEY

On the first occasion on which Lady Lentraethen visited the village, she stept into the dwelling of Evan Munro, to inquire after his welfare. The outer door stood ajar; that on her left, in the inside, was fastened, and she heard heavy footsteps pacing the floor within. The one opposite, however, stood open, as did the window to the front; within which was a small table laden with plants, whose fragrance the light summer breeze wafted around. Hearing no movement there, the Countess ventured to look within; the painful scene which met her glance, she had not anticipated. Poor Evan, now emaciated to the last degree, worn indeed to a living skeleton, lay stretched on the bed; his hollow eyes closed, and the stamp of death impressed on his features. His mother stood beside him with one hand beneath his head, which she pressed close to her bosom, while, with the other, she held a spoon containing some liquid to his parched lips. The movement at the door made her look in that direction, and seeing the Countess, she involuntarily started. The sufferer opened his glassy eyes; and, following his mother's, fixed them on the lady, who stood within the open door like an image of glowing summer beside an open sepulchre. The hectic spot glowed brighter upon Evan's cheek. By an effort he raised himself up, and, with an air of impatience, pointed with his worn and waxen finger to the door, to beckon the Countess away. She instantly obeyed the signal, and turned to depart; but just then, the door of the opposite room opened, and *the father* appeared, wearing on his countenance marks of deep distress. With a grave courtesy he invited the Countess to enter. She, on her part, expressed a regret that she had intruded at such a moment.

"No, my lady," said the good man; your visits can never be an intrusion. Your voice is not the voice of the stranger in the day of health; why should it be so in the day of trouble? If you will be seated for a while, you will give me as much pleasure as I can feel at such a time as this." Without farther dispute, Lady Lentraethen stept forward, and took her seat in the arm-chair among the younger members of the family, who were all plying some task or conning some book, but with the traces of recent emotion visible on their countenances. Not many minutes elapsed before the lady was wholly in the sympathies of the honest man, who, not without a tear coursing its way occasionally down his face, spoke of his hopes and prospects blighted in his son's approaching death. Yet, with a subdued and evidently heartfelt resignation, " Who am I," said he, "that I should murmur against the Lord? It is HE; let Him do as seemeth Him good." Then, with a feeling of re-kindling pride, he took out of his mahogany bureau a newspaper, which he handed to the lady with his finger on a list of prizes gained by his son at college the preceding winter. It was a long list. Evan had gained all the honours of his session; but, as his father said, they had cost him dear. He had taken scarce any sleep, and when he came home he was so altered that his friends hardly knew him. From that time, consumption had set upon him its seal.

The mother's step was heard approaching feebly and slowly. Her features were nearly as pinched, and her eyes as sunken, as those of her son. "Evan," she said, in a voice scarcely audible, "thought himself going soon. He wished to speak a few words to his father, and all of them; and he seemed now particularly anxious to see the lady again."

The Countess immediately rising, made the members of the family precede her into the chamber of the dying. She felt that she had least of all a right to be there; and she seated herself at the foot of the bed, shading her figure with a fold of the curtain, while the others took their places around, and the mother supported again, in a half sitting position, her dying son.

"I have thanked you, mother," he said, "a thousand times for all your love and tenderness to me, and I shall not cease to thank you till my latest moment. Father, I thank you for all your advice and all your prayers. They *have* been answered; but not in the way that you looked for. But, oh! father, thank God, thank God with me, that I have been spared the sin of being a lip-servant of the MOST HIGH, while my heart was never given to Him in earnest. When you used to question me on the progress of religion in my soul, I fear I sometimes mistook the entering in of its truths into my understanding for a change of heart, and so I may have unwittingly deceived you. Dear father, forgive your dying son, while he urges upon you not to *bring up* any son of yours for the holy ministry. *Let God choose his own*, and then let them be devoted to his service with joy and gratitude. Dear father, forgive my freedom; but since I have lain on a death-bed, the guilt of leading a life of hypocrisy has pressed fearfully on my conscience. To urge Christ on sinners as the 'one thing needful,' and yet to feel *everything* — life, friends, place in the world, any other comfort or blessing, more precious than *He* — is not that living a lie?"

"I know it, my son, I know it," said the father in a broken voice; "and God knows my daily prayer was that you might escape such hypocrisy. Nevertheless, it may be that I have sinned in that I wished to lead God's providence, and direct his sovereign grace, instead of following His will with child-like submission; and I will even now confess my sin before Him;" — and with the utmost broken-heartedness, the deepest humility, the good man knelt down, and with his son's hand in his, confessed what might have been his worldly-mindedness, the lurking pride of his heart in this his darling boy, in the offer of whom to the service of God he might not have had a single eye to his glory. When this confession, interrupted only by suppressed sobs from the little assembly, was ended, Evan addressed a few words separately to each of his brothers and sisters, and then turned his eyes — whose lustre, kindled by a temporary excitement, was fast fading away — to the Countess of Lontraethen, "I beckoned you away, lady," said he, "because it struck me painfully that youth, and beauty, and worldly prosperity, were a mockery in the last moments of such a one as I; but when you were gone, I felt that I had done wrong, and I wished you back; for, surely, you deserve that I should pray for every blessing upon you and yours, and I would have you see, too, how, on a sinner's death-bed, the Saviour can be all in all, — that so, from the dying testimony of one so feeble, you may value Him more for yourself and your people. Oh! you cannot live too much for eternity; you cannot keep it too much in view that you are a dying creature, and that those intrusted to your protection are dying, but immortal. High as you are, without a blight on your fortune, follow no other ambition than this — to know *Christ crucified* as the strength and hope of your soul, and to hear the Great Task-master's voice pronounce the blessed words,—'Well done, thou good and *faithful* servant.' Now farewell all of you — I have done with the world. Mother, stay beside me, I shall go in peace."

The members of the family pressed forward, with many tears, to kiss the hands and face of their departing brother; and the Countess, ere she went away, took the young man's wasted hand and pressed it in both hers with a kindness which brought a deep though transient flush into his face.

As she was quitting the house, one of the young ones pulled her by the skirt, and presented to her a book which he said was hers; that his brother had found it long ago, and said once that he wished it were restored. It was that she had dropped on the night of her mountain excursion — a volume of Mrs. Hemans'. The book, as she examined it on her homeward way, opened of itself at a passage which ran thus: —

> "To love in doubt and fear;
> Shutting the heart — the worshipped name above
> Is to love deeply; and my spirit's power
> Was a sad gift, a melancholy power
> Of so adoring; with a buried care,
> And with a deepening dream that day by day,
> In the still shadow of its lonely sway
> Folded me closer; till the world held nought
> Save the one being to my centred thought.
> Oh! But such love is fearful! And I knew
> Its gathering doom; — the soul's prophetic sight,
> Even then unfolded in my heart, and threw
> O'er all things round, a full, strong, vivid, light,
> Too sorrowfully clear! An under tone
> Was given to nature's harp, for me alone,
> Whispering of grief."

The page was much blistered, and many of the words almost effaced. Can *love*, too, have had its share in the early decline of this promising young man? thought the Countess, as she saw well that the words must have expressed too truly the feelings of his soul. Was it indeed so, that this young man had sacrificed himself to an ideal passion? — had, perhaps, spurred himself on to preternatural exertion by the phantom vision of some possibility, even to himself obscure? Oh! marvellous folly of youth, which will barter peace, prospects, life itself, for the painted shadow of a dream! Poor Evan Munro! His eyes were, perhaps, even then, closing in the darkness of death. But the grave will keep its secrets: the heart that has ceased to beat is at least safe from intrusion. Some consolation there was in the thought, that if he had lost his grasp of a shadow, he had found a great reality. His talents, of no mean order, though not yet fully developed, were nipped for ever in their worldly uses; but a seed of grace, far humbler to the eye of man, yet of infinitely richer promise, had been sown, which would not cease to bear fruit, both intellectual and spiritual, throughout the duration of an endless eternity.

In another part of the volume, there was a paper folded for a mark. It contained these sentences, written apparently during the progress of the student's illness, and tinged a little with the gloom of disease:—

"LIFE, what art thou? DEATH, what art *thou*? This is *life* — 'to know God, and Jesus Christ whom He has sent.' Oh! great life, perfected through death! High, divine mystery, opened up to the believer's heart. Fellowship with the FATHER, the eternal LIGHT, across the majesty of whose LIFE no shadow of darkness has ever fallen! Fellowship with the SON, the GOD enlightening humanity! — humanity exalted into Godhead! Fellowship with the SPIRIT, the mysterious kindling principle of being! Oh, great life! I would lose myself in thee! Existence here to me is often terrible. How is its glimmering track beset with pit-falls, snares, diseases — the gloomy apparitions of crimes and miseries! I would continue to live, indeed, through my crucified Saviour; to prosecute his heavenly mission, to exalt human nature, by his life and death, to the divine. Yet, oh! death, I embrace thee as a seraph crowned with amaranth; whose flaming sword no longer guards from the believer the way to *life*, but even points him thitherward.

"I have wished to find *life* within the span of this mortal, but I found it not. Mortal love! I thought that in thee it dwelt. I worshipped thee as pure, exalting, divine. Thou wert a false meteor, that led me into a wilderness of flowers, to land me in a wilderness of graves."

Cabul,----------

From HARRY: M'LEOD to his Cousin Miss HAMILTON LEGH, of Chesterlee.

"Dear Cousin, — This will reach you by a private hand, long enough, perhaps after it is written, and after your cousin Harry has gone to the land of forgetfulness. I was struck yesterday by a cannon-ball; had my leg shot off, besides a gun-shot wound which I cannot survive. It would be an awful thing to live with a wooden leg. Dear Jane, a soldier's life is not quite what I used to think when I dinned you in the days of old about battles and sieges. There are plenty of brave fellows here, indeed, and plenty of fighting; but we don't get fair play — at least we didn't, for it is all over with me now. We're knocked down just at the pleasure of an old woman; for there's not a soldier among us, not excepting your hair-brained cousin Harry (as you used to call me), that isn't more fit for a general than ours is. But never mind — it is all over with me now, as I said. Dear cousin, I keep the Bible you gave me in my hand, for a remembrance of you; but I don't look at the inside of it, for fear I should not die like a soldier. It *must* be a leap in the dark, you know, any way; so there is no use thinking about taking the leap into a disagreeable place. Dear Jane, if you were here I know you would preach me a sermon; but I would not mind it, for the sake of your kind voice. All last night, and it was dreadfully long, I thought of my father and mother, and brothers and sisters, and between every one of them you would come in. I may tell you, in a secret, that I have been thinking more about you since I thought less of my red coat; but I knew I needn't break my heart, because you would never have me; but pray marry a good-looking fellow, for the honour of the family. Dear Jane, if you were beside me, I would like to squeeze your hand, for there is a horrid twitching at my heart. I haven't been a bad fellow, after all. By the way, that affair of G. D — 's came across me confoundedly in those endless hours last night. I must confess that I think now you were in the right. If soldiers grumble because they have a leader that knocks his head against every post because he can't see it, people are not to blame because they won't have a leader on the way to heaven that doesn't know it himself. You will guess what I mean, for I am not very good at expressing myself in these kind of things and G.D — doesn't know more about them than I do. Dear Jane, I dare say this is a sad jumble, for I write by fits and starts. I have written to my mother, to tell her that I have done my duty as a soldier, and that I die like one; and now I feel my hand getting very weak. Never mind. All my comrades say that Harry M'Leod was a dashing fellow, and that he is dying as he lived. Don't shake your head. But, indeed, I wish you were here. I shall try to imagine one hand in yours and the other in my poor mother's, as the world goes away — away — away. Ugh! It's an ugly thought. I choke with thirst. God bless you, dear, dear Jane, and may he have mercy on the soul of your poor cousin HARRY."

CHAPTER XXVI

Such were the days — of days long past I sing,
When pride gave place to mirth without a sting;
Ere tyrant custom strength sufficient bore
To violate the feelings of the poor;
Destroy life's intercourse — the social plan
That rank to rank cements as man to man.
                                                        BLOOMFIELD

Hurrah for merry England! The last sheaves of autumn have been borne home, and there must be some farther cause for rejoicing within the smiling boundaries of Chesterlee, for a week has elapsed, and the preparations for a grand festival are not yet completed. Every village and farm-steading has been astir early and late — every house-wife has had her hands doubly full of business — every child has got into it a double infusion of life and glee. Such steaming kitchens, and merry parties assembled round jovial boards; such roasting, brewing, and baking, and making of preserves and pastry; such training of flowers, and trimming of gardens; such preparing of presents, and laying out of gala-dresses; and such boastings of greater things yet to come, never was on the estate of Chesterlee within the memory of the oldest inhabitants. At length the important day has arrived, and cars and carriages of many kinds are tending towards the manor-house, bearing joyful crowds, and making fragrant and beautiful the dusty highway with innumerable crowns and bouquets, and pyramids of flowers. The grounds and gardens of the manor-house are to be thrown open, and a STRANGER — the welcomed of all hearts — the idolized of all eyes, is to appear in public for the first time — the lately-born heir of the young Countess of Lentraethen.

Three cheers for merry England! Had all the sylphs and naiads of antiquity come to life in walking dresses, and met together for a gala-day, they could not have shown more radiant beauty and breathing grace, than beamed in the faces and moved in the footsteps of those groups in this one happy spot! The manor-house itself is thrown open, and halls, and dining-rooms, and housekeeper's and butler's rooms are laid out brilliantly with elegant refreshments fit for noble guests. No plum-pudding like dough, and sour beer, and that called a refreshment; for there are no half-starved beggars to feed. No, no! the housekeeper of the manor must show the superiority of her knowledge in all culinary and confectionary arts to the many excellent house-wives who are come to taste her cheer.

And the Earl and Countess stroll about the grounds in the rich sunshine, and greet the merry parties, adding an honest pride to their joyousness. But where is the fairy monarch of the scene? For a while, in his unconscious slumbers, he rests in the arms of fair May Morrison, within a bower gorgeous with the richest flowers of autumn, entwined with vine-leaves; and the passers-by look upon him, and bless him, and lingering, cannot satisfy their eyes with gazing on his little face, till they are obliged to give place to the impatience of others. Talk of kings and queens! No king or queen for these many long years has had half the power for life or death, for human happiness or woe, that the owners of the soil have had. *They* can do what no king or queen can! So felt — yet felt it all in hope — the tenantry of Chesterlee. Under the shadow of the ancient barons, their forefathers had sat, and, on the whole, it had fallen pleasantly upon them. A noble race they had been for the greater part — full of generous sympathies and social humours; but it was felt with deep thankfulness that now humour was exchanged for a higher principle, and that the child of their expectations would not be let loose, with all his unbridled caprices, to work among them the will of an ignorant schoolboy or an unprincipled tyrant. They knew that his lisping voice would mingle with the voices of their children, that his tiny footsteps would be familiar with their thresholds as with his own, and that their interests, until death, would never be separated from his. Happy education! like the quality of mercy — twice blessed! And ought it to be, that while every professional man, every tradesman, has the training adapted for his business, *the proprietor of the soil* shall have none for one of the most important spheres which God has assigned to men ?

When the tenantry had for a long time enjoyed themselves in the grounds, and in the manor-house, they returned home to enjoy themselves still further at the social parties previously arranged between themselves. The humblest on that evening did not remain uninvited or solitary. The joyous laugh and song, and the merry tale, went round in many a homestead of farmer and hind; and as the evening wore on, bonfire after bonfire sprang up, till, from the balconies of the manor, the whole horizon became illuminated, while, now and then, some elegant device in fireworks would rise high into the air. Night long to be remembered by youth and maiden and happy children, who chased each other in uproarious glee round the joy-fires, and supplied them with fuel, or made the air resound with shouts, as a successful rocket rose to the sky and displayed its device, without fail, as it reached the ground. Could they have seen the fires that burned on the far Highland mountains too, they would have confessed that they were not a whit less bright, neither kindled by hearts less grateful. See that glorious one on the farthest heights. Weeks have been spent in gathering together loads of fir-wood and dried heather; and during this live-long night, from evening dusk till morning twilight, did Annie, the black-eyed girl of the mountains, and her mother, watch beside it for fear its light should for one moment grow dim; while they sang at intervals Gaelic chants, once, perhaps, sung around the *Baal-jen* of the Druids, as they threw on the dark branches of the fir, and heavy loads, which required their united strength to carry, of its resinous roots.

One other fire vies in brilliancy and duration with this; — it is that on the distant moor, kindled by Kenneth Ore, and the young companions of his exile, whose feet have *that very day* pressed again their native soil. No time did they lose in re-embarking, with the help of the funds supplied them by their benefactress. Their voyage had been prosperous; and after having knelt down within sight of their homes, and thanked the Giver of all good for his care over them, they discovered with gladness that this was the day appointed for celebrating the birth of the infant heir, the son of their well-beloved lady. With feelings too deep for shouting, Kenneth and a youthful band stood around the night-fire, and pledged a bumper to the health of the young LORD ARTHUR, the last drop of which they emptied with grave ceremony into the ascending flame. And then and there they bound themselves by a vow, solemn and deep, to traverse sea and land, to lose life and limb, to drain the last drop of their life-blood, as they had now emptied that pledge, rather than harm should come, while they might do aught to prevent it, to the "lady of the light," or those dear to her.

The graver men of the returned emigrants, including Samuel the catechist, were assembled during the whole of that night round the fireside of the Munros. They recounted their providential escapes, their feelings, and experiences; while, not unfrequently it was proposed that one and another of the party should offer up a thanksgiving to HIM who had tried them, only to set their feet in a large place. Nor were fervent supplications forgotten for her who had been God's instrument to them for good, for her husband and her child. The multitude of joy-fires that night pointed to the skies, but they could not ascend thither. The vows and the blessings of merry hearts might truly indicate an increase of temporal good; but the prayers of men who walked with God on the earth, and such alone, might find their way to the ETERNAL THRONE, there to be offered as becomes an offering to the MOST HOLY, on a golden censer, by angel-hands, and with much incense!

Before Kenneth Ore went to rest on the morning succeeding that night, he had penned to his friend, May, the following letter:—

"Dear May — Oh, May! we are here once more! and if only you was in it, the happiness would be too great for me; but I am not going to tell you any thing just now, because I am better at speaking than writing, and I mean, God willing, to set out on my journey shortly to your place; so I will tell you the whole that befell us on our travels, and how we happened to come home on the very day of the rejoicings, when I see you. And I hope, May, you have not forgotten your own language, for the English has a cold taste after it. We have got beautiful crofts and materials for houses from the lady herself (God Almighty ever bless her!), and I am to farm the bit of land, and maybe to follow a trade; but I will say nothing till I see you. I can get a cast of a trading ship from — , and the distance inland will be nothing to travel on foot. — Dear May, your loving friend, KENNETH ORE,"

And where was our young Countess on this eventful evening? Exhausted with the fatigues of the day, and after having watched for some time from the windows the distant rejoicings, she lay on a couch in the drawing-room at Chesterlee, beside her own hearth-fire. The room was illuminated by lamps of a beautiful silver filigree, fed with perfumed oil, according to the taste of one of the ancient barons, which had never been departed from. Rich silver draperies of a pale sea-green, hung around, as if to exclude every breath of chill air which might find its way from without; and many gems of art covered the walls, and costly luxuries from the courts of foreign princes lay thickly around, as if to banish from the imagination everything mean and grovelling, and to suggest only the noble and the graceful. Thank God, there were here no keen bitter blasts for the heart — in this world the coldest of any, for neither gems of art, nor treasures of man's thoughts, nor all lavishments of princely wealth and splendour, can shut them out.

The Countess lay with eyes closed and lips apart, as in a light slumber. Julia sat on a low stool, her cheek leaning on the side of the couch, her silken ringlets falling negligently from her head, her soft eyes fixed on the face of her adopted mother, whose hand she held clasped in hers. Close by, on the hearth-rug, was a beautiful casket, holding a living gem. It was a cradle of mother-of-pearl, shaped like the shell of the nautilus, and sculptured all over; an exquisite piece of art, in which the young Lord Arthur lay sleeping; its silken curtain so disposed as to shade his little face from the light, and yet to permit his mother's eye to rest on it on her first awaking. Julia's hand had so arranged it. Lord Lentraethen silently paced the room, stopping now and then to gaze upon the lovely group. It dwelt upon each alternately, with an expression of the deepest tenderness. At length, unable to suppress his emotion, he sunk on one knee beside the couch of the sleeper, and took the hand of which Julia had not possessed herself in his own. This movement disturbed the Countess. A shade passed over her countenance as she awoke; which, however, immediately brightened into a heavenly smile. "Ah! I am still rich! she said; "I dreamt this moment that I was rambling alone, as if just two years ago, along the pathway beside the stream, and its banks had been overflowed; my feet were wet, and an uneasy shivering was at my bosom: and now, when I awake, I find you all beside me! "I trust you are well, Jane," exclaimed Lord Lentraethen, a shade of alarm passing across his countenance. "Oh, quite well." she replied; "my hand is cool, and my pulses quite equal; but I may have been a little fatigued and excited to-day" "It is no wonder," replied her husband; "I have been so although better able to bear it than you. God grant that we, and our little one too, may prove worthy of the deep love of our people! God grant that their hopes may not be disappointed!" "Ah, Frederick," said the Countess, carrying the hand which had clasped hers to her beautiful lips; "we understand each other. Is not *that* a blessing? Shall we not, then, be strong in heart and purpose?" "Yes, dearest," said her husband; " if it had been otherwise, life would have been to us — I dare not as a Christian say, a *dead* thing; but surely it would have been *another* thing. Yet, even as Christians, may we not draw strength from a blessed union? Does not God the Saviour present it to us as the type of the highest and most enduring love; and will not our babe draw from your breast the life of holy duty and blessed charity? Will he not be cradled in it, and drink it as the air he breathes? And such nurture does not the Highest promise to bless? With His blessing our Arthur will not squander your heritage of your people's love!"

Lady Lentraethen smiled as she turned her eye on her babe, and putting her hand on Julia's head, she said, "Your Scotch estate, however, is to be Julia's; that, you know, we have already settled." "Assuredly," said the Earl; "Julia has lived there, she knows it, and, moreover, has been brought up with that expectation. I rejoice, with all my heart, that the law of entail does not attach to either of our Scotch estates; for I dislike exceedingly the vesting of many properties in the person of one individual. In the variety of interests, all interest, except the personal one, is lost, and a man becomes a selfish cypher among the herd of vulgar proprietors. Instead of being a chief of *men*, he is supreme merely among cattle and game, or it may be is lord of some dreary-cultivated wilderness." "But, again," remarked Lady Lentraethen, "the French mode of subdividing property between all the members of a family is attended with many evils." " Quite true," continued the Earl; "on the other hand, the dignity of property should be preserved. If, for example, God should bless us, Jane, with another son, I think we shall endow him with Rosemount; and if with more, we shall train them for the honourable and learned professions of their country. It is doing injustice to the aristocracy of a great nation to condemn it to a kind effeminate sectarianism, by shutting out its sons from the arena on which men earn fame by their talents alone. There they ought to be purged from false pride and prejudice, by coming in contact with those who hold their seal-patent of nobility from Heaven itself. Nor will they serve their country the worse because they have drawn their nurture from its soil. Do you agree with me, my love? If we differ in any thing, tell me, that we may understand each other again."

A smile and a flitting blush played on the features of the Countess as her husband addressed her thus philosophically on the training of their future family. But as she raised her snowy lids, and as the soft glance of her violet eyes met the eloquent truth of his, the passing smile might have changed into a passing tear. At that moment her babe awoke, and Julia, its little tender nurse, raised it and placed it on her bosom. If tear there was, it fell in the caress which she bestowed in receiving it.

CHAPTER XXVII

"The verity of God is of that nature, that one time or other it will purchase to itself audience It is an odour that cannot be supressed; yes, it is a trumpet that will sound in despite of the adversaries. It will compel the very enemies, to their confusion, to testify and bear witness of it."

JOHN KNOX

Four years have now passed by since the disruption of the Scottish Church. It has since exhibited the spectacle of a body rent in twain. Part of it has existed in connection with the State, contented with the surrender of its freedom. The greater portion has preserved its independence, believing the promise, "Seek ye first the kingdom of God and his righteousness, and all these things *shall be added* unto you." Of the State portion of this once united Church, the enterprise has been small — the resources few. Without having to support its clergy, it has not progressed — it has not even made the attempt. That Church, on the other hand, which has dared to wave the banner of spiritual freedom in the face of Christendom, is covering the face of the land with her churches, her schools, her ministers' houses. She has opened up to her people the privilege of bringing their gifts into the treasury of the temple, and they have poured into it nearly a million and a half of their money. In all this they have somewhat whereof to glory before men, but nought before God. Something is done, yet every thing is to do. The camp of the tabernacle is merely set in order for the onward march. There is yet no rest. Abroad — at home — around — in the abysses of human misery below, Christ calls this Church to be a fellow-worker with himself. The progress of Popery on one side of the kingdom — the creation and vital energy of the Free Church on the other, are the grand antagonist movements of the powers of good and evil in our day. Compared with the giant bulk of the Papacy, her strength indeed is small — her territory insignificant. But she possesses *the light* and *the life* which God reproduces under various forms in different ages, to maintain his warfare with the powers of darkness. It is but from concentrated points in this world of ours that truth yet shines.

Eighteen hundred years ago seven specks of light shot forth their rays over the blue waters of the Mediterranean from its far distant shores. They were seven solitary Churches — small assemblages of singular men; yet, *who* watched over them with tenderest care, and tended their flickering beams? The great HIGH PRIEST, the SON OF THE ETERNAL — whose eyes, as a flame of fire, saw their blemishes; yet discerned their purity of doctrine — their labours — their patience — their works — their charity: these were the rays which shone forth afar to distant lands. The Free Church of Scotland is now sending forth these divine rays with a peculiar lustre. Not content with self-support, she is a missionary Church, consecrated for the redemption of mankind. Not in wealthy districts only does she plant her ministers. With a noble zeal, and in the spirit of her special apostle, she is gathering, under the warm shelter of Christian charity, the outcast and the miserable; she has begun, out of her poverty, to supply the necessities of those famished prowlers on the outskirts of society, whom Churches and States have alike neglected — the heirs of exile — the doomed victims of the executioner; while she is striving to impart to them the light and the love, which is the nourishment drawn from her own bosom.

Churches and schools are set down where missions of mercy have been unknown — among those whom society has trampled out of her pale, or whom she holds but by the slenderest ties. And what voice has not ceased to pound in the ears of the pale and care-worn victims of six days ill repaid toil? those whose Sabbaths have long been spent like the Sabbaths of the lost? whom poverty and misery have made to shrink back from the sanctuaries of the wealthy? Who is it tells them that God has not cast them off — that society has not cast them off — that even the titled and the noble yet feel for them as for fellow-creatures, and would stretch out a hand to help them, *if they but knew how*? Who is it that thus acts as a mediator between the far estranged classes of the commonwealth, and lends his arm to the support of the social fabric tottering at its base? It is he whose name and cause *the great* have maligned and persecuted. It is one whose energies have not been turned aside from their beneficent career, either by disappointment or by the follies and contradictions of those whom he would serve. Thank God, that in the hearts of a few great ones his words have found a response. He has stirred them up, by God's blessing, to pour forth of their abundance where it will not return void; and for the sake of the ten righteous, the doom of their order may yet be averted. May it so be!

Orders may be overthrown — nations may run their downward career of ruin; even Churches, when they cease to be fed with the sacred oil, may pale their brightness and fade away — but, blessed be God! He who holds *the stars* in his *right hand*, is alive for evermore. He it is who wields the empire of nations, and the final destinies of man. "HE HAS THE KEYS OF HELL AND DEATH."

A FEW THOUGHTS
ON
CHALMERS' BURIAL-PLACE

The pages of this book had already been printed off; they lay waiting the completion of some business arrangements regarding them. Little did the writer imagine that, ere they had seen the light, they were doomed to be blotted with tears of deepest sadness.

Chalmers is no more! Scotland mourns! A shadow of darkness has fallen on the earth! Who, of all her teeming myriads, is now arrayed in like manner with the godlike attributes of grace, and truth, and love? What living genius of the same magnitude is devoted so faithfully, so unreservedly — alike in theory and practice — by high and holy unremitting daily labour — to its noblest end, the service of the Highest? Of Chalmers it might be said, if of any of the sons of men, that he was *wholly* sanctified, in soul, body, and spirit. Great writings spread throughout the world — great schemes for his country and humanity — great labours for his God; — these were the parts of his existence.

And *this* man, this large and beautiful embodiment of the divine life, sustained by the Spirit of God, has gone from us. We shall meet him no more, seeking with unwearied footsteps the abodes of misery, bearing the glad tidings of everlasting hope; we shall gaze no more on that countenance so fraught with the light of heavenly love; we shall no more feel the warm pressure of that hand which thrilled the heart with the sympathy of so exalted a goodness. Surely if, by God's grace, man has ever enriched his fellows with the knowledge of himself, that man is THOMAS CHALMERS! The heart is divided between that bereaved and yearning love which folds the beloved image closer and closer within itself, drawing around it the veil of the inner sanctuary of affection, and that profound admiration which places it at a distance, and elevates it to the most commanding position, in order that it may receive a mute and distant homage.

Even in dying, what a series of pictures has he left us, all in exquisite harmony with himself! Let us recall them for a little in this cemetery where he sleeps — this quiet spot so beautiful that *he* coveted it for a last resting-place, but a few days before his departure. The bright summer scarce pours its tide of sunshine into a fairer nook. Here it lies, nestling in a hollow, girdled with beauty as with a living framework. Rich pastures, noble trees, luxuriant with the foliage of high midsummer, form of this framework the inner border. Above them rises the picturesque city, its outlines clear against the sky. The Castle-rock, with its time-worn battlements, occupies the middle distance, its features rugged or softened, according to the changing humour of the sky. The Athenian profile of the Calton is just retiring into the shadowy horizon; while green, and bold, and beautiful, Arthur's Seat and its sister Crags stand out on the nearer verge of the city. On the opposite side rise the swelling heights of the Pentlands, clothed with verdure; the nearer and softer slopes of the Braid Hills are here gracefully wooded, and there rich with corn and pasturage. Between these opposite landscapes there is a view of a wide and noble campaign.

All this the eye surveys from the acclivity, scarce more than a man's height above the spot where Chalmers rests. Below, the mind is not disturbed even by nature's beauty. It is a lonely place of graves, *lowered*, as it were, a few feet beneath the level of the gorgeous landscape. Here one can without difficulty gather all memory, and thought, and fancy, around the shade of the illustrious departed. All of his great life with which one has been privileged to come in contact — his looks, his words, his accents, so vivid that it seems as if they could not die; — his mind of such wonderful variety, uniting so many opposite qualities of the greatest men, that it becomes in itself a profound intellectual study. For the poet, or the philosopher, or the man of contemplative science, lives in the world without being of it. His mind, like a plant, draws its nourishment from a grosser atmosphere than that in which it lives. The histories, the doings of other men, the aspects of the external world and society, must needs be revealed to it. But its expansion is above these, and not in the midst of them. Between that mind, dreaming and still — searching, combining, transforming, like the fine and hidden processes of nature, and that other, living in passing events, attaining its end by a constantly varying adaptation of means — there is a native antagonism. Stillness — a certain kind of inertia, is the condition of the one; movement is the condition of the other. Yet who has at once dreamt, thought, learned, and *done* as Chalmers has? Let us adore Jehovah in his noblest work — a man great by nature and renewed by grace — that lamp of exquisite construction, the workmanship of Deity; that sacred and brilliant flame, which was the breath of his Spirit!

And "he was not, for God took him." The last evening he traversed his garden pathways, made fragrant by the breath of summer flowers, his soul went out in longing aspirations after God. "My Father, my heavenly Father." And God was there to reply. " No longer," said He, "shall this child-like spirit be exiled from a Father's bosom. This night it shall find its home." And in the silence and darkness of night God came. He smote the stern waters of Jordan — they parted hither and thither — and the feet of the saint felt not their icy chill as he passed. No human hand wiped the damps of death from that expansive brow. No affectionate bosom received the last sigh of that heart, loving as great. An awakening — a call — the thrill of being's transition — one ineffable glance on earth and heaven, recorded in the majestic smile which sat on the countenance — all with him is over.

With the morning in that dwelling come confusion, distress, dismay. There is a family, whose hearts, wrung with anguish, can neither realize the blow nor separate themselves from the beloved remains; there are friends who come, gaze, depart with souls bewildered, yet entranced by a wonderful vision; there is a Church in the city, which meets in solemn assembly, to separate stunned, heart-stricken, well-nigh abased, as if smitten of God. In the midst of all is that half-upright figure, reclining majestically in its last repose — the materials for early labour placed around, while the hand that should have used them was lifeless, yet disposed with a graceful ease, as if it regretted not that its work was done.

Again, another day we see a mourning city — a long dark procession, the half of which the eye cannot embrace. This churchyard and all around is veiled with a grey, softened light; the funeral fills it as with the ranks of an army. Adown the midst a coffin is borne, while the multitude stand with uncovered heads. Men of God do honour to God's servant; men of genius render homage to genius; and there are few who do not pay the tribute of their tears.

Behold the sum of mortal honours ! Dust to dust. Chalmers is not.

Yet let us take comfort. Here all is not over. God likewise has a part to perform, and it is yet to come.